A SWIMMER'S ODYSSEY

From the Plains to the Pacific

UYLESS BLACK

A SWIMMER'S ODYSSEY
From the Plains to the Pacific
BY
UYLESS BLACK

Available at on-line booksellers and local bookstores

Communicate with the author at:
www.UylessBlack.com, Blog.UylessBlack.com
or BlacksStreets@gmail.com

Additional works by Uyless Black are available at:
www.UylessBlack.com

IEI Press

Information and Entertainment Institute
9323 N. Government Way, #301
Hayden, Idaho 83835

Library of Congress Control Number: 2011909662
ISBN 13: 978-0-9800107-1-8
ISBN 10: 0-9800107-1-3

Cover & Book Design by
Arrow Graphics, Inc.
info@arrow1.com
Printed in the United States of America

Outlier: Out-li-er [ówt li ər]: Someone who does things out of the ordinary; not slightly out of the ordinary, but way out of the ordinary.

Dedication

To those outliers of the frogman world:
The members of UDT and SEALs.

With salutes to my two favorite frog girls:
my niece Britnee and my swimming prodigy Jan.
With gratitude and admiration to my swimming mentor, Tudy.

Recent and upcoming books by Uyless Black

See pages 311-312 for essays and other books

Lea County Museum Press

The Light Side of Little Texas

SAMS

Teach Yourself Networking in 24 Hours

IEI Press

A Swimmer's Odyssey: From the Plains to the Pacific

The Nearly Perfect Storm: An American Financial and Social Failure (available 2012)

The Deadly Trinity (revision available mid 2013)

Networking 101: An Introduction to the Internet and Social Networking (revision available 2013)

My Capital, My America (available 2014)

Cold Wars, Hot Wars and America's Warm War (available 2014)

Table of Contents

Preface

Early in this book, I trust its themes will become clear. For this introduction, I wish to state the book has a positive slant but its messages are not feel good gospels. I have grown weary of claims about the supposed direct physical power of happy, positive thinking. One popular falsity currently making the rounds is the idea that mental images can transport themselves through the atmosphere, even across the universe, and come back to affect our body movements.

Mental images can do wonders if they are translated into physical actions, such as speech, a slam dunk, a powerful swim stroke, a written phrase. But to claim they can change a person's life and circumstances just by being thought smacks in the face of common sense and science.

One writer tells a story of driving his car around a corner and coming across members of a gang who were beating up an old man. The writer thinks positive thoughts—real hard—and the gang members suddenly begin smiling and walk away from their battered victim. Another author tells of the power of thoughts that can cascade out into space and bounce back to earth. The thoughts are beneficial or harmful, depending on their positive or negative energy respectively.

These ideas do a disservice to those gullible enough to believe them. They tell their victims (and they are indeed victims) success can be achieved with mental machinations alone. Unless one hits a jackpot or encounters some other wildly improbable pot of gold—there is no easy way to an achievement; or for that matter, the happiness that comes with the accomplishment. Both take work and many hours of mental and physical effort. Exceptions exist to this rule of life; but they are just that: exceptions.

Nonetheless, our society traipses through these fantasies of feel good mental vibes, balancing ourselves on smiley faces. If we dare posit a negative view on our blog, we are inundated with emails about our needing a counselor or an attitude adjustment.

I know how important a mental attitude can be toward solving a problem or overcoming a challenge. This book tells the story about my belief and faith in mental strength, motivated effort, and tenacity. But it disavows the brain wave charlatans who now permeate TV talk shows, mega churches, and other Dale Carnegie wannabe rip offs. The theme of this book is simple: Unless you are a very lucky and rare human, there is no short cut to success.

Notes

For the first chapters of this book, references will be made to my initials, U.D. because for the first years of my life, I was so-called. I am now called Uyless. It is a minor point but can be confusing if not explained beforehand. In later years, I began using my name; my publishers preferred it and it is now my moniker.

A few passages in this book (in Chapters 1 and 4) can be found in an abbreviated form in *The Light Side of Little Texas*. I hope you will not find them too repetitious, as they are meant to convey continuity to both stories.

I have given considerable thought to the use of quotation marks for conversations that took place decades ago. Since my twenties, I have been making notes about some of the events in this book. They helped in reconstructing many of the dialogues. Nonetheless, a quote from, say, an interview I had with an Underwater Demolition Team (UDT) evaluator in 1963 is not a word-for-word reconstruction. Given this latitude, I have attempted to be accurate, as well as to reflect the spirit and meaning of these conversations.

The photographs I made while in Vietnam and on the South China Sea (Section III: The Hot Cold War) were snapped with a Minox camera. I also used this camera to take the shots in Thailand, the Philippines, and other places described in Section III of the book. I was fortunate to have been in Hong Kong early in my tour in the Western Pacific, where I purchased the Minox. If I had not had this small and readily available camera in my pocket, I am sure I would not have been able to take these pictures.

The Minox "spy" camera—made famous in James Bonds films—was ideal for my use during times when larger cameras were too bulky for carriage or one of my hands was needed for other activities. My duties were that of a Line Officer in the U.S. Navy. I was not expected to traipse around Asia with a 35 mm camera dangling around my neck. If I could take a shot on the side, fine. But they had to be muted actions, secondary to the tasks at hand.

Today, we take for granted small cell phones that take photos and videos. Not so long ago, these capabilities (and only still photos) were available in only a very few devices. In hindsight, thank you Minox.

On page 9, I mention swimming in dirt tanks along with frogs, catfish, and water moccasins. After the first printing of this book, my book agent informed me water moccasins do not reside as far west as the locale of these ponds. I had been under this mistaken impression for over fifty years. As best my brothers and I can reconstruct, the basis for my illusion was our father. Dad put one over on me to discourage my venturing alone around these waters. I informed my agent I would correct this error on the next printing. She responded that I should leave the story as it is, because I was under the impression water moccasins were indeed my swimming mates.

I look forward to hearing from you about *A Swimmer's Odyssey*. You can reach me by sending an email to UBlack7510@aol.com.

Section I

Learning the Ropes

Chapter 1

Early Water Life

You never see a frog so modest and straightfor'ard as he was,
for all he was so gifted.
—Mark Twain

The dive marked his passage from a world of noise and heat into a sphere of cool translucent silence. The next few seconds—coasting from the dive's momentum, gliding underneath the water's surface, flexing no muscles—left the swimmer with a sensation of an effortless soar though a chilled quiet ether. The water's mass disavowed flying. It did not matter. His aqueous exploration was more exhilarating than flight.

For those brief moments, the swimmer knew why he swam, why he loved the water. These brief escapes into his underwater world were as fulfilling as anything he had experienced in his young life.

As the water's resistance began to work against the forward thrust of his dive, the swimmer's momentum slowed. He pulled his legs forward, spread them beneath his body and executed a frog kick. With his arms resting at his sides, the leg movement thrust him suddenly through the water, as if he were shot from a water cannon into yet more water. The kick carried him several yards and gave him another gliding respite through his water world.

As he slowed again, he combined his next leg kick with a frog-type arm movement. These actions propelled him to the other side of the swimming pool, where he surfaced—once again hearing the clamor of the public swimming pool and feeling the dry heat on the plains of a New Mexico summer day.

Learning to Swim

I learned to swim when I was six years old. In the 1940s, swimming at that age was considered to be a precocious event. Today's toddlers, recently wrinkled from their stay in the womb, are now executing Australian Crawls in swimming pools—their new aqueous habitats. It may not be too long before a newborn babe sidestrokes its way through mom's birth canal.

The first day I floated in water was also the first day I swam through it. My brother Tom and I were working and playing in a metal water tank. The tank was located on the Wagon Pasture at Dad's ranch, an expanse that spread out over the vast prairies of southeastern New Mexico. The pasture was so-named because many years ago, several horse drawn wagons had been left in the pasture, near the tank. A chuck wagon and several buckboards made up the inventory.

The wagons were falling apart and rotting away. The staves of the chuck wagon, designed to support a long gone cover, were now curved belts of rust. The wagons' large wheels spoke to a fine past, yet their age-dried wood—grey in its hue—foretold their inevitable future. Whatever their past may have been, they offered venues for my fantasies. The wagons were one of my favorite places on the ranch. They were second only to a nearby aquatic playground: a water tank and an adjacent pond.

The water tank was made of steel. Its sides stood about five feet high. Dad kept the water brimmed to the top of the tank. Its overflow was diverted into a nearby dirt pond, where cows, horses, and sheep drank the precious liquid.

On this day, the tank's water level was only two to three feet deep. The water was being drained in order to clear algae from the tank's sides and bottom. Tom and I were removing the green residue and waiting for the remaining water in the tank to empty.

Even though I was not yet a swimmer, I was a student of swimming. Even more, I had met the perquisites for learning to swim. First, I had watched my older brothers swim. From these observations, I formed a key idea about swimming: stay afloat. Second, I was not afraid to hold my breath under water. Third, for hour after hour, I had watched frogs swim in the tanks, ponds, and rain puddles that were spread around the ranch.

The half full tank provided an opportunity to prove if my observations of the frogs had been effective. Without much ado, I lay face down in the water and started floating. At the same time, I initiated a rookie frog kick and propelled myself forward a few inches. Not only could I float, I could swim! I was hooked.

After this fantastic experience, I surfaced, stood on my feet and shouted to my brother, "I can swim. Can you?"

Sibling competition, I knew Tom could not swim. I had bested my brother in an athletic event for the first time in my life. I recall Tom's surprised look after he witnessed my aquatic launching. I had succeeded in an endeavor my brother had not yet mastered. Even more, I had accomplished this feat without help from anyone, except some frogs.

Success breeds confidence. It helps build one's ego, especially when facing the everyday accomplishments of five talented, older brothers. On a summer day in 1946, in a water tank located on an obscure ranch in New Mexico, I carved out a place for my own identity. I forged a tool that helped me build confidence in myself. As I proceeded through life, I held on to that moment and found ways to reinforce it.

I'm now an old man. Upon reflection from this distant platform, one could question the significance of one's life to a single event in one's youth, such as mine in the Wagon Pasture water tank. Yet how our lives unfold can be determined by a solitary experience, a chance encounter with a kind soul, the succoring and encouragement of a gifted teacher, the unexpected meeting with a long lost friend, with the forging of a new relationship. They can change a person's destiny. I would wager you can come up with your own moment.

Earlier that morning my father had instructed my brother and me to drain and clean the tank. Had that tank been its usual depth, I doubt I would have learned to swim at such an early age. This episode set the path for much of my life.

My First Role Model

As you may have guessed, frogs were an important part of my childhood. As silly as it may seem, they were my teachers for learning how to swim. I admired and envied them. Granted, most people have more popular models for excellence. Abraham Lincoln, Mother Teresa, and Michael Phelps come to mind. But I was not looking to frogs for political or divine guidance, I was looking to them for swimming guidance.

Thus, my first stroke was not the dog paddle or crawl. It was the breaststroke, also known as the frog kick or the frog stroke. By studying the frog, I learned how to execute the breaststroke leg movement as well as anyone I encountered who swam this stroke.

I watched how frogs gained their acceleration through an outward, downward, and then backward thrust of their legs, pushing the water away with their webbed feet. It occurred to me that some of their power came not only from their large feet, but also from pushing the water with their legs, especially their inner thighs. For a human, whose feet surface area is relatively small, an added emphasis on pushing and compressing the water with the inner thighs can create a lot of thrust. I practiced this idea until it became an unconscious part of my stroke.

I received no formal swimming lessons until several years after I learned to swim. I did what came naturally to frogs and me. I also learned about swimming and the crawl stroke by watching Johnny Wiesmuller in Tarzan movies. For a while, I did not know the crawl was executed more efficiently with my head in the water. I assumed Tarzan swam with his head up in the air for the practical reason of searching for resident crocodiles. For several years, I swam the Tarzan crawl.

Later, I invented what I call the "frog crawl" or "breaststroke crawl." (I think I was the first. I never saw anyone else do it.) It is swum by combining the American Crawl arm movement with a frog kick. The head remains out of the water, looking forward while using a breaststroke leg thrust. Try it. It is a very powerful stroke. If you can swim this stroke a couple of laps, you can rest assured you are in fine shape.

I named another possible invention the "over-arm sidestroke." This stroke is the same as a conventional sidestroke except the arm that is closest to the water surface is *taken out* of the water when it reaches out past the head. With this method, there's no water resistance to work against this forward arm movement. I've never understood why anyone swims the conventional sidestroke. It's clearly inefficient.

Let me know if you would like some swimming lessons. I'll have you streaking across the pool in no time. But I digress.

The lack of formal training and my observations of frogs (and Tarzan) allowed me to evolve into a natural swimmer. The situation might be similar to professional golfers who learn their trade mostly by playing and practicing—without a lot of intervention from anyone. The mechanics of swimming or hitting a golf ball become part of our motor skills. Thinking too much about a breaststroke kick or fretting about hitting a ball from the tee can sometimes be counter-productive. These actions must become part of our muscle memory, somewhat automatic.

But Tiger Woods did not become a gifted golfer by himself. He had guidance. As did I with my swimming, which I will recount in this book.

Other Swimming Venues

Dad's ranch spanned 32,000 acres. It was divided into large pastures. Each of these fields had a windmill and an adjacent pond. These ponds were built to provide water for our cattle, horses, and sheep. In addition to swimming in the metal tank near the house,

I also played in these "cattle tanks." During those early days, I sometimes used these ponds instead of the five-foot-deep metal tanks because I could touch bottom in all but the middle of these (very) small lakes. I also liked the pond near our house because its length was longer than the nearby steel tank. I could swim farther without stopping.

The downside was the presence of catfish. Dad had stocked a couple ponds near the house with these fish. When I was fishing, I had some painful experiences with these creatures. I learned the hard way of how to take a catfish off the hook. The so-called "whiskers" extending from each side of the fish's head are not gentle feelers. They are sharp spines and can inflict wounds to the skin.

I don't recall their "nicking" me while I swam, but they did come around to check me out on occasion. If I were standing still or in a motionless float, I could sometimes feel them come near my body. I suppose they kept away if I were thrusting through the water with a frog kick. But after suffering nicks to my hands while fishing for catfish, I never felt at ease swimming among them.

Another logistical problem was the mud on the sloping sides and bottoms of the ponds. They were enriched with many years of cow, horse, and sheep droppings. The critters would wade into the water, get a drink, and often make their contributions to the food chain. I paid no attention to them or their donations to the pond. I was blissfully unaware of the risks. I was six-years old and having too much fun to be burdened with grown-ups' hang-ups.

My parents and brothers did not know I was swimming in the pond near the house. Dad imposed a strict schedule on our recreational times. After work was finished in the afternoon, we boys and our hired hands were allowed to hunt, fish, swim, ride, and practice roping and steer wrestling. (Dad had built a small rodeo arena in the House Pasture.) Following lunch, we were required to rest for a while, after which we could go swimming. Then, it was back to work for everyone but me. As the runt of the litter, I was given a few chores, but not many. I had a lot of time on my hands. Getting into the metal tank required scaling a ladder, which made my profile too visible to the adult population. The pond was low on the horizon. Hiding behind reeds and bushes growing around the banks, I could easily slip off my clothes and take a swim almost anytime during the day. I had no watchdog or bodyguard to monitor my movements.

If my parents had known of my swimming in a cattle tank, I suspected they would have stopped me. Thus my stealthy swims. Nonetheless, Mom and Dad refused to wrap a cocoon of security around their children. Dad would caution me sometimes. ("Son, stay out of the Bull Pasture.") But they left us to our own devices. Such was ranch life. In hindsight, it's a wonder I didn't come down with some human form of hoof-and-mouth disease. I've always been pretty hardy. Maybe these early experiences built up my immune system.

Another disadvantage accompanied my swimming in the ponds: the presence of water moccasins. These snakes could be found around the cattle tanks, leaky windmills, and especially the ponds. They liked to dine on the smaller catfish and frogs. They are poisonous but their bite is rarely fatal. I was afraid of the rattlesnakes on our ranch, but I found the water moccasins to be shy and unaggressive. They would retreat if they saw me coming. Nonetheless, they could do serious damage if threatened. Once again, I was armed with a child's naiveté. I'm sure the snakes and I occasionally shared the pond but I don't recall seeing one swim near me.

My Frogman Dreams

In the early 1950s, after I had learned to swim—and it had become my obsession—I experienced another life shaping event. I attended a WWII movie featuring the Underwater Demolition Teams (UDT), the forerunners of today's U.S. Navy SEALs. I recall sitting in the movie theater, watching the frogmen leave a submarine and make their way to a beach to lay waste to the Germans' underwater obstacles. I said to myself, *I can do that! I don't even need those flippers. I can swim my frog kick.* I left the movie with one goal in mind: I was going to become a frogman. From that time forward, my swimming efforts were directed toward becoming a member of the UDT.

Before I saw that movie, I had become a bit of a frogman myself. I think it accurate to say I wanted to be a frogman before I knew such a person existed. But the movie sealed my fate. As I walked out of the movie theater, my boyhood imaginations crystallized into a focused goal. When I grew up, I was going to be a Navy frogman.[1]

The movie's swimmers demonstrated the skills I would have to possess to be a frogman. First, I would need to develop stamina. The frogmen in the movie swam for miles without rest. Second, I would need to swim underwater. After all, "underwater" was part of their name. Third, I would need a lot of strength. The UDT swimmers carried heavy gear and explosives. Fourth, I would need to be a quick swimmer, at least on some occasions. Actions such as eluding an enemy or reaching a beach at an allotted time would require a fast swim. Hmm, they used those strange looking flippers. I had never seen them before. No matter, my frog kick would do just fine.

Even more, I was called by my initials U.D. I was U.D. Black, as in Uyless Delton Black. For now, in my childhood fantasy, I would become Underwater Demolition Black. What could be better? I could picture it now: "UDB of the UDT!"

The danger these men faced never occurred to me. For some reason, it never entered my mind until my later years—even into adulthood—how risky it was to be a member of the UDT. Such is the folly of youth.

A Dubious Role Model?

After I decided to write this story, I asked myself, will a reader consider me a bit off center because of the role frogs played in my childhood life, of the influence they had later?

As a child I never thought of myself as being a frog, nor did I dream of becoming one. I was a fanciful boy, but not delusional. Nonetheless, I was taken by these powerful amphibians. In my quest to first learn to swim a yard or two, and then to continue to stay afloat as I struggled across Dad's cattle ponds, I kept the frog's leg kicks in my mind. I mimicked the frog's stroke. As mentioned, it became my model for swimming.

In a sense, the lowly frog became my role model in general. (Even to this day, I watch a frog swim with a sense of wonderment.) Of course, most boys of those days took on Roy Rogers or Gene Autry as their idols. I liked these drugstore cowboys well enough but I never saw them swim.

Later in my childhood, I learned the frog was held in low esteem by adults. I recall hearing grown-ups make disparaging remarks, such as "What a toad." Another putdown was, "She's meaner than a Bullfrog." And granted, they are not all that attractive. If you watch a frog eat, its eyes sink into the eye sockets to help push the meal down its throat. Who cared? I was not out to emulate their eating habits; just their swimming styles.

Nonetheless, I was puzzled by the adults' prejudices. None were held by any child I knew. How could they not admire frogs? If my Dad and brothers could revere horses, bulls, and ram sheep, why couldn't I choose my own role model? I did.

---

[1] This book uses the term "frogman" to describe this writer's legacy with frogs, the UDT, and SEALs. The word is used to describe many other people and groups. As examples (source Wikipedia), in the U.S. military, divers trained in scuba gear for assault missions are called combat swimmers or frogmen. This term refers also to the Marine Recon swimmers, the Army Ranger swimmers, Air Force Pararescue, and the Navy Explosive Ordnance Disposal (EOD) units. In Britain, police divers are called police frogmen. In Denmark and Norway they use the terms *Frømandskorpset* and Norway's *Froskemanskorpset* respectively.

CHAPTER 2

THE ENTRANCE OF A MENTOR

Unconsciously we all have a standard by which we measure (others), and if we examine closely we find that this standard is a very simple one, and it is this: we admire them, we envy them, for great qualities which we ourselves lack.
—*Mark Twain*

After learning to swim in Dad's tanks and ponds, I was able to hone my fledging skills at a local swimming pool in my hometown. During this time, and during my junior high school years, I had the good fortune to come under the tutelage of a talented swimming instructor. Her nickname was Tudy. Her real name was Dorothy Osburn, shown in a high school yearbook picture in Figure 2-1. Tudy displayed a patch on her black swimsuit that spoke volumes about her status: a Red Cross Water Safety Instructor (WSI). In my rankings of admired swimmers, a WSI was tops.

Tudy taught me to have assurance about my emerging skills. She gave me confidence in swimming crawls, backstrokes, and sidestrokes. (She offered no advice on my breaststroke, declaring it to be satisfactory the way I swam it.) Tudy provided the training that led to my becoming a Red Cross certified lifeguard and a WSI. She paved the way for my six summers of life guarding and three summers of teaching swimming.

The Red Cross did not teach the butterfly stroke. The stroke had no role in its life saving routines. Thus, Tudy did not think it appropriate to explain it. I asked for hints on how to swim the butterfly but she offered no help. I never learned it but I wish I had. I think I would have enjoyed swimming the butterfly as much as the breaststroke.

Figure 2-1. Tudy.

Anyway, for a boy who loved swimming and who was striving to swim well, I began to view Tudy as my idol. She was a powerful swimmer and executed an effortless American Crawl. And just underneath that flimsy black swimsuit was one lovely hunk of feminine muscle—a 10 in today's rating standards. If I grew weary of listening to her lectures, it was easy to tune out the air waves and watch her body in motion. Truth is, I looked at her as much as I listened to her.

As the summers rolled on, Tudy became my mentor. I think she understood how much swimming meant to me. I was at the pool almost every day and she often gave me extra lessons. She was a fine sprinter and taught me how to execute a racing dive from the side of the pool.

Nevertheless, the Red Cross did not train swimmers to be sprinters. The front crawl (also called the American or Australian Crawl, or simply free style) was taught in Red Cross swimming classes, but was not emphasized for the sole purpose of swimming fast. For the life of me (not to mention the life of a drowning person), I could not understand why speed was not emphasized more in the Red Cross manuals and classes. In hindsight, I suspect the reason was that the sprint crawl required the forehead of the swimmer to go underwater, thus losing sight of the victim. Nonetheless, Tudy was big on conditioning and required her students to swim lap-after-lap as fast as we could manage. Our arms, legs, and chest drowned in lactic acid.

One day, during one of her luscious lectures, walking before us displaying the WSI patch on her upper thigh...eh, swim suit, she asked the class, "What's the most important aim during the rescue of a drowning person?" In one form or another, our answers were: *swimming to the victim quickly, never losing sight of the victim during the swim, keeping a firm grip on the victim while making the rescue.*

Tudy, "A swimming rescue is the last resort. Try to use buoys, hooks, boats, or ropes before entering the water. Okay, assuming you must swim to the victim. The aim is *not* to end up with *two* drowning persons, the second person being you." As she proceeded to teach us the defensive skills needed to be an effective lifeguard.

These maneuvers became an important part of our training. She taught us how to approach a panicked stricken, drowning person, how to grapple and subdue the victim, how to take him to shore. She drilled into us, *You cannot save your victim if you cannot save yourself.* This lesson resonated into other aspects of my life.

Although Tudy was a fine diver, she did not teach anything but a Red Cross flat racing dive and especially the lifeguard jump, described later. Nonetheless, after her lessons, she would stay around the pool and give us hints on other dives. Two of my favorites were the cutaway jack knife and the cutaway one-and-a half. They required the diver to stand at the end of the board. Facing the board, the diver pushed away, executing a jack knife or one and one half flips before entering the water. Mrs. Camp (introduced next) took a photo of me executing one of these dives from the 10-foot board, shown in Figure 2-2. (For the readers who also dive, I was coming out of a tuck, and had not yet straightened my body. I acknowledge it wasn't a 10, but it ended up better than the photo might suggest.)

Figure 2-2. Additional lessons.

By the way, the swimming pool builder (introduced in Chapter 4) also constructed the diving platforms to his own specifications. He had no regard for Olympic meter heights. His boards were "1-foot," "2-foot," and "10-foot."

A Lifeguard Test with Mrs. Camp

Toward the end of Tudy's tenure at the pool—before she left town to parts unknown—she had taught me skills sufficient enough for my enrollment in a Red Cross Lifeguard certificate program. To pass this test Tudy enlisted the aid of the manager of the pool, Mrs. Camp. If I were to earn my badge, I had to "rescue" this woman. The problem was Mrs. Camp weighed in at 250 pounds; maybe more.

Her physique presented pros and cons. The pros: She floated as if she were inflated, thus making it easier to tow her to the side of the pool. The cons: She was so large I could barely get my arm around her.

To complicate matters, Mrs. Camp purposefully lathered up with a slick lotion. She told our lifeguard class the lubricant was not for tanning, it was to make it even more difficult to get a hold on her. I will never forget Mrs. Camp's baiting us about her Coppertone bath. There she floated, in the middle of the pool, lubricated and ready for action. *Come on in children!*

Even though she did not look particularly adept, the woman was a strong, adroit swimmer. She was also feisty, and during our training sessions, more than once she pulled me under the water as I grappled with her.

But for the day of the test, I was pumped. My "victim" was treading water in the middle of the pool mimicking a distress cry of "Help! Save me! *If you dare.*" I am happy to report I rescued Mrs. Camp on the first try. I also admit, as one of her (new) lifeguards, she had a motive for me to pass the test.

I loved that woman. During the summers at the swimming pool, she became an important part of my daily affairs. She was also a significant factor in my life. Between my freshman and sophomore high school years, she took me on as a lifeguard. Her selection meant that several other boys were not chosen. They were older, bigger, and higher up in the high school hierarchy than I. Mrs. Camp chose me over juniors and seniors. I never knew why. I never asked why. I didn't care. I was just grateful.

Mrs. Camp was an unusual person. She had her quirks. She liked control but her hegemony never expressed itself in a mean way. And after all, it is the quirks of our makeup that make us interesting, not the bland aspects of our behavior.

I loved her children as well. They became my friends and supporters. They had a hand in nurturing my swimming skills.

Lie Backwards and Spread Your Legs

In those days, the Red Cross protocol for bringing in a distressed (but non-panicked) swimmer was to calm them; then—if deemed safe—coax them into a floating position on their backs. Next, they were instructed to place their hands on the rescuer's shoulders, open their legs wide, and let the rescuer swim the breaststroke while the rescuer was positioned between their legs. This aquatic inter-twining became a convenient way for me to do some on the job courting:

"Delores, let's work on the tired swimmer routine."
"OK, how does it work?"
"Just lie back in the water a bit...That's good. Comfortable? ....Good. Place your hands on my shoulders. Spread your legs....That's also good, actually very good. Now, relax, I'm going to start swimming to keep us afloat...How does it feel?"
"Nice. Very nice."
"My thoughts as well."

In a nonsexual rescue, this operation was a dangerous process because the victim was scared, not thinking about sex, and could not see where she was headed. On more than one occasion while using this method, the semi-panicked person would panic and lunge toward me, often taking me under the water.

Tudy's solution to this situation was to go even deeper and, if possible, push away from the person. If they continued to hold on, she said all a rescuer could do was to continue to stay under the water and to fight to get away. Fine, but I came up with a solution not covered in the Red Cross manuals.

If you are ever in dire straits, if you have a panicked drowning person clinging to you and taking you down into the briny, grab the victim's crotch. Not gently. Not foreplay-like. Make it hard and painful. Male or female, they will loosen their hold and try to push you away. Their reactions are instinctive. Momentarily, their genital jewels are more important than their lungs.

For extreme encounters (which occurred a couple times-or-so each summer at the pool) I executed a Red Cross hold on the victim. I would wrap my left arm around his (or her) chest, placing my left hand underneath his right armpit, with his left shoulder under my left armpit. I would place my body slightly underneath his, thus giving him a sense of buoyancy (very important). I would execute a sidestroke kick to take him to the side of the pool or lake. My leg kick, along with one arm, was sufficient to pull the victim out of harm's way.

From these activities and experiences, I began to think I was a fast swimmer. But my only competition came from July 4th contests at the local pool, most likely, not much of a challenge. Nonetheless, my training for speed swimming was secondary to my efforts to build strength and stamina, a legacy of my mentor.

Wisdom, beauty, prudence and wit. These traits were part of Tudy, a swimming sage. She dispensed pearls of intelligence on the deck and demonstrated this knowledge in the water.

Other Role Models

Many people enter into an effort because they want to emulate someone who excels in that endeavor. The idea of role models is a powerful one. We see it every day: As a child, Andre Agassi posing for a photo with his hero, Bjorn Borg. The youthful Tiger Woods witnessing the exploits of Palmer and Nicklaus. Your youthful writer wanting to emulate frogmen and Tudy.

I had other heroes in my childhood. I was a fan of movie Westerns but as a kid who lived on a ranch, I was skeptical of the cowboys' antics. It never made sense to me that Gene Autry could ride his horse Champion and sing a get-along-little-doggie song, while accompanied with an orchestra in the background. An orchestra with violins no less! For what it is worth, even as a kid, I paid attention to details.

The real life heroes were my brothers. I watched them perform their athletic feats in awe. *How can they do that? Yes, they did that!* Perhaps in a touch of irony, I came to the conclusion their accomplishments were so far beyond my ability to achieve that I looked to other ways to spend my time, to try my hand at something they did not do.

I was afraid of being a failure in the eyes of my brothers, especially for an endeavor in which they excelled. None of my brothers were into swimming. I was. The stars were aligning.

Boy Scout Aquatic Camp

For a while, I was a member of Troop 44 of the Boy Scouts of America. I liked the BSA (I still do). We went on frequent hikes and attended weekly meetings during which we learned knot tying, the Morse code, and other essential life saving skills. Be prepared! That was our motto.

The highlight of my membership was the annual one week camp-out on the Pecos River at a BSA aquatic school located about 100 miles west from my hometown. There, I gained my merit badges in swimming, life saving, canoeing, rowing, and fishing. I failed to pass the test for the sailing merit badge—perhaps that's the reason I don't like sailing today.

My friend Jack was my tent mate for this week. He was a great buddy. I had known him since I was five years of age. He lived only two blocks from our home in town, so we saw each other often. He was also a terrific swimmer. That week Jack and I easily won a distance swim race. We represented Troop 44 and were pitted against several troops from nearby towns. It was no contest. The other boys were not up to the task. Here's why:

"Training"

During these summers at the pool I sometimes became bored with the routine of swimming laps and diving. At times, my school classmates came to the pool and we would have fun kidding around. But other times, except for the weekends, the pool was almost deserted in the afternoons. (In the mornings, it was crowded with kids and adults taking swimming lessons.)

It was during those afternoons that I devoted myself to honing my skills. Skills that I thought I needed from watching a Hollywood movie. How grand are the illusions and delusions of our youth! Reality is what we think it to be, not what it is. For me, the reality of becoming a frogman was to be a great swimmer, to be better than anyone else.

To that end, I began swimming with my legs or hands tied together, not both at the same time. I was motivated but not demented. Jack became a partner in these exercises. After mastering these Houdini routines, we contested each other for how long we could tread water with only one set of our appendages.

We took turns being a drowning or panicked swimmer and his rescuer. It became a contest of who could subdue the other. I am surprised we never came to blows because these routines became combative.

Swimming, even swimming in odd circumstances, was becoming as familiar to me as walking. Even these routines became boring. Jack and I would often swim or tread water in the pool for hours without touching the sides or bottoms. While treading water, we would pass the time making jokes and sharing fantasies about tired swimmer rescues on various girls in our school. We had already fantasized about executing other kinds of rescues. The tired swimmer carry was just another position.

Dibble-Dabble!

Another fortunate and unforeseen "training" routine helped prepare me for UDT. It was not really training, as we boys did it for fun. Nonetheless, it was a rough game. Here is how it is played. First, the goal of the game is to capture (fetch) a small piece of wood that is floating in the water.

A swimmer dives into the water and takes the wood, such as a half a match stick or a half a tooth pick, to the bottom of the pool. The swimmer quickly surfaces, swims to the edge of the pool to join other boys, who are standing at the side. All are waiting for the wood (the Dibble) to become visible.

If a boy jumps in before the Dibble reaches the surface or near the surface, he usually fails in securing the Dibble, as he loses the value of an elevated view of the position of the Dibble in the water. Timing is important. Too soon into the pool, no Dibble. Too late into the pool, no Dibble.

Unless it was a cloudy day or we were using a very small Dibble, we could spot the piece of wood making its way to the surface. Resembling metal, it glimmered as it reflected the sun's rays. At which time, all hell broke loose! We jumped for the Dibble, often colliding with each other in the air, occasionally hitting each other as we entered the water.

No holds barred. No rules. No referees. While vicious aggression seldom took place, ferocious aggression did. We could swim over a person, or push him aside. More often than not, as we swam after the Dibble, pushing it farther to the other side of the pool, we would jostle with each other, but we would always be swimming for the Dibble. The result was often the same as an outright dunking. It required strength, speed, stamina, and determination. The game was not for the meek of muscle or spirit.

The boy who captured the Dibble would proudly shout, "Dibble-Dabble!" He would announce his score of perhaps, "I now have three points," and then take the Dibble back to the bottom of the pool to begin the next round.

I have no idea who came up with the game or its name. But I have treasured memories of my friends standing with me by the side of the pool, waiting for the next melee. I can picture my buddies Delbert and Bobby (wonderful divers and good Dibble-Dabblers) dripping and panting from the previous Dibble fetch, waiting for that glimmering baton to appear. Eddie Mack—another fine diver—was in the crowd. So was Jack. Silence, except for hard breathing. Concentration, looking for the Dibble. An occasional joke as we waited for the wood to surface, and then hell broke loose again!

The first to reach five points won the game. The winner's prize was to push the losers off a diving board into the water. The push was often from the 10-foot board. The losers were required to bend down and grab hold of their ankles. Thus in a semi-fetal position, the winner would push against their butt and off they would go. The losers were not allowed to release their ankle grip, which made for some funny and occasional painful water entries.

This uncontrolled descent led to some of the boys developing the ability to turn a flip and enter the water with their feet breaking the surface...and not their face. Delbert, Bobby, and Eddie Mack turned this good natured put-down into a controlled plunge.

We would play Dibble-Dabble for a couple of hours, never taking a break. Absorbed in teenage play and competition, it conditioned our bodies to a different way of swimming. Not the predicted strokes of swimming laps, but the sudden bursts of energy, the need to swim over bodies, to stay focused on the Dibble, with little rest, to go at it again, to develop stamina. The perfect training for combative UDT encounters.

Tag

I recall some of my high school classmates left me in the dust on the tracks and fields of sports. I was a quick-start runner with good acceleration, but I did not have sustained speed. I think this trait helped me in tennis, which only requires a few steps of velocity.

I could beat most boys out of the blocks. I would hold the lead for a short distance. Then, they would pull away. But not in the swimming pool. The boys who could outrun me on the ground could not keep up with me in the water. I am certain my carving out this aquatic turf as my domain helped my teenage ego and encouraged me to continue working.

The game was tag. We played it if the pool was nearly empty of other swimmers and if Mrs. Camp gave us permission. Like any game of tag, a person was "it" and had to chase (swim-down) someone else, then touch (tag) him. Then, this person was it. He had to tag someone.

We used the entire pool, the diving boards, the water slide, even the baby pool. We could surface from the water but Mrs. Camp's rules forbade running. During these games, she sat at a table, with a whistle in her hand. If a boy tried running to overtake another boy while they were on cement, Mrs. Camp would whistle them to a dead stop. "You boys do that one more time and you're outta' the pool for the rest of the day!" Mrs. Camp kept a clamp on running on the cement. So the contest relied on swimming and diving. (Thank you Mrs. Camp.)

During this time, Tudy's racing dive tutorials came to my rescue. The swimmer's dive, especially for short sprints, is a big part of the overall package for speed swimming. Delbert, Bobby, and Eddie Mack could easily out-dive me on the boards (I was a mediocre board diver), but given Tudy's racing dive instructions, Ms. Camp's restrictions on running, and my swimming ability, I was seldom tagged by these otherwise superior athletes.

Swimming Underwater

I preferred swimming underwater to swimming on the surface. Its quiet plane was more peaceful than the noisy exterior. For a moment or two of being underwater, I was immersed in an ambulatory aqueous cocoon of serenity. I also initiated play routines to test my ability to hold my breath for longer times while I swam. Jack did not participate in this drill. He preferred the crawl, which was not executable underwater. (If you want an exercise in futility, try it.) Unless the swimmer is using fins, the breaststroke is the most effective method for swimming underwater, so Jack sat this one out.

As a novice I could swim underwater across the width of the pool, about 35 feet. I began to extend this distance and after some practice, I was able to stay underwater for four laps. The frequent turning-around slowed me down, so I decided to swim the length of the pool (around 100-110 feet.)

Holding one's breath over an extended time triggers what is appropriately called "air hunger." To help combat this condition, the practice is to hyperventilate before going under, which lowers the level of carbon dioxide in the bloodstream. As the swim continues, the level of carbon dioxide in the body increases, leading to the hunger. If the swimmer stays under too long, he may black out. I never blacked out but many underwater swims left me so dizzy I had trouble re-orienting myself to where I was in the pool. I practiced most of these underwater swims alone, before the pool opened, before other swimmers were in the pool, and before I came to my senses about the danger of extended underwater immersions.

I used a different form of breaststroke underwater than on the surface. The reason was to preserve oxygen, and make the most of each part of the leg kick and arm pull. The process went as follows: Hyperventilate, go underwater and push off from the side of the pool, execute an arm stroke, then leave the arms to the side, glide for as long as the body has momentum, execute a leg kick as the arms are brought forward underneath the body to the front, glide for as long as the body has momentum. Repeat the process.

This technique worked well underwater. For the surface it also worked fine, but it was not appropriate for competitive speed swims. The gliding part of the routine wouldn't work for a sprint effort.

I set a goal to swim underwater for a distance of 300 feet. I chose that number because it was the length of a football field (100 yards), something easier to visualize than successive lengths of a pool. My best distance was 2 1/2 times the length of the pool, which was close to the length of a football field—about 90 yards. I never met my goal and my dizziness spells convinced me to wise up and be content with what I had done.

For a non-underwater swimmer, 90 yards might sound like a long distance. It was considered a long distance back in the 1950s. Today, it is hardly close to what world class underwater swimmers can do. I surfed the Web to learn more about the subject.[1] As best I can determine, the world record for swimming underwater without aids, which is called dynamic apnea without fins, is 166 meters. That's 181 yards! More than twice my distance. I also found the world's record for an underwater swim using aids (dynamic apnea with fins).[2] It is 244 meters, or 266 yards.

It is easy to see the advantage a swimmer has by using fins. Strangely enough, to this day, I am more comfortable swimming without fins than with them. Perhaps I am not as fast or efficient, but old habits die hard.

Putting in the Time

During these times, I was preparing to be a frogman. Sometimes it was purposeful, such as swimming with weights attached to my body. Other times it was play, such as Dibble-Dabble. All of it had value.

I hope I am not leading you to think I was possessed by swimming, that I was an aquatic geek. I had other interests and the New Mexico winters kept my swimming confined to the summer months. Even though this memoir is about one facet of my life, in my defense, I had other interests.

Notwithstanding my well rounded personality, during those years, little did I know that putting in these hours and efforts would later be the subject of academic studies about excellence, that nothing comes without effort and putting in the time.

Lucky Me

Little did I realize I was a fortunate lad to have almost unlimited access to Dad's tanks and ponds, to have Tudy enter my life at my young age, to be allowed to stay at the local swimming pool for many hours every week of the summer, to be reared in a small town, where the recreational diversions were limited, to grow up before television came along to dull my appetite for getting off the couch. As they say today, I was one lucky dude.

Putting in the time was one key to my success. Living in an environment that permitted me to put in this time was the other key. If the environment had not been there, I could never have put in the time.

---

[1] http://www.koreus.com/video/apnee-record-du-monde-166m.html.

[2] http://www.worldrecordsacademy.org/stunts/longest_underwater_swim_world_record_set_by_Dave_Mullins_70865.htm

CHAPTER 3

THE 10-YEAR AND 10,000 HOURS RULES

The trouble with being intelligent is assuming you are smart.
—anon

Thus far, my story might be seen as self serving. I have not hesitated in using the pronoun I. In addition, the story has been upbeat, similar to a *Reader's Digest* composite about life in America. If one were available, I might have inserted a Norman Rockwell swimming scene picture to have the tale further suffused with positive images. But I have written the first two chapters accurately. They portray events of my youth as well as I can recall them.

So, the book is egocentric—it is after all an autobiography—and strikes upbeat notes about life. I am not into writing stories with an *Angela's Ashes* theme. Still, I hope you will stick with me. Later, I will bring in some angst.

Regardless of my self-compliments, the truth is I had no more natural ability for swimming than the average child in my hometown. It so happened I fell in love with the sport, had a lot of time on my hands, and spent a lot of that time swimming. It also so happened that my brothers' athletic prowess intimidated me. Consequently, I looked to do something they did not do.

Recently, I have read about studies that correlate a person's ability in an endeavor with how much time the person spends practicing the endeavor. I thought these studies were stating the obvious. How can anyone be good at something if they don't practice it in the first place?

Nonetheless, I have read about people who defy this "put in the time" concept. A professional golfer who stays in the big money, but rarely goes to the driving range. The gifted pro tennis player who does not train much, but wins big tournaments based on her natural physical skills. The unpracticed gourmet cook, who has a flair in the kitchen.

These people exist, but they are unusual, even rare. I know for certain I am not among these lucky folks. For each aspect of my life in which I might have excelled it came because I put in the time. In sports terms, I would be known as a "grinder."

The Place, the Circumstances, the Time

There's another essential and required piece to the competence puzzle. I introduced the idea at the end of the previous chapter: Being in the right place, under the right circumstances, at the right time. One cannot become a fine swimmer if one has no water in which to swim.

Tiger Woods is creating places for young Black Americans (and other inner city children) to learn the game of golf. His efforts will reap bountiful rewards. The kids will benefit from this time in their lives. It is safe to bet they will not become a Tiger Woods. That's not the point.

They will be given temporary sanctity from their urban streets. They will walk on grassy meadows, a respite to the narrow gravel mazes winding through congested city parks. They will be introduced to a program allowing them to grab hold of something positive and tangible. My Tudy is their Tiger.

As we say in the Navy, *well done*, Mr. Woods. I do not play much golf, which leads to most of my rounds on the links being "good walks spoiled." Regardless of my handicap, I watch you play golf for three reasons: You excel. You have put in the time and continue to put in the time to maintain your excellence. You put your immense wealth to work in order to help others excel.

Tiger Woods and I were fortunate to have been born and reared in circumstances allowing us to have the opportunity to succeed. What we did with these opportunities was another matter.

In no way am I equating my swimming exploits to Mr. Wood's golfing accomplishments. My level of excellence pales to that of Tiger's. As mentioned, that is not my point. My point deals with the thoughts expressed in this chapter and the remainder of the book. I will bring Tiger into the story, as well as other role models, such as Julia Child, Bill Bowerman—the legendary coach of 16 sub-four minute milers at Oregon—and my brothers. Andre Agassi and the pro football player Michael Oher will be highlighted in Chapter 14.

With the outline for this chapter in mind, we examine several studies about the idea of putting in the time. They usually (but not always) meld with the idea of being in the right place at the right time. Their conclusions surprised me. I'll bet they'll surprise you, too.

The 10-Year Rule

Research has been conducted on chess prodigies to try to answer the question of why are they so good at what they do. I had assumed most of them benefited from the genetic roll of the dice; that they had innate talent to begin with. Second, I assumed they put in the time to exploit their native skills.

Regarding the genes endowment idea, it is reasonable to conclude mentally challenged people will likely never be very good chess players, regardless of how many hours they may play the game or how many books they may read about the subject. A physical clunker will never be a superior athlete. The actor Jack Lemmon spent many hours trying to learn to play golf but was never able to advance past the duffer stage.

What surprised me about this matter were the conclusions of the researchers. In the 1960s, Herbert A Simon, a professor at Carnegie Mellon University, came up with the 10-year rule: "It takes approximately a decade of heavy labor to master any field."[1] That makes sense. After all, "practice makes perfect." But these studies go further.

Experience unto itself will not lead to more competence. A golfer may go to the range every day, hit buckets of balls and never break 100. I could have swum lap-after-lap in my dad's water tank. I could have taken scores of Tudy's classes and might have never become a competent swimmer. The key to success is what researcher K. Anders Ericsson calls "effortful study,"[2] and what we might also call "motivated effort."

Ericsson's idea is to continually tackle "challenges that lie just beyond one's competence." I agree and add: to be motivated and to establish goals. Here's his view of this process:

> Even the novice engages in effortful study at first, which is why beginners so often improve rapidly in playing golf, say, or in driving a car. But having reached an acceptable performance—for instance, keeping up with one's golf buddies or passing a driver's exam—most people relax. Their performance then becomes automatic and therefore impervious to further improvement. In contrast, experts-in-training keep the lid of the mind's (and body's) box open all the time, so that they can inspect, criticize and augment its contents and thereby approach the standard set by leaders in their fields.

The leaders in my field were the WWII frogmen and Tudy. During those early days of swimming, I had no idea about the ideas put forth in this quote. But I did know I had to practice. In addition, it turned out that my watching the UDT movie provided the incentive and desire to engage in "effortful study" and "motivated effort."

Recent research shows that attention (effortful study) actually alters the brain and "enlarge(s) functional circuits" in the brain.[3] Even more:[4]

> A skill you focus and train on improves, and even commandeers more neuronal real estate, with corresponding improvements in performance.

Re-wiring the Brain

The science of Neuroplasticity deals with how the brain changes its structure and operations in response to input. The scientists in this field state, "...attention is almost magical in its ability to physically alter the brain and enlarge functional circuits." They further claim, "...(a stimulus) produces a (result and eventual change in the brain) depending *only* on whether attention is being paid." Their research has found that a "cognitively demanding activity", such as trying to improve on what we do, is "...likely to strengthen synapses, and expand or create functional networks."[5]

As an aside, but an important point to consider, these studies show that physical exercise improves "episodic memory and executive-control functions" of the brain by 20 percent and stimulates the production of new synapses. Potato, off that couch!

It really was that simple. I had no more ability than my peers. I just happened to like frogs and happened to see a movie about frogmen. From those inputs, I unconsciously went about building my muscles and my muscle memory. It's funny how our lives can be affected by seemingly trivial events and experiences.

Is Innate Talent Overrated?

The studies we have examined thus far hold to the theory that innate talent is not all that important to success. I have been skeptical of this stand but the experts say:[6]

> Thus, motivation appears to be a more important factor than innate ability in the development of expertise. It is no accident that in music, chess, and sports—all domains in which

> expertise is defined by competitive performance rather than academic credentialing—professionalism has been emerging at ever younger ages, under the ministrations of increasingly dedicated parents and even extended families.

What's the secret? It comes down to three things: An interest in an endeavor such as playing golf, cooking, or swimming, being motivated to do well in the endeavor and not just "tread water", being committed to putting in the time. Perhaps the equation needs a fourth variable of having at least some basic natural skill for the endeavor. But maybe not. Maybe all it takes is an intact brain, an intact body, and perseverance.

I've been wrong about my belief that innate talent is more important than interest, motivation, and practice. I don't know why I could have overlooked this truism. I'm its role model.

Outliers

Malcolm Gladwell has written a book titled, *Outliers*.[7] The title itself might be confusing because more than one definition of the word exists. The first definition states outliers are a separate part of a system. Alternatively: an outlier is someone who chooses not to be part of a group, or an outlier lives far from his or her workplace, or an outlier is a statistical value that is outside other values in the same set of data. Gladwell's definition is: Someone who does things out of the ordinary, not slightly out of the ordinary, but way out of the ordinary.

Gladwell's premise is that, "People don't rise from nothing. We do owe something to parentage and patronage."[8] He cites several studies and his own observations that claim:

- Getting a start early in life will place a person at an advantage over his peers. For a youngster, a variation of a few months often makes a big difference.

- Having the first opportunity to practice something leads the child to gain a slight advantage over his later-practicing peers. Consequently, for team sports, this child is selected to play more, which translates into further widening the gap between him and his classmates.

- The initial advantage persists, even into later years.

- People who grow up in a culture promoting hard work and excellence tend to take on those traits. (Compare Chinese, Korean, and Japanese students to their American counterparts.)

- These cumulative advantages are also dependent on having an environment that fosters participation, growth, and practice. Gladwell says, "But what truly distinguishes (outliers') histories is not their extraordinary talent but their extraordinary opportunities."[9]

- The relationship between IQ and success does not mean much beyond a score of around 120.

Initially, I was surprised by this last point. But Gladwell cites studies to back his claim. Upon reflection, I am certain he's correct. I'll bet you are, too. Think of your friends and colleagues. Some have raw IQs that rival Einstein's (150), but they can't think their way out of a paper bag. They never quite make it. They are intelligent but they are not smart.

Gladwell's focus on "extraordinary opportunities" seems to be common sense. Tiger Woods' dad made sure Mr. Woods had those opportunities. And Tiger himself is making sure hundreds of disadvantaged children are given opportunities that they otherwise would not have without his help.

Gladwell states, "Outliers are those who have been given opportunities—and who have had the strength and presence of mind to seize them."[10] But he goes further, "I am explicitly turning my back on, I think, these kind of empty models that say, you know, you can be whatever you want to be. Well, actually, you can't be whatever you want to be. The world decides what you can and can't be." This Gladwell quote is taken from a David Brooks article and one that I think bears attention.[11]

Something Else is Involved

Notwithstanding my agreement with Gladwell's earlier ideas, as I reflect on this last thought, I become uneasy with his assertion, "The world decides what you can and can't be." It seems a variable is missing from his outliers' equation. I think it deals with his lack of concern about a person's *inherent* traits *vis-à-vis* a person's surroundings. I don't want to over-emphasize my criticism because certain points are obvious: Tiger's efforts notwithstanding, a ghetto child will most likely never learn to play golf well enough to make a living at the trade. In this situation, Malcolm's ideas hold true.

During my time in the computer software business, I worked with an assortment of people who displayed varying skills. Two traits I found in all my successful employees and contractors (as well as students during my part time teaching) were perseverance and resilience. However, these attributes were not sufficient unto themselves to make for a successful software programmer. One of my students was as tenacious as a billy goat in his efforts to write executable code. I tutored him on weekends and after working hours. He did not possess the pistons to drive his determined wheels. He eventually left the field of software engineering for other pastures.

On the other hand, I had programmers under my supervision who were of average intelligence and were effective employees. They got by fine. They were not software rock stars but they contributed to the project because they were motivated and resilient. David Brooks says it well:[12]

> Most successful people begin with two beliefs: the future can be better than the present, and I have the power to make it so. They were often showered by good fortune, but relied at crucial moments upon achievements of individual will.

It's the old story about a father encouraging his son to reach for the stars. The son is fearful he will never be able to accomplish such a feat. But he tries. As the fable goes, he never reaches the stars, but he does reach the moon.

In relation to the thoughts of Gladwell and Brooks, the philosopher Rene Descartes said, "I think, therefore I am." This concept seems to be close to Brooks' idea, as well as mine. In contrast, Gladwell appears to claim, "They think, therefore I am." For Gladwell, social determinism is the preemptor. For Brooks and this writer, it is something more than one's surroundings.

How to Explain the Exceptions?

I knew kids in my home town who came from deeply dysfunctional families. Their childhoods were chaotic. They received no positive reinforcements inside their homes. They were left to themselves and had to make their own way. Their parents were late-night rabble rousers. After generous intakes at the local bar, they came home with their buddies to finish off the early morning with bouts of drinking, gambling, and fighting.

I've read about children who live in the back hills of West Virginia or on the streets of urban ghettos. Some begin their lives as hillbilly hoboes or crack cocaine babies. They usually become drop offs into society's netherworld. But some of these children somehow go to war against their environment. Perhaps their parents and other people in their milieu become reverse role models: these children do not want to emulate the lives around them. They look at the disorder and say to themselves, "I can do better."

Some social scientists tell us these kids never overcome their past; that they live in a perpetual state of inadequacy. I disagree. They may be quite aware of their inadequate past, but they carry a sense of pride and accomplishment by overcoming their once dangerous surroundings.

They do not accept Gladwell's premise that "The world decides what you can and can't be." They make this determination on their own. They bootstrap themselves up beyond their supposed deterministic circumstances. They possess the rare qualities of self-imposed intelligence and emotional fortitude. Fate might have consigned them to failure, but they determine their own future. They find a way to carve out their own identity. They are the direct opposite of Gladwell's claim.

Positive Deviants[13]

A famous example refuting Mr. Gladwell's hypothesis took place in Yemen during 2008. A 10-year old child named Nujood Ali was forced by her father to marry a man in his 30s. Child brides are common in many parts of the world. While illegal, the custom is embedded into the cultural mind-sets of both sexes. The law is often skirted.

As expressed by a Yemeni member of parliament named Mohammed Al-Hamzi, "If there were any danger in early marriage, Allah would have forbidden it. Something that Allah himself did not forbid, we cannot forbid."[14]

That remark highlights a tremendously powerful force behind child marriages in Muslim societies. But Nujood Ali, supposedly consigned by her surroundings to deterministic circumstances, broke the mold that had been pottered by her world. She did not allow her world to determine what she was going to be.

Nujood walked alone to a courthouse, found legal officials, and requested a divorce. No "empty model" here. A book about this story has been translated into 30 languages: *I am Nujood, Age 10 and Divorced.*

Another term used in social science circles to describe people who Mr. Brooks and I believe lie outside Mr. Gladwell's theory is *positive deviants*, "...the single actors within a community who through some personal combination of circumstance and moxie are able to defy tradition and instead try something new, perhaps radically so."

Beyond Social Determinism

The "They think, therefore I am" social determinism mentality is an affront to what Brooks' says is, "...the centrality of individual character and individual creativity. And it doesn't fully explain the genuine greatness of humanity's outliers."[15] I agree. The notion of, "I think, therefore I am" is what makes an outlier an outlier.

In the universe of grinders, there lies the outlier. In a fine touch of irony, grinding appears to be an essential trait to become an outlier! Hang in there. Keep grinding. Put a brick in the mortar here and there. Before long, it becomes a wall. We may reach for the stars. We may never quite make it, but we may reach the moon.

How? Once again, by putting in the time. Let's see what Mr. Gladwell has to say about this idea, with which I do agree.

The 10,000-Hour Rule

Gladwell discusses an issue that has been debated for years: Is there such a thing as innate talent? As introduced earlier in this chapter, his research concludes, "...the closer psychologists look at the careers of the gifted, the smaller the role of innate talent seems to play and the bigger the role preparation seems to play."[16]

As suggested earlier, it is not just rote preparation. It is focused preparation, how hard a person works, how intelligently the efforts are applied. Nonetheless, he emphasizes that it takes the brain a long time to assimilate what it needs in order to achieve mastery of something. The researchers and Mr. Gladwell say ten years is how long it takes to put in 10,000 hours of hard practice. They say 10,000 hours is, "the magic hour of greatness."[17]

I have already taken issue with Gladwell's omission of what Brooks and I believe to be a quality of humans that cannot be measured. I accept many of Gladwell's positions, but he has missed a key point—perhaps because of his background and experiences. He has not seen first-hand the socially and environmentally deprived children in my home town. I'd wager he has not walked around the dumps of the hillbilly hoboes, or tried to collect overdue bills from folks living in Watts, California.

I suspect his retort would be, "Yes, but even those downtrodden souls had a tether, a mentor, a model from which they could expand their horizons." Maybe he is correct. But I want to believe there is something in our beings that cannot been measured, something that Gladwell and the studies he cites cannot calibrate.

Perhaps it is silly to think we humans are not social automatons, that we cannot break the mold that was pottered by our past. I choose to think otherwise. I will not argue that we are a product of our environment. But I also argue that each of us adds to that product. The addition may be good or bad but it remains part of the product.

This addition to the product comes from our creativity. It is not preordained by social determinism. Perhaps it's akin to a Darwinian mutation, leading to something different. Whatever it may be, it is part of our makeup. Some bring it to the fore. Many do not. But it is there, waiting to be tapped. Just ask Nujood Ali.

Muscle Memory or Lack Thereof

On a more practical plane, I would add that it takes a long time for the brain *and* muscles to accomplish this assimilation. The partnership is known as muscle memory. *I would also add that even motivated repetition may prove futile to achieving muscle memory.* During the times I was giving swimming lessons, I came to understand the complexity of muscle memory. It was one thing to explain, say, a rather simple part of a swim stroke. It was another to execute it.

I made use of swimming boards during my lessons. They were (are) light-weight pieces of Styrofoam, about twelve inches wide and twenty-four inches long. My students used them to practice five leg movements: the sidestroke kick (also called the scissors kick), the crawl flutter kick, the backstroke flutter kick, the breaststroke kick, and the inverted breaststroke kick (floating on the back instead of the stomach).

After explaining the mechanics of a leg kick and then demonstrating it while out-of-water, the students would practice it on shore while lying on their sides, backs, or stomachs. I found this terrestrial task to be a useful tool. It was difficult to perform and was quickly tiring. I did not ask the students to spend much time on the side of the pool doing these routines; just enough for them to say upon entering the water, "Wow, it's much easier than I thought!" Aquatic bribery.

During the drills, a few of the students, holding onto their boards, would kick the daylights out of the water but remain immobile. One of my students managed to execute the frog kick and propel herself backwards! Others held on to their boards, executed the breaststroke kick but stayed in one place.

Their futile actions were amazing to watch. They executed the motions of the frog kick. Mechanically, they made the movements, but to no avail. It was obvious, even to me (a teenager at the time), that they had no idea of what they were supposed to be accomplishing. They were going through the motions. They could have held on to the swimming board executing the frog kick for 100,000 hours and never have advanced an inch.

No amount of repetition would alter their muscle memory of non-performance. It would only reinforce their inabilities. Perhaps the difference between enjoying, say, a sport and finding misery in it lies in accepting that sometimes, try as we may, we are destined to be average. I'm sure the acceptance of this fact of life would lead to fewer smashed golf clubs and tennis racquets.

Case Study: Julia Child

Julia Child was a cooking whiz. She is best known for her book *Mastering the Art of French Cooking*, and her how-to-cook TV shows. She has become a legend in American culture, not just for the ingredients in her recipes but the way she wrote them. How did she come to write such lucid, entertaining, informative, practical recipes? By determined study, motivated effort, and continuing to raise the threshold of excellence, by practice and repetition.

She also became an expert by paying attention to the details of her craft. As one example, because French flour and butter are made up differently from American flour and butter, Child discovered the French recipe for *béchamel* (white sauce) did not work in an American kitchen.[18] After many hours of experimentation and analysis, she came to understand that U.S. flour had much of its fat removed in order to extend its shelf life, and that U.S. butter had different levels of salt and fat than French butter. Eventually, she changed the ratio of flour to butter by a slight margin, resulting in a fine American *béchamel.*

Julia spent thousands of hours in the kitchen and in food markets. She spent time taking lessons. She taught Americans in Paris how to cook with French techniques. She learned French and became part of the French culture. She sought out fine cooks and learned their secrets. She graduated from the Cordon Bleu cooking school.

She said, "Sometimes...it takes me an entire day to write a recipe, to communicate it correctly. It's really like writing a little short story."[19] Yes, just for one recipe, perhaps consisting of a page or less of text.

Case Studies: Hometown Heroes

I have mentioned how talented some of my brothers were on the athletic fields. Three of them were high school "all-state" in one or more sports. Some had college athletic scholarships. One was named Athlete of the Year at his university. Two were voted all-conference in their college sports. Another was an All-American in junior college track and field.

They too served as role models, but in a different way. Perhaps one story will explain what I mean. My brother, Ross, played on a high school basketball team that won the New Mexico state championship. In those days (1949), the state's athletic programs had no divisions based on population or enrollment. Lovington, a backwater town, defeated school teams from large cities. This championship became the stuff of legends, and I recall watching the team play its games with this thought, *Can I do that?*

Our home had a backyard court. I practiced and practiced on this court. My brothers also played there. They were much older and bigger than I, so I was not allowed to play with them. The same situation existed for football, and track and field. I was on the periphery, watching my heroes in action, but never able to participate.

I don't mean to write sour grapes about my bothers. In comparison to them, I was inept. They had no idea of how much I wanted to play with them. After all, they were teenagers, how could they know much of anything? Nonetheless, watching Ross's state championship team play, I knew I also wanted to be something special. I was proud of my brothers, and I wanted them to be proud of me. Fortunately, I was into swimming by this time, and determined to carve out my own place in our family's trophy case.

Effortful Practice. My brother Tom is a naturally gifted athlete. As he grew older, he decided to replace pole vaulting and steer wrestling for hobbies that were easier on his body. At the age of 41 he took up the game of golf. During his first years of learning the game, he would practice so much he developed bloody calluses on his hands. He may not have made it to 10,000 hours, but he did put in the time. And it was not rote practice. He thought about the swing. He spent hours watching the pros.

When he was 65, he shot his age on a tight course, (The Cochiti Golf Course, Santa Fe, New Mexico, rating: 68.6-119). I played a round with him in Hawaii a couple years ago. On a difficult course (The Big Island Country Club, rating: 73.9-135) he shot one under his age: 71.

Does Tom have that magic touch? I suspect so, but he took no short cuts. He became a student of the game, and a frequent visitor to the driving range.

Motivated Practice. When my brother Ross was a teenager, he developed a love for track and field. His favorite events were the high jump and pole vault. He wanted to practice after hours on the school's fields, but they were in continuous states of disrepair.

Across the street from our home in town was a vacant lot. On this small pasture, Ross constructed a vaulting/jumping pit and a runway. He built a vaulting box and the supports for the cross bar. He borrowed the school's (Swedish Steel) vaulting pole and went to work.

In those days, synthetic foam had not yet been invented. The high quality vaulting and jumping pits located at major track and field venues were filled with sand. New Mexico had an abundance of sand, but Ross had no way to haul the sand to his private stadium. Without any other alternative, he broke dirt clods into smaller pieces and piled them up where he thought he would land.

Ross worked-out at this private arena almost every day. I watched him jump and vault—over and over again. He was motivated to work on technique, the approach, the lift, repetition in order to excel. If he could do it with a vaulting pole, I could do it with a frog kick.

Ross won a scholarship at a major university for his track and field abilities. He became a successful coach. He coached a U.S. National team that journeyed to the former USSR for a meet. His team won.

Smart Repetition

Bill Bowerman was the famous track and field coach of Oregon. (He was also the inventor of a runner's shoe that led to the creation of the Nike Company). His approach to training was revolutionary.[20] He gave his runners rest! Up to his time, the rule for coaching was to run the athlete ragged. The more exhausted he was, the more the athlete was learning. I can attest to this philosophy being prevalent in the sports industry. Some of my junior high and high school football coaches ran us into the ground. We had two-a-days under a hot New Mexico sun. No water until the practice was over. It is a wonder some of us didn't die. A lot of us became very sick.

Bowerman was different. He had his runners "practice smart." After a long run, or a series of sprints, he required them to rest:[21]

> Repetition work was revolutionizing running, as least in Eastern Europe. (Researchers) showed that dozens of repeated 200s increased the pumping power of the heart better than any other exercise....So, yes intervals worked. But there was a catch. Runners often improved their times dramatically for a few weeks or months.

Then, they would succumb to injury. Bowerman spent months analyzing the problem, and came up with solutions. He knew the "...answer had to include not only the right type and amount of work but also the right type and amount of rest to keep a runner from illness or injury."[22] Before long, he had tailored a program for each of his runners. Before long, his teams were winning national championships. He coached 16 sub-four-minute milers at the University of Oregon. He was the head U.S. Olympic coach. Sure, put in the time. But do it intelligently.

Another Case Study

Without realizing it at the time, my childhood and teenage efforts to emulate and master the frog stroke bears a close resemblance to Julia Child's passage from a non-cook to an accomplished chef. Forgive the stilted metaphor, but I went from a non-swimmer to a breaststroke gourmet. I will repeat a few thoughts about frogs that I have spoken-to earlier. I'll amplify these ideas with other observations.

After I had learned to swim, I began watching frogs even more closely. I was amazed by their leg power. With one thrust, they would shoot through the water as if they had pushed-off from the side of the tank. Even on land, their legs gave them great leaping ability, but it was their water work that held my interest.

Leg Kick. I could not come up with webbed feet and could never match the frog's kick. Thus, I began to experiment with my kick to at least make it more effective. I began with the positioning of my legs under my body as I began the kick. Laying face down in the water, I kept my arms to my sides, and tried different leg movements. After a while, I discovered that dropping the knees too deeply in the water pulled down my back and butt, thus negating some of the thrust of the kick. By bringing my legs forward toward my body in a more shallow position, I not only kept my body from sinking but I also expanded the arc of my leg thrust, resulting in more power and better acceleration through the water. However, if I made the arc too wide, the wide-spread legs slowed the momentum of the previous kick. I also discovered an excessively wide arc of the first part of the kick was not effective. There was too much angle and not enough leverage to generate power.

Arm Thrust. For the frog stroke, it matters a great deal how far the swimmer pulls his arms toward his body. Initially, I was taking my arms all the way to my legs. As I experimented, I found a better technique. As with the leg kick research, I took a face down floating position in the water. I kept my legs motionless, only using my hands and arms to provide power. I found I could gain more efficiency by bringing my arms inward and forward before they came to my sides. I made this discovery easily, as taking the arms all the way to the body was clearly inefficient. But it took time and effort to learn the technique. (This method is not favored by breaststroke swimmers who specialize in underwater swimming; a topic covered in Chapter 2.)

I kept a record of my experiments by tracking the distance my thrusts carried me. I placed markers on the bottom of the pool to record my experiments with kicks and arm pulls, and their resulting momentum. These efforts took a long time and a lot of practice to first discover and then incorporate into my muscle memory.

The Lifeguard Jump. The lifeguard jump is used by a swimmer to enter into unknown waters feet first, or to enter any water in order to keep sight of a distressed swimmer. I learned early the folly of diving headfirst into a place where I had never swum. I know of people who are paraplegics because of these dives.

The jump is executed by entering the water with the legs spread apart; forward and backwards, not side-ways. The arms are extended at a 45 degree angle from the armpits. As the jumper enters the water, he thrusts his legs together and pushes his arms to his sides.

It's a simple maneuver but to do it well—to keep the head above water and the eyes on the victim—requires coordination. For one thing, the best technique is to not create a splash in front of the jump that might obscure the sighting of the victim. The key is to *never* lose sight of the distressed person.

My swimming mate Jack and I practiced this jump off the side of the pool until it became routine. Then we tried it from the mid-height diving board (about 2 feet high). After a while, we were able to keep most of the splashing down and our heads up. With this success behind us, we worked on the lifeguard jump from the high board (ten feet high). This setup was much more difficult. The speed of our descent made it a challenge to keep our heads above water. In addition, it was difficult to prevent the water splash contained to the sides and back of our entry.

We tried and tried again. We never conquered the splash in front of us, but we were able to contain it somewhat by making a more vertical entry (a straight downward plunge) into the water. However, this trajectory, in contrast to an angled entry, resulted in an increased acceleration directly into the water, which made it almost impossible to keep our heads above the water.

But lacking television and MTV to divert us, we kept at it. Eventually, we were able to drop from ten feet, almost vertically, and keep our necks and heads above the water. Jack did it okay, but he was not a frog-kicker. I mastered the technique because of my frog kick. My frogs once again came to my aid.

No Short Cut

It took time and effort to learn to combine the leg and arm movements to gain the best possible combination for a breaststroke. It took Julia Child time and effort to learn the best combination of flour and butter for an American *béchamel.* It took time and effort to learn the lifeguard jump from a high dive board. It took Julia Child time and effort to learn to make a French-like pie crust from American flour. It took time and effort for Tom to learn to shoot his age on the golf course. It took time and effort for Ross to become the athlete of the year at a major university. There's no short cut.

---

[1] Philip E. Ross, "The Expert Mind," *Scientific American*, August, 2006, p. 69.

[2] Ross, ibid., p. 69.

[3] Sharon Begley, "Can you Build a Better Brain?", *Newsweek*, January 10 & 17, 2011, p. N43.

[4] Begley, ibid., p. N44. On the other hand, just because you have trained yourself to be a whiz in, say, basketball does not mean you will be a whiz in baseball. Competence from motivated repetition of shooting baskets does not generalize to competence in swinging bats. (See Michael Jordon).

[5] Begley, ibid., p. N43.

[6] Ross, ibid., p. 71.

[7] Malcolm Gladwell, *Outliers,The Story of Success*, Little, Brown, and Company, New York, 2008.

[8] Gladwell, ibid., p. 19.

[9] Gladwell, ibid., p. 55.

[10] Gladwell, ibid., p.167.

[11] David Brooks, "Lost in the Crowd," *The New York Times*, December 16, 2008, p. A37.

[12] Brooks, ibid., p. A37.

[13] This section and the next footnote is sourced from Cynthia Gorney, "Too young to Wed," *National Geographic*, June, 2011, pp. 79-99.

[14] And defenders of the practice state that an "elephant and rat" sexual act will never occur, because the groom promises to wait until his bride is "older." Even though the word older is not defined, it makes no difference. Nujood's new "mother-and sister-in-law examined the (wedding night) bloodied sheet approvingly before lifting her to give her a bath." The repulsive practice of child-rape is common in certain parts of the world.

[15] Brooks, ibid., p. A37.

[16] Gladwell, ibid., p. 38.

[17] Gladwell, ibid., p. 41.

[18] Julia Child, with Alex Prud'homme, *My Life in France*, Anchor Books, 2006, pp. 136 and 146.

[19] Microsoft ® Encarta ® 2006. © 1993-2005 Microsoft Corporation. All rights reserved.

[20] Bowerman did not invent these techniques, but he did refine them.

[21] Kenny Moore, *Bowerman and the Men of Oregon*, Holtzbrinck Publishers, 2006, p. 89.

[22] Moore, ibid., p. 90.

Chapter 4

Easley's Twin Lakes[1]

I am sufficiently young enough to know everything.
—anon

Wisdom is sparse. Why waste it on youth?
—anon

If I were not swimming in Dad's steel tanks and mud ponds, I was at the local pool at the idyllic Easley's Twin Lakes, a small marine resort three miles east of my home in town. I alternated my habitat. Sometimes, I lived at the ranch with Dad and my stepmom. Sometimes, I lived with Mom in town.

If Mom permitted, I would walk these three miles in the morning, swim all day, and walk back to my home in the late afternoon. By this time, I was usually red-skinned toast, leading to my body eventually becoming a fertile garden for basal cells. In those days, sun block did not exist. We kids rubbed baby oil and iodine on our bodies to attract the sun's rays. No umbrellas and few hats. I was often in the sun from 8 am to 5 pm.

I use the word idyllic to describe the Lakes. In my youthful, naïve eyes, they were that and more. I spent as much time as possible at the swimming pool or in one of the lakes at Easley's, often staying in the water all day.

John Easley was as important to my swimming life as Tudy and frogs, the models for my swim strokes. He was instrumental to my becoming an accomplished swimmer, because he created Easley's Twin Lakes. These lakes were my Disney Land, Sea World, Water Park, and Lake Mead, all rolled up into two tiny bodies of water and a swimming pool.

Easley's lakes would be classified as ponds by most folks. Each measured about two football fields across their widest parts. But to Lea County citizens, having no other significant bodies of water nearby, we were proud to call them lakes. The lakes formed natural pools of water and over many centuries, they evolved to become leak free reservoirs. Nonetheless, their surface water evaporated in the county's arid air, so John kept them full with a frequent infusion of fresh water.

The swimming pool was a large one. As mentioned earlier, it measured about 110 feet in length, with a depth of 10 feet in the diving area. John positioned the pool as a peninsula into one of the lakes, as shown in Figure 4-1. The citizens called this lake the ski lake because it was used for boating and water skiing. Notice the lake at the top of the photo, surrounding three sides of the pool. (A small circle has been drawn around a metal rail next to steps at the shallow end of the pool. In Chapter 6, I will explain why I highlighted the rail.)

I began swimming at John's pool as a customer. Later, I had the good fortune to be employed as a lifeguard and swimming instructor. Still later, I became the manager of the pool. As I unfold the experiences and adventures at this fanciful place, I will describe them in the context of all four of my roles: swimmer, lifeguard, instructor, and pool manager.

Draining the Pool

Originally, the pool had no chemical, filter, or heating systems. (Later, John added a dangerous, jury-rigged Chlorine system to his list of inventions.) We lifeguards kept the pool fresh with frequent, cold water recharges, straight from the earth through one of John's irrigation pumps. But this system was inadequate for keeping the water fresh. On Monday, after refilling the pool, the water was as clear and fresh as it could be. But with each day, the swimmers' suntan lotions and skin oils gradually contaminated the water and stained the sides of the pool.

As a consequence of these emollients, each Sunday night we drained the pool's murky water and scrubbed down the pool's sides. Afterwards, using John's irrigation pumps, we filled up the pool during late Sunday night and early Monday morning.

The task made for a tiring day. Every inch of the oily water line on the cement sides had to be scoured with a brush and Comet Cleaner. The bottom had to be swept down to remove dead leaves and other offerings from Mother Nature and the swimmers. We rarely finished the draining and cleaning before midnight.

Figure 4-1. The swimming pool.

The draining of the pool began late Sunday afternoon. The weekend crowd had departed for evening church services, but a few malingers stayed in the water until we chased them away. During this time, John's powerful drainage pump was working full time, pulling the water from the pool and pumping it into the lake.

During the later hours of those Sunday afternoons, we kept a closer watch on the swimmers in the deep end. The suction of the pump could pull an unwary person down to the drain, which was located at the bottom of the pool. A reasonably competent swimmer with an engaged mind could easily overcome the suction and make his way out of the whirlpool. An unwary, weak swimmer was in danger. As the water was drained from the pool, the confined swimming areas increased the chances of a swimmer encountering the pump's pull down effects.

We lifeguards, acting as a prototype OSHA, would whistle or shout people away from the drainage area. No one drowned. We had a few minor scares, but nothing serious. Common sense came to the fore. People, not Uncle Sam, assumed responsibility for taking care of each other and themselves.

Risky Business

On these Sunday afternoons, after the swimmers had left the pool, one of the other lifeguards and I would play a game of "I dare you." (The boy was named H. P. Harris, and plays another role in this story shortly.) With the water reduced to a low level and becoming lower with each passing moment, we would dive from the 10-foot board into about four feet of water. Because of the low water level, the dive was closer to 15 feet in height. My friend came across this idea after watching a movie of a circus performer diving from a high platform into a small tank of water. He suggested we could do it, too.

I was skeptical. The high distance dive into four feet of water did not concern me. A flat dive, even though it might sting when entering the water, would not require much water to absorb the acceleration of the plunge. However, as Figure 4-2 illustrates, John's design of the pool bottom placed the steep slant of the floor underneath the landing zone of a dive (shown with the dotted line). Granted, this example shows a far-reaching dive from the board, but with a shallower depth (bold wave lines in the figure), a dive would direct the diver toward the slanted floor.

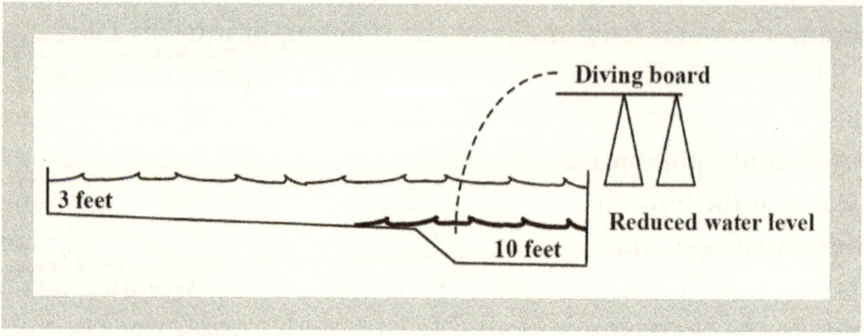

Figure 4-2. Diving into shallow water.

Looking back on these times, I question my intelligence, if not my intelligence, certainly my judgment. I write this part of the book, not in bravado, but in wonderment of a young person's foolishness. H.P. was a small, compact boy, and he had an uncanny ability to dive shallow from high heights. I was not big, but a bit gangly. Try as I did, I could not keep my dives as shallow as those of H.P.

One Sunday afternoon, H.P was feeling his oats. After each spectacular circus dive into yet shallower water, he would surface and shout, "Your turn!" *Shit.*

I should have said, "H.P., you're crazy," and went about the business of scrubbing Coppertone from the sides of the pool. But I was the *head lifeguard*. And I was a better diver than H.P. Even though I was risking losing my face, how could I risk losing face?

As the water depth dropped, it became necessary to make *very sure* we kept our arms in front of us at all times during the entry. We used our hands to brace our head from hitting the pool's bottom. How stupid is that? I am almost embarrassed to write about it.

I've read something to the effect that, "Pride precedes a fall." On that Sunday afternoon my pride got in the way of common sense. As H.P. made each successful plunge, I hurried up the ladder to the diving board to take another dive before the water became even shallower. On my last dive, the force of my acceleration collapsed my arms and my face hit the bottom of the pool. It is a wonder my neck was not damaged. I came out of the water with a broken nose.

I was very lucky. The danger was past but not forgotten. I never played dare-devil-diving again. To this day, the cartilage between my two nostrils resembles a corrugated piece of tin with resultant labored breathing. I deserved it.

Cold Water and a Dangerous Bridge

For the next two days after the cleaning, the pool attracted masochists, the physically comatose, profoundly hung-over drinkers, and people who were unaware of how cold water from the earth was. As I recall, the water came out of a pipe into the pool at a temperature in the mid-60 degrees range. Whatever the temperature, my most difficult teaching day was Tuesday. It was not an unusual occurrence when students refused to enter the water (especially the younger children). They were not necessarily afraid of the water; they were afraid of its temperature.

In addition to the hypothermia-inducing water, another unique feature of Easley's was a small island placed in the ski lake with an elegant suspension bridge connecting the island to the main shore. The island measured about 100 feet across and was graced by a large Weeping Willow tree. Figure 4-3 does not do justice to this lovely bridge, but my rendition is sufficient to draw your attention to the height of the tallest part of the bridge to the water: about six feet, perhaps a few inches more. The restricted clearance meant a skier had to exercise caution and ski directly under the bridge in a stooping position. If the skier were on either side of this center, bending-down was not an option, it was essential for survival.

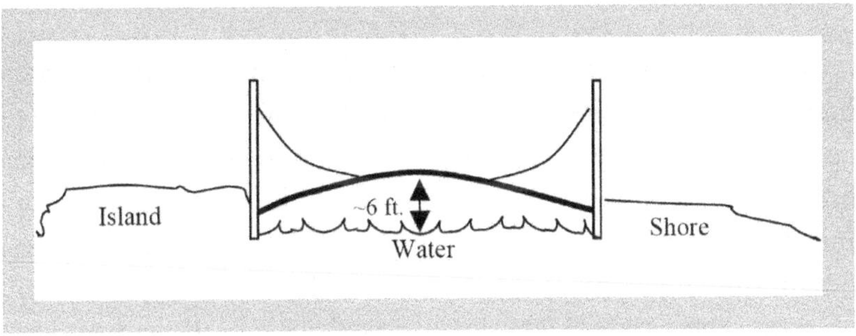

Figure 4-3. The suspension bridge.

A Dangerous Lake?

John charged a fee for the use of the lake. A boater would pay the money to an attendant and gain an all day pass. During the weekends and on holidays, the ski lake was crowded with boats and skiers. It was dangerous to be on the lake during the busy times. Keep in mind the small size of the lake. Take into account that ten to fifteen boats—piloted by beer drinking helmsmen—would be circling the lake, one behind the other, most of them towing a skier.

Accidents were not unusual. I witnessed several serious injuries during my summers at Easley's. The lake sometimes resembled a scene from an aquatic Keystone Cops movie. Here are examples of accidents:

- A downed skier was hit by a trailing boat; the boat's blade cut deeply into his shoulder.

- A skier ran into the suspension bridge; he suffered severe head injuries.

- A boat and its skier collided into the island, minor damages to the driver; the skier escaped unscathed.

- A boat collided with another boat, injuries ranged from bruised pride to broken bones.

- A boat crashed into the swimming pool area.

The latter accident occurred while I was sitting in the lifeguard chair at the end of the pool—the end that jutted into the lake (see Figure 4-1). Imagine my surprise when a high speed boat crashed through the wooden fence surrounding the pool—BAM!—and landed on the pool's deck, about four feet from my chair.

After the flying pieces of the fence had settled, I looked over to the boat. Three passengers slowly raised their heads and peeked a view. They saw surprised swimmers and hundreds of pieces of wood, floating in the pool or resting on the pool deck. The driver was the last to emerge. His grin disappeared when he discovered several gaping holes in his boat's bow.

A Dangerous Swimming Pool?

To further enhance the recreational risks at Easley's, John installed a water slide on the north side of the swimming pool, at an oblique angle to the pool's side. Figure 4-1 shows the bottom of the slide on the left side of the picture, as well as a typical Sunday afternoon crowd.

The baby pool is at the bottom of the picture. The lifeguard chair where I watched the boat crash through the fence is at the upper right in the picture. Your writer is the boy standing at the baby pool looking out over the big pool. A fellow lifeguard is to my right, kibitzing with me but not watching the baby pool, which was his duty.

This slide was not like those you see today in amusement parks. It was a playground slide—no sides, no protective awning—nothing to prevent a person from falling off the slide onto the cement deck of the pool. The sliding area was kept wet with a rubber hose, extended to the top of the slide, about 18 feet high. The water ran down into the pool, keeping the sliding area wet and slick.

Several of the swimmers at Easley's became accomplished slide "jumpers." We would stand at the top of the slide and leap down toward the water, with our knees bent to receive the slide. A good jump carried us almost to the end of the slide. The resulting acceleration catapulted us almost into the middle of the pool. Because I hung out at the pool for many hours, I had a lot of time to practice these jumps and I became an adroit slide performer.

Serious injuries occurred on the slide. I am surprised no one was killed. Several times, we lifeguards had to take care of people who had fallen off the slide onto the pool deck, "U.D., break out the Iodine. Wayne fell off the slide...left most of his skin on the concrete."

"U.D., Get on your clothes. Jimmy broke his arm on the slide. Take him to the doctor."

I am not exaggerating these injuries. Serious accidents also occurred on the high diving board. We kids used it as a surrogate trampoline, bouncing on it four to six times until we were suspended some three feet above the ten foot diving platform. Then, executing varying numbers of somersaults, we entered into the pool's ten foot depth. On more than one occasion, we broke the board in half, much to the chagrin of John and Mrs. Camp—and perhaps to us as well, depending on how and where we came down.

One boy broke his ankle and suffered head and body lacerations by missing a jump on the board. After several springs, he came down a bit crooked. Losing his balance and falling backwards, his body hit a hand rail positioned on the side of the board. He rebounded off this railing, allowing gravity to fulfill its job description, to land partially in the water and partially on the side of the pool. Sitting on the lifeguard stand, I was a witness to his aerial maneuvers and crash landing—a messy scene.

In spite of our injuries, and without the supposed wisdom that comes with adulthood, we kids kept performing our daredevil jumps from the water slide and our trampoline jumps from a non-trampoline. To this day, I carry marks on my knees that are the result of my hundreds of water slide jumps.

The Baby Pool

The baby pool is shown at the bottom of Figure 4-1. Notice the children playing in the pool. A cheerful aquatic ambience: Small *Homo sapiens*, rekindling their primordial dispositions toward liquid environments. Not to mention vetting their bowels and kidneys in accordance with Mother Nature's dictates.

On more than one occasion, I would scoop up the toilet deposits of one of the children, who had exited the baby pool, dropped his pants, and made his contributions to the food chain cycle.

However, my poolside pickup was better than making retrieval from the pool water itself—a task requiring closing the pool, draining the water, and refilling it with a fresh supply of John's almost icy water. On two occasions, nocturnal troublemakers sneaked over the pool fence and made their offerings to the water of the big pool. I had the job of cleaning it up. Who said the job of a lifeguard was glamorous?

A lifeguard was required to watch the baby pool even though only one baby might be in it. To see why, Figure 4-4 shows a side view of the pool. John had not attended the OSHA School for Keeping Americans Safe. His baby pool bottom was the same design as the large pool: A shallow end, gradually tampering down to more depth, followed with an abrupt, steep slope. The large pool started at three feet, gradually tapered down to five feet and suddenly dropped-off to ten feet. The baby pool started at 12 inches, tapered down to 18 inches and suddenly dropped-off to around two feet. The children often walked down the gradual slope, unaware of the sudden decline, and then toppled-off into the deeper water. We lifeguards rescued more victims from the baby pool than from the main pool.

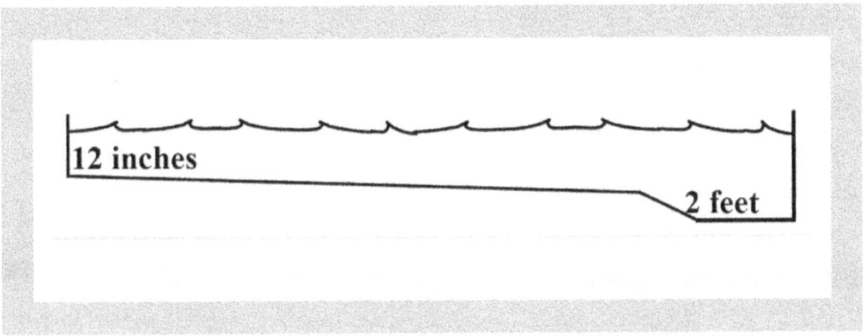

Figure 4-4. Sideview of baby pool.

Fourth of July Festivities at Easley's

Many Lea County citizens spent the July 4th holiday at the lakes. They arrived early in the morning to reserve choice spots and stake their claims around the lakes' shores. The goal was to secure a prime place for viewing the evening's fireworks display. By midmorning, the shores, the swimming pool, and all picnic tables were packed with people.

The pool manager (Mrs. Camp) organized swimming contests and awarded medals to those who won a race. Ribbons were also given to second and third place finishers. A lifeguard colleague I mentioned earlier was named H. P. Harris. He was a short boy with undersized legs, but his shoulders, chest, and arms were huge. H.P. swam with no lower body movement whatsoever, as if his legs were trailing, useless pieces of string. I instructed him on how to use a flutter kick but he responded that a foot kick slowed him down. He demonstrated, and sure enough, he swam faster without the use of his legs—faster than anyone I had met.

H.P.'s style and strength almost propelled him out of the water. Watching him sprint across the pool reminded me of a Saturday afternoon movie cartoon in which a character boosts himself onto the water's surface with his arm actions. I never knew what his initials meant but I called my friend Horse Power Harris, because of the phenomenal strength of his crawl stroke. I admired that man's uncanny swimming ability almost as much as I admired Tudy's swim suit.

On one 4th of July, H.P. won the freestyle race and I won the breaststroke contest. With two other lifeguards hired for the day, we also won medals in the relay races. Our opponents complained to Mrs. Camp that the lifeguards should not be allowed to compete in the holiday contests, but to no avail. We had the home field advantage.

As the July 4th day came to an end, we would close the pool and head for a place to watch the fireworks. I usually drifted over to the island or to a location populated with some of the girls who had just left the swimming area.

John shot-off the fireworks in such a way that they would ignite and explode over the middle of the ski lake. The scene was reminiscent of a Norman Rockwell painting: Cars parked around the lakes, folks sitting on blankets next to the water, some munching on chicken, others drinking soda and beer—gasping, shouting, and laughing at each incendiary display. It was a happy, tranquil, and yes, idyllic time in my life and the lives of those celebrating the 4th at Easley's.

Hazards but no Lawsuits

In today's culture, Easley's pool and lakes could not exist. They would have been closed down by OSHA-type agencies or forced to shut their operations due to exorbitant insurance fees. No question, skiing, swimming, diving, and boating could be risky ventures, but the customers accepted the risks. I know of no injury related lawsuits brought against John and his tiny resort.

Comparing the Jobs of Roustabout and Lifeguard

One summer, I asked Mrs. Camp for a week off from my swimming pool job. I wanted to work in the oil fields. Even now, I wonder what possessed me to seek such a diversion. I worked for two days with a seismograph crew and for the remainder of the week I toiled away as a roustabout, the lowest position in the oilfield social register. The roustabout was a jack-of-all-trades position. The work was dirty and exhausting. The job consisted of digging ditches, assembling or disassembling pumps and tanks, and cleaning sludge from the bottom of the oil tanks. After the week was over, I happily returned to my job at the pool, and continued my so-called "work" as a lifeguard.

Words cannot describe the differences between the jobs of a roustabout and a lifeguard. But I will try. The table below provides a summary of why I stayed away from the oil fields as much as possible and why I stayed in the lifeguard business for as long as possible.

Leaving Home and Coming Back

I worked as a lifeguard in my home town through parts of my high school summers and several of my college summers. After Mrs. Camp left the swimming pool, I was hired by John Easley to manage the pool. This promotion gave me the authority to hire lifeguards, manage the concession stand, and create my own swimming lesson program. The program introduced me to teaching, writing, and public speaking. It also provided a perverse amount of money for a college lad. During these times, I kept up my swimming exercises at home and college, stories for later chapters.

---

[1] Parts of this chapter are also in *The Light Side of Little Texas.*

Job Attribute	Oil Field Roustabout	Country Club Lifeguard
Danger to life and limb	Above the national average.	Very little, as long as I stayed out of the water.
Sanitary conditions	Far below the national average, but above that of garbage collection.	Excellent, given all that Chlorine.
Calories burned per hour	Far above the national average for menial work.	Perhaps a few hundred, just to keep my eyes open, and lungs and heart pumping.
Ambience of work place	Below the jobs of garbage collectors and dog catchers.	What can I say? It was a country club swimming pool.
Chances of encountering the opposite sex	Very high, if one was not too concerned about the species encountered in a pasture.	What can I say? It was a country club swimming pool.
Chances of doing any good once the opposite sex (of the same species) was encountered.	Non-existent.	What can I say? It was a country club swimming pool.
Remuneration	About the same as dog catchers.	Who cares? It was a country club swimming pool. Anyway, for swimming lessons: obscene rates of return.
Status of job	Between that of dog catchers and garbage collectors.	Higher than investment bankers —admittedly, a low bar for comparison.

Chapter 5

Water Safety Instructor

Those who lead often make the least noise.
—anon

After Tudy had moved away from Lovington, and after I secured the head lifeguard job (boss of one other lifeguard, except on weekends), four people paid me a call. They were Red Cross representatives from Roswell, New Mexico, a community 100 miles west of Lovington. They had come over to evaluate my swimming program.

Figure 5-1. The WSI badge.

By this time I was giving private swimming lessons but they were not sanctioned by the Red Cross. I was not a certified Red Cross Water Safety Instructor (WSI) and that was the reason for their visit. They invited me to spend a week in Roswell to train and take the WSI test. I was dumbstruck. I might become a Red Cross Water Safety Instructor! I could wear the same badge as Tudy. (See Figure 5-1). I accepted their offer and hired a high school friend to help my (only) assistant lifeguard to protect Easley's Twin Lake swimmers.

My First Encounter with a UDT Frogman

While at the pool in my hometown, one of the Roswell couples joined me for a swim. We chatted while we took some leisurely laps. They asked how I became a swimmer. I told them about my frogs. They seemed to be amused by the story of my amphibian breaststroke teachers. I told them about the swimming exercises Jack and I invented and my wish to join the UDT. They were pleasant enough, but offered no feedback about my ambition, at least not on that day.

As the week in Roswell unfolded, my four mentors and I became friends. I was a guest at the home of the couple who had swum with me. They worked me hard each day and fed me generously each night. The husband was named Steve. He was a quiet person, but a pleasant sort of guy. I asked him a couple times about his swimming background but he did not have much to say.

One morning Steve asked if I wanted to go for a run. We did. The next morning we went to a gym. There, we worked with weights, and carried out rope climbs and chin-ups. After these workouts, we would head for the swimming pool for more training.

At the end of the week, after the tests were successfully completed, the three of us were having a celebratory dinner at my hosts' home. At this time, Steve informed me he was a former member of the UDT. I almost dropped my fork! I had been showing off my skills all week, thinking I was more froggy than anyone nearby. Yet, very nearby was an honest to God live UDT warrior.

I asked, "Why didn't you tell me about your background when I told you about my plans?"

Steve, "I didn't want to make it an issue. It might have made you nervous."

An understatement.

Steve, "Your telling me about your goal is the reason we took a run and worked out at the gym. To make it in UDT, you have to be a good swimmer, a strong runner, and be able to make it through a tough obstacle course. You need a good head about you and you must have a lot of stamina. That's another reason I've not told you. I wanted to observe. You were slated to stay (at the other couple's house), but after my swim with you at your pool, the four of us talked it over and made the switch. We were impressed with your WSI test today."

I had been under the microscope for almost a week. I said, "If I had known I would be rescuing a UDT swimmer this morning, I don't know how I would have handled it."

Steve, "You and your classmates had enough pressure as it was. Anyway, if you decide to go into the program, your swimming will be your strong suit. Your crawl is strong. Forget about your backstroke. You won't be tested on those strokes anyway."

"Really?"

"Your trials will be in the breaststroke and sidestroke. (My strongest strokes.) Your run was fine. The rope climb was good (I had executed a lot of rope climbs in PE classes). The obstacle course requires a lot of upper body pull ups, not only from ropes but poles and bars as well."

"I'll start doing chins and buy some weights."

"Don't worry about the weights. You did okay at the gym. Many muscle bound guys don't make it through UDT. They're too bulky to run and swim. The chinning bar pull ups will help you with the obstacle course. They're important."

"You keep mentioning the obstacle course."

"For good reason."

Steve continued, "The UDT program puts the week you had here to shame. I wouldn't encourage you to pursue it if I didn't think you had it in you. But don't think it will be easy. Your 'rescue' today is a piece of cake compared to what you will go through."

"I'll be ready."

I returned to Lovington as a Red Cross Water Safety Instructor. The day after my arrival, I installed a chinning bar at the swimming pool.

The Distressed, Panicked Swimmer Rescue Test

Before moving on, I'll describe one of the tests the candidates had to pass to be awarded a Red Cross WSI certificate. It was the rescue of a distressed, panicked swimmer. The victim was Steve. Now you may appreciate why I was thankful I did not know his background.

Three other students were in the class. Two men were from Roswell. Another was from Artesia, a small town nearby. After taking written tests and several in-water trials on strokes and the tired swimmer carry, Steve entered the water and we began the distressed, panicked swimmer rescue test.

While Steve treaded water in the middle of the pool, his colleagues explained he would sometimes resist being approached, sometimes not. He would sometimes challenge us after we had him in our grasp, sometimes not. We did not know what to expect. While we were given these warnings I watched Steve watching us. I will never forget this moment. He had a slight grin on his face; his treading was effortless. *I'm waiting—come on in suckers*! He was a big man and this was a big deal in my life.

Lucky for me I was not the first victim of the victim. The first candidate jumped into the water (a lifeguard jump) and swam to Steve. After some rather easy looking jousting, Steve was taken into tow with the man's arm around Steve's chest, a technique described earlier. Without warning, Steve rotated the top part of his body, taking himself out of the grasp of the rescuer. Just as suddenly, he grabbed the former rescuer's body and pulled him under the water. Next candidate.

For the second rescuer, Steve did not allow the man to gain a hold on him. As the lifeguard was about to engage him, Steve executed a powerful leg kick, almost catapulting himself out of the water onto the startled rescuer, who just as suddenly had a new job description. Next candidate.

I was miffed at Steve for his actions against the second student. It was unfair to assume any drowning person would have the wits, strength, and ability to make the maneuver Steve made against this man. The first man's failure was fair. From my training with Tudy, I learned how difficult and dangerous it could be to maintain a hold on the victim while swimming to the shore. I said to myself, *If Steve tries that on me, I'm going to grab his balls.*

Next candidate. Into the water I went, adrenaline working overtime. I approached Steve as he mimicked a panicked person, splashing and yelling a lot. As I was wondering what to do, what type of approach maneuver to make, Steve helped my decision by lunging at me. The second candidate made a mistake when Steve made this same move. He tried to keep his head above water while contending with Steve.

As mentioned, Tudy taught her lifeguards: If the victim gets a hold on you, go under the water. Fast! (She did not cover the balls-grabbing protocol; that was my own invention.) The last thing the drowning person is going to do is follow you under the surface of the water.

However, this maneuver is more difficult to execute than it might appear. How do you go under the water when another person is using you as a life buoy? You put your legs together, if possible place both your arms to your side, then do a arm-like frog stroke, thrusting your arm(s) upward. Without exception, you will go down.

Almost without exception the victim will let go, as he or she will choose to stay on the surface. I say "almost." Mrs. Camp was an exception. During the drills at my home pool, on more than one occasion, she succeeded in grabbing me. Try as I did, my downward trusts had no effect. This woman would not only maintain her grip, she would remain on the surface. It was akin to forcing a balloon under the water. The good news is that as long as Mrs. Camp had a hold of me, neither of us was in trouble, because she acted as a floating dirigible.

But not Steve. He was lean. He and I could not float on our backs without our noses going under the water. (To have that body mass index now.)

Steve made his lunge. I went down but he did not bother to go underwater with me (which he could have done, but would have been unfair). With a couple strokes I was able to get around behind him. I came to the surface and secured the cross-arm hold around his chest. He made my day, "Good work." That is, he almost made my day. He followed his compliment with, "Now tow me in if you can."

You bet I will. I was not going to allow Steve to get out of my grasp. The side of the pool was only 20 or so feet away. So, I placed *both* my arms around *both* sides of Steve's chest. Instead of swimming a modified sidestroke with one arm, I swam on my back with just my legs, executing an inverted breaststroke kick, while I kept Steve under lock and arms.

I surprised him. Just as soon as I had secured my second (right) hand underneath his left armpit, he tried to rotate, but he couldn't. I had him. He thrashed about but he had no leverage. He could not reach up to my head. His legs and hips could not twist his body around without assistance from his upper torso. It was not all that difficult to swim to the nearby pool side. I could not have kept this up for a long time, but we were in a pool, not a lake. I made it to the side with Steve still kicking up a fuss, but defeated!

At the side of the pool, we coughed and hacked our way to aerobic recovery. Steve was smiling but it was a perplexed smile. He asked, "Where did you learn that?"

Jack and I had practiced this hold for hours. It had evolved from our good spirited, aquatic combats with each other. We had discovered that after either of us gained this hold on the other, it could not be broken.

I responded to Steve, "Just something I picked up while fooling around."

The truth is, I carried off this feat because I had a worked for hundreds of hours developing a strong leg kick, and I had practiced the cross hold many times.

There's no short cut.

Chapter 6

College Days, Water Polo, and Overcoming Handicaps

None is a fool always, everyone sometimes.
—George Herbert[1]

Because I competed against untrained swimmers in my youth, I reached a possibly faulty conclusion that my abilities were well above average. Not outlier-like, maybe on the periphery. Nonetheless, I earned my growing self confidence. I like golfer Gary Player's answer to a heckler, who accused him of being "lucky."

"Yep," he replied, "and the more I practice, the luckier I get."

I graduated from high school and headed for the University of New Mexico, in Albuquerque. As mentioned, during my college days, I returned to Lovington during the summers to work as a lifeguard and swimming instructor. For this part of the story, I'll tell you about my first day at college. Later in this chapter, we return to my hometown swimming pool and recount times I spent there between college years.

Swimming with the Freshman Swim Team

After stowing my gear in the dormitory, I made my way to the swimming pool, an outdoor facility located behind the university gym. My attention was drawn to one side of the pool, which had been roped off. Several boys were swimming warm up laps. I walked over and introduced myself to the group.

The swimmers were members of the freshmen swim team who had recently arrived on campus. Two of these men were from New York and were attending UNM on swimming scholarships. They automatically assumed position number five on my list of admired swimmers, just behind UDT, Tudy, Steve, and frogs.

After chatting a bit, I was invited to join the swimmers in their reserved area. Before long, they began to swim competitive sprints and I was asked to join. My unexpressed thought was, *yes, absolutely!* My response was, "Sure, thanks."

I readied myself to embark on my next swimming challenge. I was excited about testing my skills against gifted swimmers—collegiate athletes, some with swimming scholarships to a major university. I knew I could swim long and hard. I knew I had stamina. I was eager to learn if I could also swim fast.

Our first races were one lap. The crawl (free style) started the contests. Tudy had taught me the racing dive and I got off okay. Four swimmers were in the race. I finished a respectable third. Fine. The crawl was not my specialty. I was waiting for the breaststroke.

The butterfly was next but I did not participate. The swimmers were puzzled, so I explained my Red Cross training and my teacher's bias against the butterfly. I think they were more puzzled by my explanation. They had not been trained by the Red Cross and were able to swim all the strokes. I watched them swim this race. I had never seen anyone execute the butterfly so well. It is the most beautiful stroke of any, and I wish I had learned it. I admired and envied their versatility.

The butterfly race was over. The last two races were to be the breaststroke, followed by the backstroke. My backstroke was barely passable and I finished last in this race. It is the breaststroke race that serves as the climax to this part of the story.

Four of us lined up on the pool's edge to begin the race. Off we went, hitting the water at about the same time. I took an early lead and never relinquished it. I won the race. I was well ahead of two swimmers as I touched the other end of the pool. The second place swimmer was about a half-body length behind me.

As we caught our breath and got out of the pool to walk back to our towels, one of my competitors put his hand on my shoulder and said, "You should be on our team. You just beat the man who has a breaststroke scholarship." The defeated breaststroke specialist who had come in second was equally gracious.

Fantastic! My dedication, my training, my thousands of weight laden laps had paid off—not to mention the contributions of Tudy, John Easley, Jack, Mrs. Camp, Steve, and of course, the frogs on a ranch in Lea County.

Later, we swam a two lap breaststroke race and I lost. I did not know how to execute a racing turn and relinquished the lead on the return lap. I finished second behind the breaststroke specialist. My swimming mates were puzzled by my racing turn, or lack thereof. I suspect they were amazed by my one dimensionality.

It was of no importance. The UDT did not need swimmers who swam the butterfly or executed fast sprint turns. The Team needed swimmers of strength, stamina, and speed. When this afternoon was over, I knew I possessed all three.

And Tudy? My black suited beautiful, powerful, lovely hero. Where are you today? I would like tell you how much you helped me overcome my doubts, how you helped me learn I could indeed excel. I learned I could fanaticize in more ways than one.

Swim Team Tryout

At the suggestions of these men, I looked-up the freshman swim team coach. I told him about my background and the impressive medals I earned at the Easley's Twin Lakes July 4th Swim Meet. I explained my Red Cross background. He was not impressed and obliquely offered he did not know why I was in his office. I then understood the swimmers at the pool had not told him about our races. I was a walk-in wannabe. Were the swimmers just being polite? I never knew.

I think of myself as a contradictory blending of competitiveness and lethargy. For some of the time, I consider being competitive as little more than tiring. Why bother? But for other times, I get stoked. Part of the stoking can occur when I think someone is dismissing me without seeing what I have to offer. My competitive juices kick in and I want to show them that I am better than they think me to be. Maybe not the best, but at least a bit better.

For this encounter, I was puzzled by the coach's behavior. I had bested his freshman breaststroke swimmer. I mentioned the races to him, but he still seemed uninterested. It could have been that he was preoccupied with something else and was not paying attention to this uninvited stranger. Nonetheless, I did not want to walk out of his office without some sort of resolution, however small it might be.

But I was confused. I wanted to become part of a fantastic swim fantasy. A whole pool of Jacks and Steves! It was almost beyond my comprehension that I could be part of such an assemblage.

But I could. I had put in the time. And time expended in New Mexico waters was no different from time spent in New York waters. Regardless of the location, it was the effort spent in the water that mattered.

I asked the coach if he would at least time me on a swim test. … "Do you have your suit?"

"Yes."

"Okay, let's give it a go."

Knowing my racing turn problems, I asked for a one lap test. I aced it. The coach responded, "Okay, let's try 50 and 100." I did not do as well. I would come up to the end of the pool and execute an inefficient delay in getting my body turned around.

The coach, knowing of my Red Cross training, told me, "I can teach you the turn; it takes some practice to get it down, but it's not very difficult to execute. I'd like you to start swimming with the freshman team. But I've no more scholarships for this year."

Nothing ventured on his part, no money out of UNM's pocket for a prospect that might make the team. What's one more swimmer? Nonetheless, I was excited to be invited. I was in a state of disbelief.

But logistics got in the way. I had to keep my part time jobs.

The coach told me the freshman swimming program consumed around two hours of training each week day and two to three hours each Sunday afternoon. During the week, the members would swim in the early morning or late afternoon. I was working in the cafeteria to earn my meals and delivering flowers to earn money. I had almost no free time except to go to class and study.

I did not respond to the coach's news. I should have known the program would be time consuming. After all, that is what I had done—put in the time to become a swimmer. I was not thinking clearly. I was taken with the prospect of belonging to a college swim team. Teenage befuddlement.

I left the gym and made my way back to the dorm. I asked myself why I had not thought of seeking-out a college program, say, a year ago? But such a notion was not on my horizon. I never conceived of it, and I'll never know why. Perhaps it was because my limited small town horizons constrained my vista of options. It's been said, "We should not constrain ourselves because of our circumstances," but how are we to know what might lie beyond them?

Tudy might have proctored me to do so. So might have Steve. But they were temporary presences in my life. They were out of my sight and I was out of their minds. (I have not seen them since my teen years. After a classmate sent Tudy's address to me, I tried to correspond with her. She never responded.)

I had no choice. I had to eat and I needed pocket money. My father had paid my tuition and books for my first year in college. After that, I was on my own. That was our agreement. I would never have asked him to come forth with more support.

The next day I called the coach and told him I would not be swimming with the freshman team. I explained the situation. He listened and responded, "How's your crawl?"

"Not bad. I beat one of your team members."

"You might think of water polo. There's some teams in Albuquerque, part of the AAU system. They're always looking for new talent." He added, "And the sport doesn't require a racing-turn." Ha.

"What's their training schedule?"

"Pretty much what each man can do. Most of the swimmers have full time jobs. Many aren't students. Interested?"

I had never played water polo. I had never seen water polo being played.

I answered, "I think so."

The coach gave me the phone number of a man who had put together one of the teams. I thanked him, we said our goodbyes, and I headed for the school library to read up on water polo.

As the semester progressed, I watched the freshman swim team members go back and forth between the dorm and the gym. As it turned out, I was not all that disappointed about not swimming with them, especially after getting into water polo. I did not like the regimen required of the swim team program. But I have learned something about myself in this regard. I don't like anyone's regimen but my own. As I went through life, my professional jobs gradually culled down occupations that entailed other people setting my agenda. I am sure that is one reason my final job was occupying the single position of a one person company.

Water Polo

Water polo is a contest of throwing an inflated ball into a net that is positioned at the end of the pool. To understand the idea, think of a field soccer net. The water polo net is much smaller, but the strategy is the same. Two teams (one goalie and six field players) try to advance the ball toward their net. The other team tries to stop them and steal the ball in order to turn the tables.

The field players are not allowed to use the sides or bottom of the pool for support. (No racing-turns.) The man in possession of the ball can place only one hand on the ball at a time. He advances the ball by passing it to a teammate, or by swimming a heads-up crawl with the ball floating between his moving arms. The technique was one of my specialties: my Tarzan crawl.

If he passes the ball to a teammate, the receiver must catch the ball with one hand, or have the ball drop down near him, by deflecting it with one hand. The ball cannot be pushed under the water.

The ball is put into play by a referee tossing it into the middle of the pool. The opposing teams swim toward the ball. The first man to reach the ball usually throws it back to a teammate. This action initiates the tactics to try to score a goal. The game is divided into four 7-minute quarters, with a 2-minute rest break between quarters.

A Water Polo Adult League

I made contact with the "coach" of a water polo team. I place the word coach in quotation marks because he was not a coach in the conventional sense. He organized the team's workouts and games so he himself could play. In our (rather rare) practices, he would occasionally offer a comment about tactics. But the team members were casual about it all. We were not out to win a gold medal at the Olympics. The team was similar to the night league teams in other sports. The coach put the players in and out (including himself), but the arrangement was largely egalitarian.

I liked the setup, the loose schedule, and the game itself. No boss to speak of. If I could not make a practice, it was no big deal. But most of us did not miss a match, which was the sole purpose of participating in the first place. If necessary, I would find a substitute for the cafeteria or flower delivery jobs.

Dibble-Dabble, but with a Ball and Net

The game itself? I had been playing a version of it for over ten years. Water polo was a variation of Dibble-Dabble. It required the skills I had been learning in my hometown pool as Delbert, Bobby, Eddie Mack, Jack and I fought to capture the tooth pick.

The water polo ball was our Dibble. A goal scored was our Dabble. Granted, the water polo contestants did not launch themselves from the side of the pool, but I rapidly discovered this wonderful fact: Water polo was a wimpy form of Dibble-Dabble. (Use caution if you offer my opinion to water polo players. They may take offence.)

Water polo has this rule: A swimmer cannot impede the movement of another player unless that player has possession of the ball. No jousting of each other. No swimming over each other. In a nutshell, a water polo match is a respectful Dibble-Dabble match. I took to water polo like a frog takes to water.

To be fair, the game was not always respectful or polite. While the AAU water polo program in New Mexico in the 1960s might have been somewhat off the cuff, the matches could be ferocious affairs for the man holding the ball. He could be semi-assaulted. The only rule I recall about this part of the game was that a swimmer who was attacking the man with the ball could not use a closed fist.

A rule violation came in different levels of severity. For example, swimming over a person without the ball was a minor infraction, and allowed the opposing team one uncontested pass. A major infraction, such as punching an opponent in the face, resulted in a 20 second expulsion of the offender and a free shot at the net. Only the opposing goalie could defend against this shot. It was taken from a 13-ft marker. Free shots were big deals; they could turn the game around.

Because of my Dibble-Dabble mentality, I was a frequent rule violator. It had nothing to do with anger or aggression. I was just playing a game I was conditioned to play: swimming over the other guys. I was expelled in my first game for three fouls (the limit). Later, I wised up and settled down.

The water polo/Dibble-Dabble relationship was a fortunate coincidence. Once again, I was lucky to have been doing repetitions of a sport (Dibble-Dabble) that would contribute to my ability to participate in another sport (water polo) that would contribute to my ability to become a frogman.

The stars seemed to be lining up for me. But UDT was still far away. I had to finish college, join the Navy, complete Officer Candidate School, and make it through UDT training. Still, I was on track.

An Injury

As I completed my first three years of college, I continued swimming and became interested in gymnastics. My hometown high school had a fine gymnastics program and I learned some basic skills there. I was never much of a whiz, but one of my fraternity brothers took me under his wing and taught me the basic movements for the parallel bars.

My favorite part of gymnastics was the trampoline. It reminded me of using a diving board. I especially enjoyed the routine of running up to and then springing from a mini-trampoline, which launched me over a vaulting horse. I would open my legs and spread eagle over the horse, using my arms and hands to push me over the barrier. It was almost like flying, if only for a few feet.

During one session, after taking some routine jumps, I asked the spotters to place the trampoline about three feet farther from the horse. I had never made a leap this far; in fact, far from it. A more measured approach (no pun intended) would have been to make an incremental extension, say a half-foot; working up to longer distances—just as I had done with my effort to swim longer distances underwater. I was ignorant of what I was trying to do. I was also foolish. Benjamin Franklin said, "Most fools think they are only ignorant." I was both.

The spotters moved the trampoline and returned to the sides of the horse. Their job was to protect a jumper from an errant vault. I was eager and nervous to meet the new challenge, but my ounce of concern was outweighed by a pound of foolishness. My next leap from the trampoline was not well executed. My uneven jump onto the trampoline's webbing propelled me forward at an angle toward the horse. With my legs spread wide apart, I planned to place my hands on top of the horse, then straddle and propel my body across it, thus landing feet-first on the floor. But my flight was off course.

The spotter on the right side of the horse was not prepared for my wayward body—he was startled to see me coming in his direction. He moved away from the horse and let gravity take its course. His spotting was, charitably speaking, spotty.

The result of the jump was an ugly collision with the vaulting horse. The impact of the crash into the horse was concentrated in my groin area. I then landed on my head as I fell to the hardwood floor. My next coherent recollection was lying in a college infirmary bed. I had suffered a concussion and had injured my groin area. My left testicle was badly bruised. My right one was partially crushed.

There's an old adage I've heard bandied about: *Few things make us feel better than having our judgment proved sound.* And a variation:

Few things make us feel more foolish than having our judgment proved faulty. The trampoline jump changed my life.

Summer Days during College

During the summers between college semesters, I returned to Lovington and took over as manager of John's swimming pool. My first chores were to clean up the place, hire another lifeguard, stock the concession stand, run checks on the Chlorine system, wax John's boat, cleanup the boat house, and organize a swimming lesson program. For the latter, I knew I could bring in lots of students. The summer swimming program had been a mainstay in Lovington since John first opened the pool.

But after Tudy left, the program languished for lack of a guiding hand. As a lifeguard in previous summers, any lessons I gave came under the direction of the pool manager (First, Mrs. Camp, and later, some other people who had no training in the field.). I was certain a pent up demand existed for swimming lessons, and I was in the position to create the program. My first business was about to be formed.

John took none of the teaching fees. For the first time in my life, I would know how it felt to have extra cash, so I wasted no time. I purchased an ad in the local paper and that was all it took. In one morning of registration, most of the classes filled up.

The pool was reserved for swimming lessons from 8 am to noon on weekdays. If students were not in a class, they were allowed to swim in one section at the shallow end of the pool before or after their lessons. Thus, I also became a baby sitter. Mothers would drop off the kids for their lessons, and come back two or three hours later to pick them up.

I divided the four hours into eight 30-minute lessons. I registered up to eight students per class. (All but one class was always full.) I charged a modest fee per student per week, which was one reason the program was so popular. In addition to John paying me as a pool manager, he also gave me money for two lifeguards, as well as extra money for the weekend lifeguards. I told John I needed funds for only one regular lifeguard, as I was the other and he was already paying me to be the manager.

John, "You're doing two jobs, right?"

"Sort of, pool manager is far from a full time job. The lifeguards do most of the work."

John, "You must manage the concession stand and take care of the boat house. You have to rent my boat and skis and collect fees for lake usage from other boaters. You must collect the fishing fees." (The profits for the concession stand went to me, not John. He received the fees for boat rentals and fishing in the lake.)

"John, I can take care of those tasks from the swimming pool stand. I can do maintenance on the boat and boat house after the pool closes. I can post signs at the boat house and boat ramp directing them to the concession stand. That's what Mrs. Camp did when Mr. Camp wasn't around."

"That's fine with me. It may be that you'll need extra help. I pay for the manager, two regular lifeguards, and for two weekend lifeguards. You take care of things as you see fit. How you dispense the money is up to you. You've worked for me for five years. I know I won't have to come over here to fix anything. You know the Chlorine system better than anyone." (Amen, it nearly killed me more than once.)

"Just take care of things. If you have a problem, let me know, but you know the ropes."

John Easley was a classy and kind man. He was a pillar of our community. He was on the school board, and was a successful farmer and rancher. He trusted me; he was not going to nickel-and-dime the relationship. He had all the leverage but did not apply it, just the opposite.

I was clearing over $300 per week for swimming lessons, a lot of money fifty years ago. I was raking in even more from the two jobs John had so generously funded. But I had to find a regular lifeguard. Where to look? H. P. was gone; he had joined the Navy. Jack was not interested in full time work. Bobby, Delbert, and Eddie Mack were already employed.

My New Lifeguard

I had my future employee identified. He was living with me, my brother, Tom. He was not a great swimmer but he was home for the summer from his teaching duties, and therefore available. He was already drawing a salary and had a lot of idle time on his hands. He was tired of working in the oil fields during the summers.

About the swimming deficiency: He was an average swimmer, and I worked with him the first week, especially on the use of ropes, poles, and life buoys. Being an extraordinary athlete (and a fine calf roper), he learned the details quickly.

I am almost ashamed to write this part of the book. Unlike noble John Easley, I leveraged my own brother. I paid him $25 a week. But that was fifty years ago. I also gave him control of the concession stand and its profits. There, my conscience is (somewhat) clean.

Tom would show up at noon and work to around five or six. He even made some rescues. He later told me that excluding the lousy pay, the job was one of the best he had. At the end of the season, I gave a party after hours in the concession stand and presented Tom with a trophy. It was a Dixie Cup with an ink inscription: "Employee of the summer."

Midnight Swimming

Now that I was manager of John's pool, I could swim anytime I wished. Often, I would go for a swim during the night. I usually went alone, after I had taken my date home. As you may recall, the swimming pool was three miles from town. It was isolated from homes and offices.

During these times I would swim a relaxed breaststroke with my head out of the water. Entering the pool at the shallow end and executing an easy push off from the side, I would glide through the cold still water. Once underway, I would quietly make my way toward the deep end of the pool, keeping my strokes under water.

Silence. No urban cacophony to interrupt the stillness of the night. Southeastern New Mexico offers clear views of the sky. During the evening, the faraway stars appear as if they are hanging nearby, but just out of reach. I would swim on my back with an inverted breaststroke and gaze at my private observatory. Taking in the Heavens, I thought of the old saying, "There are no atheists in fox holes." The idea also applied to my midnight swims at Easley's Twin Lakes: Nor in silent, pristine night-time waters.

The only sounds were croaks from frogs who resided in the surrounding lake. Even my friends ceased their songs if I made a noise. But for just a little while. Shortly, their frog songs would accompany my frog strokes as I made my way back and forth in a serene fantasy world. What I would give for one more of those nights.

I had the good fortune to be dating a lovely semi-swimmer that summer. "Semi" in the sense that she was eligible for the tired swimmer carry, especially a midnight tired swimmer carry. On some occasions, she came with me for a midnight swim. She was not shy, nor was I. The frogs croaked in wonderment.

Teaching Myself to Teach

I was at odds about what I wanted to pursue as my college degree. Three of my brothers had gone into coaching, so they majored in education. During my sophomore year, I signed up for a class in "Education 101" and dropped it after attending the first week. I do not understand the concept of teaching someone how to teach. I think the art of teaching can be learned, but I don't think it can be taught. A gifted teacher has something going in the first place. Mr. Galdwell might disagree, but it is a Tiger Woods—Jack Lemmon situation. You've got it or you don't.

I did not know it at the time, but my swimming lessons helped prepare me to be a lecturer, an occupation I pursued in the latter part of my professional career. Luckily, learning to teach swimming proved to be easy for me. First, the surroundings were informal. We were in swim suits, no coats, ties, dresses, or wing tips in the crowd. Most of the participants were motivated to take in my instructions. After all, I wasn't demanding they diagram sentences; just float for a few seconds and see how it feels.

Oh, you're afraid of the water and you don't know how to hold your breath? The water bothers your nostrils? Fine, let's play a game. Can you blow out air through your nose? Great, stoop down with me; as your head goes down....just a little bit....start blowing air out of your nose. There! No water in the nose, right? Okay, let's try the bobble-bubble game. Bobble up and bubble down. As you come up, take a breath through your mouth. As you go down under the water and then come up, blow bubbles through your nose, then take a breath through your mouth and go down again. Watch me... Yep, your feet are always on the floor of the pool. That's right. Bobble and bubble. Bobble and bubble. See! No water in the nose.

* * *

Okay, a few more seconds. Don't worry, feel my hand under you? I've got you. Look! My hand is just a few inches away and you're floating! Okay. Good. I got'cha. Well done. Let's try a leg kick. Watch. That's right. Hold on to the side of the pool. Good. OK, let's see if we can combine the two.

* * *

I'm going to stand about five feet from you. Place one foot on the side of the pool, push away and float to me. I'll grab your arms when you arrive. ...What? OK, if you don't arrive, I'll come to get you in a New York second. ...Very well done! Now execute the push off with a flutter kick. See if you can advance only two more feet.

* * *

Yes, a headlong dive appears as if we are high above the water. Let's try this. Stoop down beside me. One foot on the pool gutter, the other on the deck...that's the way. ...Now, place your arms and hands into the swimmer's dive....Yep...then lean over to where your hands are close to the water...See there? You're just a few inches from the water. You know how to float and swim, just topple forward. Wait for me to get in the pool to be near you. ...Great!

Repetition. Before long, even most of the "scaredy cats" were bobbling and bubbling, and floating and kicking with the best of them. Intelligent repetition. Step by step, building on their confidence. The bobble-bubble game was one way of preparing them for the breathing movements required for the American Crawl.

I was not taught these tricks of the trades. Necessity being the mother of invention, they evolved as I also evolved to become a swimming teacher. I was lucky I had no one looking over my shoulder telling me I should teach the student to bubble then bobble, and not bobble then bubble. I was allowed to work this teaching technique out on my own. I don't think my students suffered because I didn't have a college degree in Teaching Swimming.

The Handicapped Help me with my Handicap

I'll even venture to say the same applied to my favorite class. I taught swimming to several people with physical handicaps. The class started with one student, but I suppose word got around, and by the end of the summer, I was working with a blind woman, a teenager missing one leg, and two kids, each missing an arm.

Toward the end of the summer, a fifth student joined the class. This young boy had all his limbs, but he was crippled and used braces to walk. His mom would help him to the pool area. There, with my assistance, he would remove his braces and enter the pool. For the last couple weeks of the summer, I separated his instructions into a late afternoon private session. He was frightfully leery of the water and had trouble keeping his balance. But he was a game little guy, and I grew very fond of him.

How was I to teach a diverse group such as this? I had no idea. I had dropped Education 101. I thought it was just common sense—not to mention expedient—to tailor my instruction to each person in the class, to make sure they were always comfortable in the water, and to make sure we became partners in their quest to swim.

And to be honest with them. Before taking on each student, I told them (and their parents if the prospective student were a child): "I've had training and experience in teaching swimming and diving, but I've never worked with someone who has lost a (leg, arm, etc.). If you're willing to work with me, I'm willing to work with you. I have some ideas about how to get you swimming but we will work them out together. I will never put you in a position where you feel the least bit uncomfortable."

Be upfront. Most people will accept what you have to say. (At least about teaching swimming. Politics is another matter.)

I started with the usual lightning quick face submersions and the bobble-bubble routines. We also (as in all classes) played a game in three feet of water where the students would hold their breath, go underwater with their feet still on the floor and try to pick up a piece of metal (painted bright red) from the bottom of the pool. This routine was undertaken after they were comfortable with head submersions and performing the bobble-bubble successfully.

We called this piece of metal the baton. Fetching it became a game. Our rallying cry became, "Capture the baton!"

My blind student was a humorous woman. As I was explaining this new drill, she offered she did not mind participating but she would appreciate a hint as to the approximate location of the baton. She offered a joke that I remember to his day, "I don't see well under water."

This simple exercise of fetching the baton was a revelation to some. As they bent down, they discovered the natural buoyancy of their bodies tended to work against their attempted submersions. Often, their legs would leave the pool bottom and they would be in a quasi-float position. Usually, this occurrence startled them.

Some of the more cautious students became frightened at this loss of control. This part of the program presented the biggest challenge to reluctant beginners: how to gain back their balance; how to get those feet back underneath the body. I discovered an effective tool to help them and me (and I used it for all the classes).

Take a look at the small circle in Figure 4-1 of Chapter 4. For those who were afraid, they could hold on to the banister of the railing (a small pipe anchored to the bottom of the pool). If they lost their balance they had the pipe as an anchor to right themselves. As they became more confident, I would lead them away from the pole. They would hold my hand as they went under. Next, I would have them go under without any hold. But I kept my hand touching theirs.

If they panicked, we clasped each others' hands and I helped them right themselves.

But how could I use this technique with the two students with only one hand? Obviously, I couldn't. But I didn't want them excluded from this important drill. So, we jointly worked out a protocol where I would go under the water with them, with my hand gently grasping their elbow. If they made the slightest movement with the hand toward anything but the baton, I pulled them to the surface. It worked well enough. One of the students eventually asked me to stop interfering and let her perform the task unaided.

As the summer progressed, as I was trying to come up with ideas and techniques to tailor for each person, I decided no one would know better the sensations resulting from my suggestions than the students themselves. I could only vicariously appreciate how a one legged person might execute a flutter kick, or how a blind person could search for a piece of steel on the bottom of the pool. I asked them, "How does it feel? What's the sensation? Are you comfortable? Why? Why not?"

It wasn't an inquisition. We were working jointly to solve a problem. I took this idea one step further. I asked the other students for their ideas. Asking a student to teach the class? Giving up control? Yes and no. I kept the participation structured, but it was amazing and pleasing to hear the one-legged woman make a suggestion to the crippled boy, for the two one armed students to help each other.

Because of their situations, I had to be careful not to have them spread out across the pool. During the lesson, they sometimes sat on the side as I worked with one or two students. I was careful not to extend this routine for too long a time, because it would lead to boredom and loss of interest. We were usually in the water together but when we were not, I would solicit input about my (newly constructed) swimming hint.

As an example, for the one armed students, I had decided a modified sidestroke would be the best technique for them. I thought they could best execute this stroke by having the single arm underneath the body. It worked somewhat, but both students had trouble keeping their head up when they pushed their arm forward.

I thought the answer to the problem might be to execute an over arm stoke (described in Chapter 2). But it was too complex at this stage of their development.

As the three of us worked on the problem, the one legged student offered from the side, "Why don't you try the breaststroke?" Why not indeed! We gave it a go, and it was a terrific suggestion. They didn't use their arm for gaining thrust, they used it more as a forward rudder, to keep themselves going in a straight line and to help add buoyancy to the front part of their bodies.

One of these students made yet another improvement on his own accord. As they progressed through the summer, I demonstrated more advanced strokes, mostly for their entertainment and my ego. As I was showing them the over arm sidestroke, the one armed boy proclaimed, "I think that would work better than the breaststroke." He got into the water, and floating on his side in which his arm was above the water (and not underneath him), he tried the stroke. It was rough, but he liked it. In a few days, he was executing it as smooth as silk. The other one armed student stayed with the modified breaststroke. Different strokes for different folks.

Let us never handicap the handicapped. Give them a chance and most of them will excel. The so-called disadvantaged have much to teach us. I am certain I learned more about strength of character, humility, and pride from these five people than I learned from anyone else in my life. Talk about motivated effort. Talk about outliers. Compared to them I was a slacker.

Not Everyone Excels

Around 90 percent of my students learned to swim in one fashion or another. Some became fine swimmers. I had one student who was what we would call today an outlier, and I will tell you about her shortly. But some of the students never learned to swim. They never overcame their fear of water. It was heart rending to see these kids, scared as could be, half shivering from John's cold water, looking up to me with plaintive eyes: *Please don't make me do this!* I know this comment is a bit maudlin, but their cold little bodies warmed my heart.

Eventually, it was just too painful for these children, their parents, and me. For as long as possible, I would keep them in the program, and have them involved in activities that did not humiliate them. But it would reach a point where the other students had passed them up to where it could not be masked. At that time, I would have a meeting with the mom or dad, and give them the bad news.

Some took it well. Some did not. Some asked me to give their child private lessons. I could not accommodate them. I was booked and I was the only qualified swimming instructor in town.

I remember one little girl who could not make the grade. She flunked out of "school" but she could have cared less. The Sunday after her dismissal, her dad brought her to Easley's, where she jumped into the baby pool and began playing with the other kids. She was seven years old. The age limit for using the baby pool was five years of age or younger.

Her dad was a class act. He said she was begging him to let her come to the pool. He knew she meant the baby pool. He asked if it would be okay? Why not? I was the manager. I set the rules. The child loved the water, she just did not like swimming in it. But for splashing and having fun? She was an outlier.

A Student Becomes an Outlier

During my last summer at Easley's swimming pool, I had the pleasure of giving private swimming lessons to a ten-year old girl named Jan. A tiny girl for her age, Jan reminded me of a tadpole. She certainly swam like one.

From the start of our sessions, Jan took to the water as if her arms and legs were fins. I taught hundreds of people how to swim or how to mimic swimming. Jan was the most naturally gifted young swimmer of them all.

She was mentally tough, too. After working with her several times a week for a month, it was obvious she could easily assimilate my instructions into her muscle memory. So I began to push her—more than I had done with any other student. She responded as if she were a miniature Esther Williams. This analogy is particularly apt. Williams was a gorgeously smooth swimmer. She could glide around a pool seemingly without effort. But she was a fast and powerful freestyler behind that synchronized swimmer façade. She won the National AAU 100 meter freestyle and would have competed in the 1940 Olympics, but they were cancelled because of WWII.

Watching Jan swim, watching her respond to my regimen (even swimming with small weights attached to her arms or legs), I came to appreciate I had a very special swimmer and a very special person on my hands. She was a swimming instructor's dream come true, a teacher's model. On one occasion, I had her swim a race against two high school boys who were not only competent freestylers, they were cocky. They needed a dose of humility and Jan waxed them!

She was a fine diver as well. Not a splash was made as she entered the water. Her only weakness was her racing dive. She had a tendency to hit the water at too sharp an angle, but once underway, she was a swimming dervish.

A few years ago, her older brother sent me an email. Here is an excerpt:

> Jan married about 1967 or so can't recall for sure. She and her husband live about 60 miles north of Anchorage, Alaska. Jan had a tumor taken off of her spine in 1985, and she has been in a wheelchair ever since. Her attitude has been great over the years considering her situation. I know she is the toughest of our family. I would not have been able to adapt as well as she has done.

Esther Williams and my student were tough cookies. Williams rarely used a stunt double. She broke her neck filming a 115 ft. dive. She ruptured her eardrum several times. She nearly drowned shooting an underwater scene that led to severe oxygen hunger.

"Young" Jan was in the mold of Esther Williams. I hope "old" Jan is as elegant, cheerful, competent, and tough now as she was fifty years ago. I would wager she is. If I once again teach swimming to the handicapped, I hope I can somehow recruit Jan. She would be star of the class. Regardless of her situation, she would once again be my model.

Teaching Lifeguards

A WSI was not allowed to make money teaching swimming. If I charged fees and issued Red Cross certificates, most of the money was supposed to go to the Red Cross. This monetary angle was one reason the Red Cross representatives came to Lovington to recruit me into the WSI program. They saw the potential for another cash flow to come their way. I decided to forego Red Cross certification for my swimming program. No one cared. They were happy to have someone in town to set up and teach the classes. The exception to this practice was the class I taught for Red Cross lifeguard certification. I charged no fees and could therefore issue Red Cross certificates.

The most demanding class for testing my mental faculties was the session with the handicapped swimmers. I was continuously thinking of techniques to teach my five students how to overcome their handicaps. I was handicapped myself. I had no training for this type of instruction.

However, the most demanding class physically was the water safety class for lifeguards. The students were my age, near my age, or older. They were fine swimmers and they were out to prove to their teacher they could handle the program. Their assertions were often challenges to me. After an hour of demonstrating carries and defensive maneuvers against boys and men who wanted nothing better than to best the teacher, I was a candidate for the tired swimmer carry. By the second lesson, I wised up and let them practice on each other.

It was during this last summer at John's pool that I became aware how much fun teaching could be. I began thinking about the process of how to convey knowledge to someone else. I had given little thought about the notion of actually "teaching." The informal and natural surroundings of the swimming pool probably helped me to become a teacher later in my life.

I'm getting a bit ahead of my story. For now, the thought I took with me from that summer is that in the ideal teaching environment, the teacher becomes a student and the student becomes a teacher. But only to an extent. An effective teacher must possess an aura of knowledge and a manner of authority. But once again, only to an extent. The gifted teacher intuitively understands that certain boundaries must be placed between the teacher and the student. This teacher knows how to shift the boundaries to meet each situation. It's little more than just having a sense of empathy toward each human encounter.

By using the phrase "little more," it may appear that I belittle talented teachers. To the contrary, truly gifted teachers have an outlier's persona. In a touch of irony, an outlier teacher does not have to put in ten years or 10,000 hours to learn how to excel at teaching. For this situation, "You've got it or you don't."

Anti-Outliers

During these summers I had an opportunity to observe a wide range of swimming abilities, as well as the amount of motivation the swimmers possessed. Some were workers, some were laggards. I didn't mind if the laggards lagged, so as long as they accepted their lower lot in life. But I made a discovery about human nature: A substantial number of untalented humans who populate this earth believe they are equal to everyone else, and if they are not equal, they deserve the same treatment as others—regardless of their work ethic.

I acknowledge my naiveté at that time in my life, but from my limited perspective, I assumed everyone believed in meritocracy, that all people believed their position and status should be based on their achievements, not chance or family wealth. Not so. A few of my students had a sense of entitlement. They were not happy with failure. Few of us are but these folks would not accept the fact that they were the reason for their failure. Mom and Dad could not pull them out of this one. Nor could I, nor did I want to. I found them to be unbecoming creatures.

Writing Enters my Life

Ms. Frances Campbell, my high school English teacher, had a commanding countenance about her. She was sharp witted and funny. With a pronounced and refined accent, she made fun of her southwestern, slow talking students. She brooked no teenage sloth. She uttered no "ehs" or "uhs" when she spoke. She may have been the first person I encountered who could be described as an articulate speaker. She was probably my first encounter with an elitist.

Frances liked to dissect the English language with the use of diagrams. Day after day she taught us how to depict the architecture of a sentence in the form of a chart.

Assuming a teenager could have this degree of discernment, I thought the idea silly and came to dislike formal definitions of language. Not so for my English teacher. For Frances, if an utterance did not fit into a diagram, the utterance was grammatically incorrect, and therefore invalid. Looking back to those times, I think this approach to English led me to be afraid of writing. When I did write, it led to wooden prose. But I was at a great disadvantage in disclosing these observations to my teacher because I was not aware of them at the time. (I was circumscribed by my circumstances.) In addition, I was a teenager who could not diagram "See Spot run." I had no confidence in myself and Frances did not help matters with her tart manner.

On the other hand, Frances contributed something quite valuable to this part of my life. She led me to understand if a writer writes too formally, the *average* reader won't read. But if the writer writes too informally the *above average* reader won't read.[2] It's a fine line.

Frances challenged us to be better writers. She did not accept mediocrity. She could have been a model for Malcolm Gladwell's outlier teacher. To this day, Frances is loved and remembered by her students.

Toward the end of my last summer at Easley's, and just before my last year in college, a reporter from the local paper paid me a call. He wanted to write an article about my classes and the students.

He stayed the entire morning. While having lunch, he asked if I would "jot down" my thoughts about teaching swimming in general and about teaching the handicapped specifically.

I was reluctant to accept his offer. I couldn't compose my way off a Big Chief writing tablet. Ms. Campbell's definitions of words had left me baffled and insecure about how to compose readable text. I had flunked or barely passed my attempts at writing essays in high school. If I did not know the difference between past participle and a past perfect words, how could I write those words succinctly and correctly?[3] I gave it a go but the outcome was not pretty. The paper's editor rewrote my "column." After some editing attempts, the project dropped between the cracks and more important local matters found their way into the paper.

Nonetheless, this failed effort was my first attempt to write about *how to do something*. Regardless of my ineptness, I enjoyed the process. I began to take notes about the goings-on around me, writing down verbatim quotes, sometimes recording my own impressions and interpretations. Some of these notes have found their way into this book. I hope they are improvements to my original mangled prose.

I eventually came to understand Frances Campbell's diagramming drills had left me with a stilted style of composition. My method evolved to what I think is a more natural style. Admittedly, I now tend toward informality (Ms. Campbell's colloquialisms), but I hope you find the prose in this book to your liking.

Sports Editor. My high school essays, subject to Ms. Campbell's editing ostracism were paper work, not work on paper. I skirted-by with them, earning the derision of Frances for my laziness and disinterest. I disliked writing but the newspaper exercise opened a gate. I discovered writing could be a pleasant experience. I wanted to improve my meager skills. During my last year in college, I was given a golden opportunity.

The University of New Mexico's school paper, *The Lobo*, was a left leaning publication. The editor, Mark Acuff, was a talented liberal student who took up causes such as "Hail Fidel Castro!" Mark's friend, Cruz Alderette (a jock in heart and soul), was the sports editor. Fortunately, both Mark and Cruz were my fraternity brothers. We knew each other well, opportunities for the good-young-boy network to flourish.

Cruz and I were running mates. I sometimes accompanied him to varsity games, where he would file a report and also type a weekly write up for "The Lobo Lowdown" column. He began to offer me space in the reports section. I would attend a basketball or baseball game, make my observations, copy the box scores and file a report. In turn, first Cruz then Mark would rewrite my work.

One late evening, on a night before the paper was to be published the next morning, Mark and I left *The Lobo* offices for a short break and a beer at the local watering hole, Okie Joes. We talked of Cruz's departure from school after the ending of the winter semester. At that time, Mark asked if I wanted some advice about writing sports reports for a newspaper.

Of course I did! I had no journalism training whatsoever. I had never taken a class in creative writing, only Ms. Campbell's class in noncreative diagramming. In concert with Frances' edits to my essays, Cruz and Mark made similar drastic changes to my reports. I could use a lot of help and was not shy in saying so.

Over our beers, Mark gave me encouragement, *You move smoothly from one paragraph to the next.* (I had no idea about these mechanics.) Followed with, *you're too formal.* (My worry about Ms. Campbell's past participles.) Sandwiched in by, *you've an entertaining style.* (Was that a compliment?) Followed by, *Make your columns shorter, get to the point.* (I was too "wordy.") And, *you're accurate in your reports.* (Yes, I took notes, which I was doing as we spoke over our Coors.)

I was grateful to Mark. He was a gifted writer and was taking time from his work to help me. This act was not to be dismissed. We fraternity brothers had dubbed Mark "the sexual intellectual." Our session at Okie's was likely intruding on his after-hours diversions.

During this session, I mentioned to Mark I would like to contribute to "The Lobo Lowdown" column. I had an idea for a series. I said I would not ask for a byline, but would like to have some space in the paper, other than summing up box scores.

Mark asked, "What's your idea?"

"I'd like to do research on UNM's past great athletes and find out where they are now, what they are doing. I'd like to talk with them to see if they are successful, and if so, why. Maybe relate their present to their past at UNM. Then write about it."

Mark, "Human interest. I think the readers would like it."

"Yeah. Light stuff, a change of pace from your editorials."

"Ha. Got a title for the series?"

"Yes, I've thought about the title. It would be 'Where Are They Now?' "

"Tell you what I'll do. Would you like to take over as sports editor for the spring semester? Your ongoing reports are okay. I'll continue to edit them. We could do a couple of your columns and see how they fare."

"You're asking me to be an editor? I barely know the trade!"

"No, not really an editor. I'll do the editing. You'll do the writing. Editing is not much work. It's the leg work that's valuable to me. You've shown you can do that. We work together as a team. You've not taken issue with my hand in your work. That's one reason I'm making the offer."

I accepted. We toasted to the new relationship with another Coors, another, and another. Much to the amusement of the guys running the printing press, we staggered back to *The Lobo* office to "put the paper to bed." We should have put ourselves to bed instead of the paper.

Once again, I was in the right place at the right time. I had gotten a break. What I did with that break was up to me.

Moving On

As recounted in this chapter, after the summer of my swimming instruction program, I returned to college to complete my curriculum and fill the job of sports editor job at the college newspaper.

UNM did not offer a degree in swimming. I had chosen to pursue a BS in Psychology, anything to gain a sheep skin and then depart for the U.S. Navy Officer Candidate School (OCS), my next step toward becoming a UDT swimmer. The days of college pranks and country club swimming pools were over. It was time to put the pedal to the metal.

---

[1] George Herbert, *Outlandish Proverbs*, 163, 1640. Secondary source: Leonard Roy Frank, *Quotationary*, Random House, New York, 2001, p. 286.

[2] Too colloquially, as Ms. Campbell would say.

[3] For example, here is the definition of past perfect: A verb tense with "had" that expresses an action completed at a more distant time in the past, that is, a time previous to the past time specified or implied elsewhere in the passage. Here is the definition of past participle: a participle that expresses past time or a completed action. It is used with auxiliaries to form perfect tenses in the active voice and all tenses in the passive voice. Got it?

Section II

Frogman Experiences

CHAPTER 7

THE UDT AND SEALS[1]

The greater the risk, the sweeter the fruit.[2]
—Francis Bacon

The Underwater Demolition Teams (UDT) were formed as an aftermath of a WWI military disaster off the shores of northwestern Turkey. During February, 1915, the Allies began an attack on Gallipoli, a city located on a peninsula extending into the Dardanelles. The initial assault failed because floating mines damaged the French and British ships. The Allies were forced to withdraw and try again later. It became obvious that any significant amphibious assault onto a foreign shore would require extensive intelligence about that shore.

For example, amphibious assault boats, those that carry men to the shore, must beach themselves onto turf for their landing. The landing sites' terrain and slope must be known. Rocky shores will not do, nor will beaches with a steep gradient into the water. Tides must be evaluated, cross currents as well.

The job of the UDT was to first, find beaches that could accommodate the landing crafts and the debarking of Marines. Second, obstructions (such as cement pilings and steel beams) had to be destroyed, especially less-visible obstacles that lay beneath the surface of the water. They were dangerous and could put a hole in the bottom of a boat. The penetration of the landing craft often resulted in men drowning because these passengers were weighed down with heavy gear.

The UDT began training in June 1943 at Fort Pierce, Florida. The teams saw action at North Africa, Normandy, and several locations in the South Pacific. In those early days, UDT personnel did not go ashore. Their operations were confined to the water and the adjacent beaches. During the Korean War, they continued to focus on beach and hydrographic surveys, demolition of obstacles, and mine disposal. But during the Vietnam conflict UDT's mission was expanded to land operations. Increasingly, the UDT adapted commando tactics and training into their tactics. This evolution eventually led the UDT to become today's SEALs (Sea, Air, and Land). During my stay in UDT, the SEALs were just being formed, a story recounted in this chapter and Chapter 8.

Forerunners to UDT

In 1942, prior to the formation of UDT, the Amphibious Scout and Raider School was established by a joint effort of the U.S. Army and Navy. This school trained both Army and Navy men in explosive ordnance use and disposal. The personnel were combat swimmers but were given additional training in beach survey operations. Later, Navy and Marine troops were assembled together and trained to become the Naval Combat Demolition Unit (NCDU). The NCDU was first employed in Operation Torch during the invasion of North Africa in 1942. This unit became the first group in the U.S. Navy to specialize in amphibious raids and tactics.

Jump-Starting the UDT Teams

During the first part of the Pacific campaign the amphibious assaults met little resistance. As well, the embryonic UDT had not yet made its presence known to any great extent. However, at Tarawa (1943) the United States faced serious Japanese opposition to the American amphibious landing. The 4,500 Japanese defenders were well supplied and well prepared. They "fought almost to the last man," extracting a heavy toll on Marines and the Navy personnel who were manning the boats:[3]

> The landings began on November 20 and immediately ran into trouble. Coming in at low tide, the assault boats were forced to disgorge their men far from shore. Wading through waist-deep water over piercing, razor-sharp coral, many were cut down by merciless enemy gunfire yards from the beach. Those who made it ashore huddled in the sand, hemmed in by the sea to one side and the Japanese to the other.
>
> The next morning, reinforcements made the same perilous journey bringing with them tanks and artillery. By the end of the day the Marines were able to break out from the beach to the inland. The fierce combat continued for another two days.
>
> The cost of victory was high for the Marines who suffered nearly 3,000 casualties. The toll was even higher for the Japanese. Of the 4,700 defenders, only 17 survived. Their willingness to fight to the last man foreshadowed the fierceness of the battles to come.

Figure 7-1. The Disaster at Tarawa.

Figure 7-1[4] shows one section of the beach at Tarawa after the initial landing. The dead and destroyed equipment litter the beach. Not shown in this figure are the dead sailors and Marines in the water and other men in the destroyed boats on the beach.

Following this disaster, Rear Admiral Richmond K. Turner directed the formation of nine Underwater Demolition Teams. These initial teams were mostly composed of navy personnel from the Naval Construction Battalions (Seabees).

Early Training Methods

The early UDT training relied on the use of inflatable boats to carry men from their ships to the shore. There was relatively little swimming involved. The men also became skilled at carrying the boats around on their shoulders and heads from one drill to the next. This training was still part of the program when I joined UDT in 1963. Although swimming became a major part of the training and the use of these boats diminished, my training school teammates and I still had to cart them around the base and on the beach.

The early UDT warriors did not have access to scuba gear. Thus, they would paddle to the beach, disembark from the small craft and go to work in the shallow water. They left the deep water demolitions to the Army. The Marine Reconnaissance units conducted the hydrographic operations from shallow water to inland, while the accompanying UDT conducted the demolition and hydrographic work from deeper water to the shallow areas.

Later, UDT swimmers were launched from submerged submarines. Using flippers (fins) and primitive scuba gear they made their way to the beach. They also carried explosives. (I still recall from that WWII movie the actors carrying packs of explosives in tubes.)

By the time I reached Coronado, California (the west coast home of UDT) the teams were being trained increasingly in commando tactics and more sophisticated explosives. Parachute training was added to the curriculum.

Getting There and Getting Back

Depending on the nature of the mission and the availability of scuba equipment, the teams would swim or paddle into the area of operations and swim or paddle back to their mother boat or ship. A faster and less dangerous option was often used to get the swimmers back to safety. A high speed boat (usually a PT boat or a small boat from a destroyer) would secure a rubber raft next to it. At an agreed time and place, the team members would spread out in the water and wait for the personnel in the raft to haul them in as the boat hurried by. If a swimmer missed the pickup, the boat would circle and try again

Figure 7-2. Speed boat pickup.

The tool for the pickup was made of rubber and shaped as a square-like oval. A picture best explains the arrangement and the pickup device. In Figure 7-2 I am being picked-up by a UDT retriever. I'm happy to say I latched on successfully with the first try.[5]

Scuba gear was used sporadically in the early days of UDT. In 1948 the first formal program using Scuba was initiated at the east coast UDT home in Little Creek, Virginia. Shortly thereafter, a successful lock out and reentry operation from an underway submarine took place. This technique became part of the training and was often used in subsequent battle campaigns.

Later, the teams initiated experiments with insertion/extraction by helicopter, jumping from a moving helicopter into the water or rappelling like mountain climbers to the ground. These operations became part of the UDT (and later SEALs) training in the early 1960s. During my training these operations were becoming part of the emerging SEALs program.[6]

Before the advent of the space shuttle the SEALs/helicopter maneuvers were seen by millions of people during the recovery of the space reentry capsule. The frogmen jumped from the aircraft and secured the floating capsule to the helicopter.

Korea and Expanded Roles

The UDT began to develop commando tactics during the Korean War. Nonetheless, their principal operations continued to focus on what they had done in the past: surveys, demolitions, and mine disposal. But their mission was expanding. They accompanied South Korean commandos on raids in North Korea to demolish train tunnels. Some UDT officers thought this activity was contrary to UDT's training and missions, but times were changing. Indeed, the UDT was used to help smuggle spies into and out of North Korea. They also were assigned to damage the North Korean fishing industry, which led to a diminished supply of fish to the North Korean Army. Not to mention North Korean civilians, but such is the nature of clandestine war and sabotage.

The Korean War represented a period of transition of the UDT from a water based combat organization to one that fought on the land as well. The changes became even more pronounced during the Vietnam conflict.

Vietnam

In 1960, the UDT became involved in Vietnam when they delivered small boats up the Mekong River into Laos. The next year UDT personnel began training Vietnamese to be frogmen. These men were called Lien Doc Nguoi Nhia (LDNN), which is roughly: the "soldiers that fight under the sea."

It was during the early 1960s that the UDT began a planned, intensive effort to become the SEALs. However, before we look at this fighting force, we go back in time to introduce an amphibious landing craft. It is part of the story of the UDT and SEALs, because these frogmen were tasked with removing all obstacles on shore that might impede the landing of these boats and their precious cargo: United States Marines.

The LCVP

The Landing Craft Vehicle Personnel (LCVP) or Higgins boat was an amphibious craft used during beach assaults. It played significant roles in WWII, North Korea, and Vietnam. Its success was owed to its simple and brilliant design. (As well as the work done by UDT and SEALs that allowed the craft to land on the beaches.) The left photo in Figure 7-3 shows a side view of the craft. I snapped this photo at the National D-Day Museum, located in New Orleans.

The boat is nicknamed after Andrew Higgins, the man who invented it and whose factories around New Orleans built thousands of them in a few months. These boats changed amphibious warfare as it was practiced before WWII because they broke the dangerous gridlock and bottlenecks of ship-to-shore off loading operations. For example, in the Gallipoli assault, it took the British and French several days to disembark men and supplies onto shore. In the meantime, their enemy, the Turks were building up their defenses against that shore.

As mentioned, the design was one of brilliant simplicity. It was mostly empty space, as seen in the right photo in Figure 7-3. This arrangement allowed Marines to climb down rope ladders from a ship's deck into the large well of the boat. If they fell, they would usually land in the boat and avoid drowning or being crushed between the ship and the boat. The large space could hold a lot of men (depending on their gear, usually 36 Marines).

The boat, being small, could be stored in davits along the sides of a troop transport. As such, many of them could be lowered into the water quickly. The Marines would then be placed in their holds in a few minutes. The operation allowed an attack force to appear off a coast and launch a full attack in a matter of hours (depending on how much preliminary softening-up was done with artillery.)

The flat bottom accommodated itself to beaches. The water proof bow gate allowed the Marines to disembark relatively easy. For example, Figure 7-4 shows a battle scene from WWII from the stern of an LCVP.

Figure 7-3. The LCVP (the Higgins boat).

Figure 7-4. Disembarking troops.

The design of the boat restricted its speed (maximum of 9 knots or 10.5 mph), which made it vulnerable to shore fire from the enemy. In addition, other than its thin sides, the boat had no protective plating.

It is easy to appreciate how important the roles of UDT and SEALs were in surveying and clearing the landing beaches. The bottoms of the LCVPs were fragile. They had no double bulkheads. They needed a clean beach to land on, which was the responsibility of the frogmen to provide.

Asymmetrical Warfare

Since WWII, UDT's missions had been expanding to include more land-based commando operations. The post WWII conflicts in Malaysia, Laos, Cambodia, and Vietnam brought home to all military thinkers that conventional forces were still effective, but not in certain conditions. An open space, such as a desert or plain, could be effectively attacked and conquered with Patton like tactics. Not so for regions populated with mountains or jungles. The WWII Finnish snow mountain battles against superior Soviet forces demonstrated the effectiveness of unconventional warfare.[7]

In addition, gone were the days when an air force could annihilate a city and bring its citizens to heel. Dresden or Hiroshima type bombings were no longer accepted as part of warfare. Indeed, the concept of total warfare became obsolete, at least to most of the democratic, industrialized nations.

By taking advantage of this new mind-set the warriors in third world countries—located in mountains and jungles—knew their locale gave them leverage. How? By conducting guerrilla warfare: Pick the time and place for a battle. Afterwards, withdraw into forests or mountain enclaves. Don't be concerned with holding a specific piece of turf against better firepower. Sap the enemy of his spirit.

The guerrillas knew they could not win a physical, tactical war against a superior force, but they were convinced they could win a psychological, strategic war. (As the Americans did in their revolutionary war against England.)

Placing the Final Straw onto the Camel's Back

On occasion, the guerilla might be placed in a position to execute a specific battle leading to the defeat of the enemy. Perhaps the carefully chosen attack would result in the enemy withdrawing from the third world country. And a strategic defeat of the enemy did not necessarily have to occur on the battle field. It might take place because of the outpourings of the media, or from the second thoughts of the politicians. It might take place in the minds of those parents who had sent their children to the third world country.

To cite two examples: (1) A supposedly superior first world army might be defeated in a single major battle by their third world guerrilla enemy (Dien Bien Phu). (2) If the resident warriors could not win such a battle, they might dissolve the will of the first world's citizenry to support the war with a set of intense but diffused encounters (the Tet Offensive).

The SEALs

The United States slowly came to realize these truths. In a May 25, 1961 speech, John F. Kennedy complimented the Green Berets and announced a plan to expand America's unconventional warfare capabilities. The president was committed to hold the line against, "the relentless pressure of the Chinese Communists." He gradually began to ramp-up American military presence in Vietnam, in spite of French President de Gaulle's warning that "Vietnam would trap him in a 'bottomless military and political swamp.' "[8]

During this period the Navy initiated programs to train and possibly deploy guerrilla and counter-guerrilla troops, to make each man an expert in hand-to-hand combat, high altitude and low altitude parachuting, beach operations, demolition, and certain languages.

The idea was to adapt the tactics that had been used successfully by the Vietnamese guerrilla forces to defeat the French. However, these forces would expand the UDT operations as well as conventional guerrilla tactics: They would operate on sea, air or land. This strategy led to the beginning of the SEALs. Many of the first

SEAL members came from UDT. Later, UDT was folded into the SEALs.

For a while SEALs participated in UDT training. Afterwards, the men would undergo a three month SEAL Basic Indoctrination (SBI) training class. Finally, they would enter a platoon and train in platoon tactics for operations in Vietnam.

The tests and screenings to be admitted into the UDT training program—not to mention the program itself—were rigorous (and are even more rigorous for today's SEALs). The UDT set a high standard for potential inductees. And once in the program, the drop-out rate was very high. In Chapter 8, I describe these tests, both for UDT and the SEALs.

In 1962, the UDT began conducting hydrographic surveys of many South Vietnam shores and beaches. That same year, the Military Assistance Command Vietnam (MACV) was formed to act as the command organization for all military forces in South Vietnam.

(During the years of 1963-1966, after leaving UDT, this writer was assigned part time duties as a communications courier. I carried classified documents between MACV in Saigon and Danang, and the command ship of the U.S. Amphibious Forces. Before leaving the ship an intelligence officer would handcuff my left arm to a brief case. I would carry a side arm (a WWII .45), but I was not armed with the key to the handcuffs. A duplicate key was held by the intelligence group at MACV. If I had been captured by the enemy the possibility did enter my mind that the Vietcong might place a higher value on the brief case than my wrist.)

In 1962, SEALs were also deployed to South Vietnam for the purpose of training the Army of the Republic of Vietnam commandos in SEALs tactics. At this time the merging of UDT and SEALs was taking place. Some of the teams in South Vietnam were UDT and some were SEALs. By the mid 1960s the former (water oriented) frogmen had been supplanted by the SEALs program. The SEALs were also nicknamed frogmen and they proudly carry this moniker today.

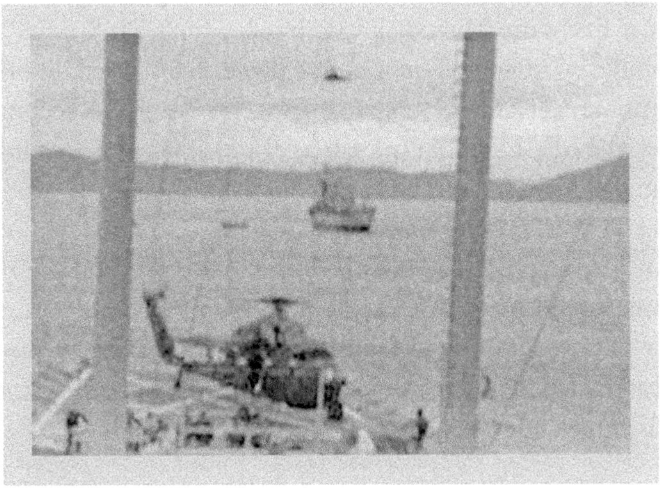

Figure 7-5. SEAL operations from helicopter.

The Central Intelligence Agency began covert SEALs operations in early 1963. Some teams were deployed from a ship to which I was assigned. The operations consisted of ambushing supply movements and capturing North Vietnamese officers, some of whom were brought back to our ship for interrogations. The drops and pickups were often made by helicopter. Three of the ships I rode while in the Vietnam conflict had a landing pad on their sterns. I snapped the photo in Figure 7-5, which shows a helo on the pad. It was waiting to board a SEALs team to take them in-country, a story recounted in Chapter 11. The other ship in Figure 7-5 was a troop carrier. Its job was to transport the Marines to the landing zones on the beaches, also described in Chapter 11.

The SEALs were initially deployed around the Danang area of northern South Vietnam to train the South Vietnamese in diving, demolitions, and guerrilla/anti-guerrilla tactics. As the war continued, SEALs were deployed to disrupt the enemy supply and troop movements in the Mekong Delta and certain areas further inland. Unknown to the public, some SEALs were parachuted into Laos and Cambodia for insurgent operations during the early 1960s.[9] I do not know where the SEALs were going in the helicopter shown in Figure 7-5, most likely the Mekong Delta or the Rung Sat Special Zone.

Combat with the Vietcong was sometimes direct. Unlike the conventional warfare methods of firing artillery into a coordinate location, the SEALs might operate within inches of their targets. In Vietnam the coordinate tactics often did as much harm as good. Gone were the WWII days of bombing blocks-upon-blocks of cities. The Rules of Engagement had changed. Television showed the damage of inaccurate pillage of supposedly targeted sites. Besides, Congress had not declared war. The United States was merely in a conflict. In a war, the soldiers fight with both hands. In a conflict, one hand is tied behind their back.

Pre GPS and Pre Frogman

The futility and Kafkaesque absurdity of the situation—one in which a country goes to a new war but fights with the mentality of an old war—is illustrated in Figure 7-6. (With the exception of figure (b), I took these photos from one of the ships participating in the "battle".) In addition to America committing combat Marines to Vietnam in 1965, the United States also conducted attacks and raids on suspected enemy enclaves along the coast of this country. One assault (with a subsequent amphibious LCVP-accompanied landing) took place as follows:

- Figure 7-6(a): Lobbing shells into a general region containing suspected Vietcong. I say general, because accurate intelligence about the enemy was sketchy or nonexistent.

- Figure 7-6(b): Continuing the bombardment into the night; maybe hitting something—other than empty thatch huts. (This photo was taken by a photographer who was assigned to our amphibious assault staff.)

- Figure 7-6(c): Assured that the enemy will not launch an attack with its own assault boats, moving closer to shore the next day to sprinkle some shells on suspected enemy enclaves near the beach.

- After the completion of these maneuvers, launching combat troops (in LCVPs) in an assault to *surprise* the enemy.

- Finding the enemy "not at home." Finding the hamlets empty. Finding tunnels where the enemy had placed themselves to escape the happenstance bombardment.

- Concluding that America was fighting a post WWII enemy with WWII tactics.

Figure 7-6(a). Softening-up the enemy.

Figure 7-6(b). Hitting something besides a straw hut.

Figure 7-6(c). Moving in for the kill.

Military Combat Outliers

I might come across as overly critical about these early efforts but I am simply arm chair quarterbacking. Adapting new battle tactics rarely occurs serendipitously. It comes about from bitter experience, from loss of battles and loss of lives. Most of us would have taken the same actions as those of the commanders described in the previous section. Trial and error eventually leads military leaders to abandon their past practices.

Figure 7-7. Ominous looks, ominous actions.

For this story the SEALs and other commando units changed the nature of how the United States fought wars in third world countries. They helped America migrate from a WWII mentality of massive, symmetrical battles to smaller, asymmetrical fights. This is to say, when these tactics were warranted.

The SEALs were successful in this new style of warfare. They out-fought the enemy at the enemy's own game. Their anti-guerrilla and guerrilla actions put the fear into the enemy. The Vietcong referred to them as "the men with green faces," due to the camouflage face paint the SEALs wore during combat missions. They looked ominous and they were ominous (Figure 7-7).[10] They would fit into Malcolm Gladwell's outlier population of warriors.

Recent SEALs Operations

The Central Intelligence Agency (CIA) recruits men from the SEALs teams into their Special Activities Division (SAD), home of the elite Special Operations Group (SOG). Joint SEALs and CIA operations go back to the MACV-SOG during the Vietnam War. As mentioned earlier, even though most of the SEALs now do their work on land, they are still sometimes referred to as frogmen.

You have probably read about the SEALs killing the Somalia pirates to help rescue a captured commercial ship. What you hear less of are the clandestine SEALs operations taking place in Afghanistan, or their lesser-known feats in 1997/1998 to capture indicted Serbian war criminals in Bosnia.[11] For the present situation in Afghanistan, these men are risking their lives in a bizarre world of religious fanatics and goat herders—often the same people. They go into hostile territory to perform intelligence operations, capture high yield Taliban leaders, and call in air strikes. They are taking the fight to the enemy, the only way a war can be won.

Osama bin Laden. The value of America's commitment to unconventional warfare—and the consistently outstanding performance of 68,000 special operations personnel (including about 2,800 SEALs)—is no better exemplified than the May 1-2, 2011 attack and killing of the sociopath Osama bin Laden. It was brought-off by a small group of SEALs, Navy frogmen—and with deep intelligence support.

In consonance with America's improved intelligence-gathering and analysis capabilities, asymmetrical warfare—once the domain only of third world countries—is no longer asymmetrical. With bin Laden's demise, I think it is fair to coin a new term: *symmetrical, asymmetrical warfare.*

We're far from success in the war against these madmen, but our improved postures are making it less attractive for the religious diehards to die.

The Collective Outlier

About the subject of bin Laden and his death, let's take a different path about one of the major themes of this book: Outliers do not come about by happenstance, but through prolonged periods of dedicated and goal-oriented efforts.

For this path and using the example of bin Laden's termination, an outlier need not be an individual—those cited thus far in this book. Outlier performance can be collective, involving many people. But the rule cited above holds true for the collective outlier: Once again—and I am admittedly becoming redundant—here's no short cut. Just look at the intense training of the UDT and SEALs introduced in this chapter and explained in more detail in Chapter 8.

For the collective outlier—such as the SEALs and John Wooden's UCLA teams—the situation is more involved. An individual outlier's world is simple: one person makes-up the single performance. The collective outlier's world is complex: more than one person makes-up the single performance.

Many individuals might be members of a collective outlier, a Marine platoon, for example. Some are competent but others may be less so. Thus, they present a more intricate situation than the single performer. That is why collective outlier performance is inconsistent (even rare) and individual outlier performance is usually consistent enough to be almost predictable (the tennis player, Rafa Nadal, on clay, as an example).

The challenge of any system containing more than one person is to brace-up the stragglers onto a higher level of performance. To try to make these plodders perform similarly to the person who is a consistently whirling dervish of superior performance.

That is one reason why SEALs (and other elite units, such as the Delta Force) are so successful. Once you are within their membership, you have already been braced-up. In contrast, the vast military and intelligence complex cannot have such high standards. If they did, they would be undermanned.[12]

We should also understand that the performance of a SEALs 6 team—members of whom are all outliers in their chosen work—may not always lead to outlier results.

During the bin Laden demise saga, America's military/intelligence apparatus displayed outlier skills. Its collective operations will continue to stumble on its skirt. It always has, it always will.

Such is the nature of the collective outlier challenge. We, in the public, should keep this idea in mind when we (often routinely) criticize the performance of the groups in our public service arena. We marvel at the performance of the *individual* outlier. We should be more understanding of the difficult achievements of the *collective* outlier.

Honor and Respect

You may agree or disagree with America's involvement in Afghanistan. If you are against this war, I hope you will not disparage the warriors who are conducting it. Vent your ire on the leaders who are orchestrating it. For what it's worth, your writer was in favor of our Afghanistan invasion to dislodge al Queda, not to install democracy into a centuries-old culture of patrimonial hierarchies, but to interrupt al Queda—which we did. I was not in favor of the second Iraq assault. It diverted our efforts from Afghanistan, which is where the real danger lies.

Dangers Ignored

The occupation of a U.S. Navy frogman was (and is) not a safe one. In WWII some of the team members were killed by machine gun and mortar fire. In the Vietnam conflict several of my UDT training team mates were killed doing their jobs. Today, members of SEALs teams are placing themselves in harm's way every day.

What compels young men to sign up for these duties? What compelled this writer to do so? Since my childhood, I had built a fantasy world about the UDT frogman. It was immune from reality. Dreams die hard.

But there is more to my story than a fixation on a WWII movie. In the early 1960s as a political activist on my college campus I had reached a decision about America's involvement in Vietnam. I believed the only options of the South Vietnamese were to be under the umbrella of America or that of Communism. In those Cold War days I did not see South Vietnam as a stand-alone, neutral country. Because of its history and geographical location, coupled with the nature of the Cold War, it was destined for either the Western or Communist camp. I was sufficiently knowledgeable to understand the woeful deficiencies of Communism. (But as recounted in Chapter 10, I was ignorant of the corrupt rules of (first) French and (later) Vietnam leaders.)

If I joined the UDT, I thought the odds favored my being shipped to Vietnam. Amphibious clandestine guerrilla warfare was "in." Its venue was Southeast Asia. If I were in UDT, I was also "in."

I accepted this possibility for four reasons: First, wherever it might be fought I supported the Cold War. Second, if necessary, I was willing to be an active participant in the military part of this war. Third, the UDT was going to be an integral part of it. Fourth, as a young man I believed myself impregnable. Death never entered my mind; it happened to someone else. I was immersed in the confidence of youth. Besides, as Francis Bacon said, the greater the risk, the sweeter the fruit.

---

[1] Unless otherwise cited, the historical information on the UDT and SEALs has been sourced from the following:

http://www.navyseals.com/navy-seal-history. Wikipedia. Microsoft Encarta Encyclopedia.

Bruce F. Meyers, *Swift, Silent, and Deadly: Marine Amphibious Reconnaissance in the Pacific, 1942-1945*, Annapolis, MD: Naval Institute Press, 2004. NavyFrogMen.com, U. S. Naval Special Warfare Archives, http://www.navysealmuseum.com/heritage/history.php.

[2] Francis Bacon, "Of Love," *Essays*, 1625. Secondary source: Leonard Roy Frank, *Quotationary*, Random House, New York, 2001, p. 182.

[3] http://www.eyewitnesstohistory.com/tarawa.htm.

[4] http://www.eyewitnesstohistory.com/tarawa.htm.

[5] This photo was made after I had left UDT 11, recounted in Chapter 8. We were doing this drill mostly for fun.

[6] My training was not yet integrated with SEALs. In 1963, during one of our sets of exercises at the Coronado, California facility, we trainees beheld a helicopter hovering over San Diego Bay. Suddenly, men in swimming gear began jumping out of the helo into the water. We declared and asked, "What is that?!" Our UDT instructor responded, " 'That' will eventually be us." He mentioned the term "SEALs." It was the first time I had heard it. I don't recall his telling us what the term conveyed, but I do recall I was both impressed and confused by the name.

[7] This type of combat has a history spanning across many centuries. For example, in the first century BC the assassination of Julius Caesar had placed the Roman Empire in civil war. Contending (Republican) Roman army factions in Spain successfully countered superior (Caesarean) Roman Legions by using hit-and-run tactics. More recently, the Taliban in Afghanistan survives (as of this writing) with asymmetrical war tactics and a complimentary "wait-us-out" patience for America's withdrawal.

[8] Stanley Karnow, *Vietnam: A History*, Penguin Books, New York, 1983, pp. 264-265.

[9] In 1964, this tidbit (classified at the time) was divulged to me by a SEALs friend.

[10] From Wikipedia. Key-in UDT or SEALs.

[11] See The Military Channel and "Navy SEALs: Untold Stories." The British SAS commandos (and U.S./British intelligence) were equal partners in this amazing episode.

[12] Thus, the group performance of, say, the FBI—who must deal with potentially recurring horrific events—is a huge challenge. The members of this organization likely contain high performers and laggards, as well as outliers. The FBI must contest for recruiting superior employees with private industry, who can pay a lot more for these skills. Anyway, in the main, group performance comes from the group's leadership.

Chapter 8

Officer Candidate School and UDT Training

Join the Navy and see the world.
—From a recruitment poster

At long last, I was nearing my goal of obtaining a university diploma. The next step was the U.S. Navy Officer Candidate School in Newport, Rhode Island. That time would come soon enough. My last semester at UNM during the spring of 1962 was a time for celebrations and preparations.

Celebrations

The celebrations were conducted almost nonstop. Ignoring our studies for final exams, we fraternity brothers and our girl friends closed the local bars almost as frequently as the bartenders closed our tabs. We knew our collegiate years of lethargic hedonism were coming to an end, that we would eventually be forced to leave the campus and go to work. But not for a few more months. I was not due to report-in to the Navy until the fall of 1962. In the meantime, we comported ourselves in the best tradition of "Animal House."

My Sigma Chi buddies gave me a going away party. None of the other brothers were honored with such a bash, but I was one of a few men who was actually "going away." Most of the others were headed for jobs in family businesses, or graduate, law, and medical schools. Anyway, Tina, the mate of my roommate, Jim, started the party speeches by presenting me a handmade card, parts of which are shown in Figure 8-1.

Figure 8-1. Tina's gift for my departure party.

Frank, one of my best friends, gave a short speech. He offered humorous comments about the Navy and UDT, and got a few laughs from the group by joking about the structured military and my happenstance ways. He polished me off with, "God speed, U.D, you're crazy as a loon!" Jim, the son of a retired Navy Captain, put my adventure in a context the other brothers may not have grasped. "To hell with 'um, U.D.! A ship's safe in a harbor, but that's not where a ship's supposed to be. Smooth sailing!" We then hoisted another Coors (the preferred beer at UNM).

As you may have gathered by now, I have been a note taker and pack rat for most of my life. Thus, I still have Tina's card, the photos from Easley's Twin Lakes, and other memorabilia. I never kept a diary but I often jotted down descriptions of events and unusual thoughts and quotes that I came across. As I reflect on those times with my fraternity brothers, I am reminded of a quote I recorded in my notebook many years ago. It's from a book titled, *Her Privates We*, by Fredric Manning, "Men are bound together more closely by the trivial experiences they have shared, than by the most sacred obligations."

Those friends of many years ago still remain my friends. Perhaps our friendships endure because of the idea behind Manning's thought. Perhaps it is because our common interests keep us together or perhaps it springs from the notion that, "friendships multiply joys and divide griefs."[1] I suspect my friendship with these fine men has lasted because of all of these reasons.

Preparations

In contrast to the college bacchanalian romps, my preparations for UDT were yielding mixed results. Since my vaulting horse groin injury the year before, my body was having trouble repairing itself. My left testicle had healed, but the right one was acting up. Not acting up in the sense of playing out its customary role. Rather, it was acting up as a result of its mistreatment from the vaulting horse. The injury was aggravated by the attending doctor at the college infirmary applying incorrect treatment. When I awoke from my concussion, I found my groin area had been taped up. The dressing also covered my buttocks and upper thighs. I could hardly move. I was feeling no major discomfort as I had been given pain killers but I could sense the tightness of the bandages.

Other than outright castration, the treatment could not have been shoddier. No ice had been applied to relieve the swelling. The tightly bound taping made the swelling worse but the swelling had no room to swell. Later, a urogenital expert at a Navy hospital offered his opinion that the taping likely made a serious but healable injury into one that was more serious.

The injury was a fickle one. Sometimes, I could exercise vigorously and suffer no subsequent pain or swelling. Other times, the right testis would rebel from the physical activity and swell to the size of a lemon. I would be forced to take it easy for a few days. The swelling and pain would go away and I could continue my normal life. As my body permitted, I kept preparing for UDT. Overall, the injury was manageable.

The Physical

As I was winding down my college years, I knew it was time to pay a visit to the Navy recruiting station in downtown Albuquerque. The process to join the Navy was almost effortless, not much more than signing on a dotted line. The threshold for admittance to Officer Candidate School (OCS) was higher but most college graduates were accepted. Without much fanfare, I signed up and was instructed to go to the nearby Sandia Base military hospital for a physical exam.

At the hospital, a doctor looked me over. After checking assorted orifices, organs, and limbs he informed me, "You have two problems that could keep you out of the service: your right shoulder (from a football injury) and your testicle. I can flunk or pass you. What do you want to do?"

I was surprised and replied I did not understand what he meant.

Doctor, "Your injuries are not serious enough to disqualify you outright, but could possibly merit a 4-F classification. It's a gray area. What do you want, in or out?"

The doctor was unaware I had volunteered for the Navy. His job was to assess physical, not mental conditions. He had brought up the idea of my not being in the service, perhaps thinking I would leap at such an opportunity. He could not know he was contending with a promise I had made to myself 15 years ago. I had not come this far to turn back now.

"I want in, doctor."

"Fine. You're in. Good luck."

It's odd how some events in our lives can take place so quickly yet affect us for as long as we live. As I reflect on my conversation with this doctor, I continue to believe my decision was the right one at the time. I'm certain if I had said, "I want out, doctor," I would have regretted it for all my days.

The relevance of these unprompted decisions and declarations is made more interesting by the fact that our lives are not just affected by our positive avowals, such as my statement, but by our naysays as well. *I want in* would have been as significant as *I want out*. It is these sorts of ironies that make life more fascinating and keep us engaged. Without question, my declaration led to some unusual experiences down the road.

Homework for OCS and Advice from a Seasoned Chief

After passing my physical and completing paper work at the Albuquerque recruiting station, a Chief Petty Officer took me aside and gave me some advice.

Chief, "I'd like to loan you this book. (As he handed me a thick book with a dark blue hard cover.) If I were you, I'd read it end to end, and I'd especially study the chapters on the Maneuvering Board and celestial navigation. Dutton's (the book's author, and still in print today) will be your main text for the OCS classes."

Recruit, "Thanks. What's a Maneuvering Board?"

"For about 20% of OCS students, it's the reason they flunk out of the program. Here's some chart paper, a compass, and a parallel ruler. Make sure you do all the practice exercises and learn to do them fast. Accuracy of your plots is the most important point, but speed in putting the plots on the sheet is critical."

The Chief had my attention. For the next week I spent most of my waking hours reading Dutton, learning about the stars and the concepts of relative motion, the latter being the focus of a Maneuvering Board. I can now add another hero to my story: a Chief Bos'un who convinced me to once again, put in the time.

California Dreaming: First Encounter with the Pacific Ocean

As a newly appointed member of the U.S. Navy, I was ordered to report to Officer Candidate School at Newport, Rhode Island. Roster call for OCS was to be the fall of 1962. For now, it was spring.

I had a full summer on my hands. The plains of New Mexico and Easley's Twin Lakes were in the rear view mirror. It was time for other explorations. I left the high and dry deserts of Albuquerque to spend the summer on the beaches and waters of southern California.

My brother, David, was living in the Los Angeles area. I hooked up with him and he was kind enough to room and board me for three months. I secured a semi-secure job as a bill collector in Watts, California, a tale for another time. For this story, the California summer provided my first experience with salt water swimming, just off the shores of Malibu Beach.

I came to prefer ocean swimming to swimming in a pool. The salt water made it easier to stay afloat. Plus, I liked the physical sensations of the waves and tides flowing around my body. Even more, ocean swimming offered more interesting scenes than the sides of a cement swimming pool.

From the waters of Malibu, I could take in spectacular views of Malibu's beaches and the cliffs behind them. I would swim away from the beach, turn myself around, float on my back and luxuriate in my new aqueous world. The sounds from Malibu's civilization were muted by the water and waves breaking across the beach. My newly discovered cocoon was not the same as the silence of being underwater, but it gave me a sense of calmness and serenity. Swimming in the Pacific Ocean was another dream come true.

Dave and I were on our way to Malibu to meet some of his friends. From his home in LA, we drove down Sunset Boulevard, through Hollywood, Beverly Hills, and the Pacific Palisades. Our route gradually descended from inland terrain towards the Pacific Coast Highway.

As we neared the coast line, we crested a hill overlooking the highway. Without warning, I beheld a vast prairie of water, flat and seemingly without end. From this distance, I thought the ocean did not resemble an ocean. Rather, it appeared to be an immense lowland containing diffused images of undulating blue-green grain stalks. But who was I to say what an ocean looked like? It was my first sighting. Nonetheless, the expanse of the water across the horizon was wonderfully incomprehensible. I could hardly wait to take a plunge.

After a brief introduction to Dave's friends, I put on my swim trunks and hurried to the beach. Without hesitation, I sprinted to the surf and took a headlong dive into the incoming waves. For the first time in my life I entered into the wonderful world of a salt water ocean. It was a fanciful and very big pond…a bit larger than my dad's cattle tank.

From my low vantage point, the water seemed to merge with the distant horizon. Looking and swimming west, I saw no cement pool sides or beaches. I only saw a fantastic expanse of seemingly unending water.

The sensations were extraordinary, so different from a swimming pool: powerful pulsating water, the pushes and pulls of its tides, its salty tastes, the sand in my mouth, the noise of the waves. I had been transported into another aqueous world of fantasy. I asked myself, *Why had I not come to see David sooner*?

With an easy breaststroke kick, off I went into the briny, swimming west, not caring or worrying about anything in this world. Why should I? I was somewhere else.

After a while, I took a rest. I treaded water and took in the somewhat distant shore line. I could make out David and his friends at the beach house. More accurately, I could only see figures of people on the deck. They were waving at me. I waved back and started a crawl, paralleling the shore line. I swam for a while, reversed my course and came back the other way with an under arm sidestroke. For my swimming readers, this stroke is ideal for swimming along a shore and taking in the sights. Your head is above water, and you are always facing the beach.

As I neared the point of origin of my parallel swim, I again spotted Dave and his friends. They were still waving at me. I decided they might want me to return to shore. I could not understand why. They conversed about films and their favorite hang-out places in Hollywood. I had nothing to offer to the dialogue.

I started my swim back. On the way, I discovered yet another love for the ocean: body surfing. But not for long, Dave had come down to the shore.

"God damn it! Are you crazy? What in the hell are you doing?"

"Swimming."

"I can see that. What are you, some fucking frogman? You could have drowned out there."

Other than carrying out occasional childish pranks, for my entire life I had been differential and subservient to my five older brothers. In their presence, I became a human Switzerland. They could do no wrong and if they admonished me, I took the fault line. Their love for me was never a question in my mind. Their respect and acceptance were.

As I grew older, I became aware of this gap between them and me. I was a late comer to the family and did not mingle with my brothers very much because of our age differences. Their sports were football, basketball, and track and field. Mine was swimming. We shared no mutual interests. Perhaps joint activities would have helped to bond our relationships, but it did not happen until later in my life.

During my college years, when our family members assembled for reunions, my brothers talked with each other and exchanged nostalgic stories as if I were not in the room. In hindsight, their discourses during these reunions were natural extensions of the past. I was there, but I was not there. That's the way it was.

I have come to understand their benevolent isolation led me to try things on my own, to entertain myself, to ignore their unconscious snubs. But I also have come to know that I harbored resentments toward my siblings for their not allowing me to be part of their world. On that day on Malibu Beach, my brother Dave witnessed my coming out party.

"Yes, I am a *frogman*! I have been for years. I can swim as easily as you can walk, knowing you, probably easier. I'm a grown man, and you're talking to me as if I were a child. I'm not. Things have changed, David."

For the first time I can recall, I saw an older brother taken aback by my statements. Dave paused, then offered, "U.D., there's no lifeguard out there. You scared me to death."

"It's none of your business. If I want to swim to Asia, that's my choice. I appreciate your concern, just don't be so arrogant."

"But I'm your big brother!"

"And I'm twenty three years old! You left home when I was six. You have no idea of who I am or what I can do. If you want to be my brother you can start by treating me as an equal."

In one fashion or another, over the next decade or so, I conveyed these frustrations and desires to all my bothers. They gracefully took it in, likely wondering, where did *that* come from? Today, they are my best friends—even if they swim like bricks.

Ocean Depths

In my exuberance to demolish sibling suzerainty, I ignored David's common sense observations. I was swimming alone, several hundred yards off shore, one that was unprotected by lifeguards. I knew very little about cross currents and under tows. I had read about them in the Red Cross manuals but like the dangers of UDT, they remained abstractions. My youth made me impregnable to hazards. Others were vulnerable. Not I. Besides, I was in less danger swimming a quarter mile off a Southern California coast than driving on a Southern California freeway.

Notwithstanding my immature hubris, on this initial encounter with an ocean I became aware of its depth. I pulled myself under water and stroked farther downward. I kept going down for a short while. Unlike John's pool in New Mexico, there was no 10 foot bottom. I was not completely corn pone to be unaware of the deepness of the Pacific. Nonetheless, to appreciate the awesome aspect of ocean water depth, a swimmer must at least try to penetrate its void. From my first swim, I came away with a cautious respect for the Pacific Ocean: *Jesus, this is a big swimming pool*!

Someone to Watch over You

During the weekends of the summer of '62, I spent some of the time at other beaches. I preferred Long Beach and Manhattan

Beach because they were easier to reach from Dave's home in the Silver Lake district of LA. The major disadvantage of these beaches was the presence of lifeguards. They imposed a limit on how far a person could swim away from the shore. I recognize I am exposing my contrary nature by recounting this next story to you. But I do so to make a point.

After arriving at Manhattan Beach and staking my claim to a spot on the sand with my towel, I entered the water and began to swim some distance away from the beach. At that time, I was not aware that the colored buoys a few yards away from the beach represented inviolate fences. My rather idle thought was that they represented warnings to swimmers, but nothing else. I paid no more attention and swam on.

Before long, I heard shouts and whistles. As a former lifeguard, I was attuned to whistles. I looked back toward the shore and noticed two lifeguards, standing on an elevated platform. They were whistling and signaling with their hands. I thought, *Not again! Why can't people mind their own business?* I ignored them and turned west to continue my swim. If they wanted me to swim inside a corral, they would have to rope me in. Roping and corralling were their intents. They launched a boat and paddled out to force me back to shore.

I was given a hard time by the guards. Fine by me, I had purposely given them a hard time. They told me I had violated a city ordinance. They dropped a ladder in the water and ordered me to board the boat.

"I'm getting in no boat of yours. I'll swim back to shore by myself."

Guard, "I'm warning you. Get in this boat."

"How do you think I got out here? I'm swimming back."

I began swimming toward shore using my breaststroke crawl. I don't know why one of the guards did not jump in the water and "rescue" me. I suspect they decided not to go to the trouble, that they saw I was proficient.

As mentioned in an earlier chapter, the breaststroke crawl is a powerful stroke but its execution expends a lot of energy. When swam properly, it displays the strength and stamina of the swimmer.

I was several hundred feet from shore, but I was determined to make it in on this stroke alone and display my skills. My ego was fully engaged.

As I made progress, I occasionally glanced back to see the lifeguards trailing me in their boat, keeping their eyes on their subject. Well done. They had been properly trained.

As I reached shore and walked through the remaining surf, I heard a smattering of hands and cheers from some of the beach goers. The "rescue" had gained their attention and the scene had become a weekend melodrama. Except for two agitated lifeguards, what a kick!

As I walked to my towel, some fellow sun worshippers came by and asked what was going on? Before I had a chance to respond, one of the lifeguards approached and ordered me to accompany him. I was out of my element. He had me roped and corralled. I followed him to a small hut located at the back of the beach.

There, I met the head lifeguard of Manhattan Beach. He informed me I was banned from swimming for the day and stated my irresponsible acts were a danger to the public and his lifeguards. The lifeguards might have had to risk their lives to rescue me. In the meantime, fewer lifeguard eyes were scanning the corral of human sardines (my words, not his). If I swam beyond their sardine can again, I would be banned permanently.

I returned to my towel. As I sat there, my eyes turned to the swimmers inside their boundaries. The scene took me into a funk. The city of Manhattan Beach had established a small swim zone within the largest body of water in the world. To do nothing more than to protect people from their own folly, without any regard to their swimming ability. To this day, the situation rankles me. I want government to protect me from others. I do not want government to protect me from myself. But that's not the way it is in our culture of irresponsibility: *Can't take a chance. You're not going to drown on our watch. We'll get sued because of your stupidity!*

I recognize I'm swimming upstream on this issue. I've had countless arguments with friends about the foolishness and irrationality of my views on this matter. Nonetheless, I remain convinced that Uncle Sam and his minions are gradually pinching off our freedoms and their associated requirements for exercising self responsibility. Perhaps my swim that day represented a youthful semiconscious rebellion.

I never swam again at a beach in southern California that had lifeguards to guard me from doing one of the things I loved to do: swimming without external boundaries, but with boundaries imposed from within. The idea is a metaphor for living one's life. I was responsible for my own actions and it was *my* responsibility to assure they harmed no one else. In my view, it is in concert with the saying, "Responsibility is the price of freedom."[2]

Reporting In

In the fall of 1962, I made my first trip to the east coast. Until that time, I was a provincial youth, confining my excursions from New Mexico to the states of Texas and California. My next stop was Officer Candidate School (OCS), located at Newport, Rhode Island.

My eagerness to be a member of UDT and the U.S. Navy was counterbalanced by the realization I was entering a structured, disciplined system. If so motivated, I knew I could impose structure and discipline on myself. Self imposed behavior was part of my makeup, but having someone dictate my behavior? I was not certain I would accept such a big change in how I lived.

The other concern was getting along in a hierarchical culture. I have always liked a flat organization. As a businessman in later years, I made certain few levels of bureaucracy kept me from the folks who burned the calories to put black ink on my balance sheet. This mode of management would not be acceptable in the U.S. Navy. As an officer, I would be expected to lead my lower-level graded men through several levels of ranks. Maybe so, maybe no, but I knew I had to make adjustments to my egalitarian mind set. My petty officers would be my key to success. I had to manage my men through them.

Figure 8-2. Reporting for duty.

On a cool fall afternoon, along with several hundred other men, I reported-in to OCS (see Figure 8-2). On the way to the base from the airport several other candidates and I shared a Navy bus. The vehicle had been assigned to transport OCS newcomers to the Naval Station Newport (NAVSTA Newport) located on Narragansett Bay. If all went well, in 16 weeks I would be commissioned as an Ensign in the U.S. Navy and could try out for UDT. If I failed I would be required to stay in the Navy, but as an enlisted man. I had nothing against being a swabee but I had not come this far to be mustered out of my dream.

Academics and Marching

The attrition rate at Navy OCS was higher than I expected. I had assumed OCS would be a cake walk, but it wasn't. I was in Kilo Company. Our platoon (Kilo One) started with forty men. Thirty three were commissioned. The dropouts became enlisted men and were sent to the Great Lakes training facility and later to the fleet. The curriculum was rigorous, but it was not the difficulty of the subjects. It was trying to absorb a lot of information in a short time.

Each week day began at 5:30 am with the sound of reveille piped into our WWII vintage barracks. At 6:30, we fell out for breakfast to march to the mess hall. We ate, marched back to the barracks, where we prepared ourselves and our lockers for a white glove inspection. Next, we sat in a study hall from 8 am to 9 am. At 9 am, we fell out for morning classes and marched to various class rooms. We marched to the mess hall for a one hour lunch break. We were allowed to return to the barracks from lunch singly; no marching. At 1 pm we fell out and marched to our afternoon classes. They ended at 4 pm, at which time we marched to the parade grounds to practice marching...which we had already practiced. After dinner, we spent another two hours in the study hall. Taps were played at 11 pm.

The worst part of this routine was the routine itself. But the rigor was necessary in order to bootstrap a bunch of immature former college students into positions of leadership. To this day, I extend my gratitude to my country for those 16 weeks. The lessons learned at OCS and the responsibilities placed on young Ensigns gave us a head start on other men of our age. I gained more from this short intense training and studies than I did from all my graduate work.

All of us were green. A few of us were tinhorns—and about to be taken down a notch or two. Our success as officers would depend largely on the understanding and competence of the men who ran the navy: Chief Petty Officers. After completing OCS and being assigned to a ship, I was fortunate to have two fine Master Chief Petty Officers guide me though the ropes.

Putting in the Time

In Chapter 3, we read about studies substantiating the idea that getting an early start in learning a new endeavor places a person at an advantage over his peers. For an intense learning situation, such as OCS, a difference of a few hours or days can make a huge difference between success and failure.

Imagine that you are the officer on the bridge of a navy ship. You are also officer of the deck, thus you are in command of the ship at that time. Imagine ten other ships are sailing in rough weather with your ship, all in a prearranged formation. (A common situation during my time aboard ships.) Imagine a man goes overboard on a ship that is in the middle of this formation. (Which also occurred while I was in the fleet.) Upon discovery of this accident, the ship sounds "Man Overboard!" Through radios and flags, this alarm is conveyed to the other ships. Immediately, the command ship (that would be yours) issues orders for all ships to take evasive actions to avoid running over the stricken sailor or colliding with one another. If all ships do not act togethr in concert, chaos follows.

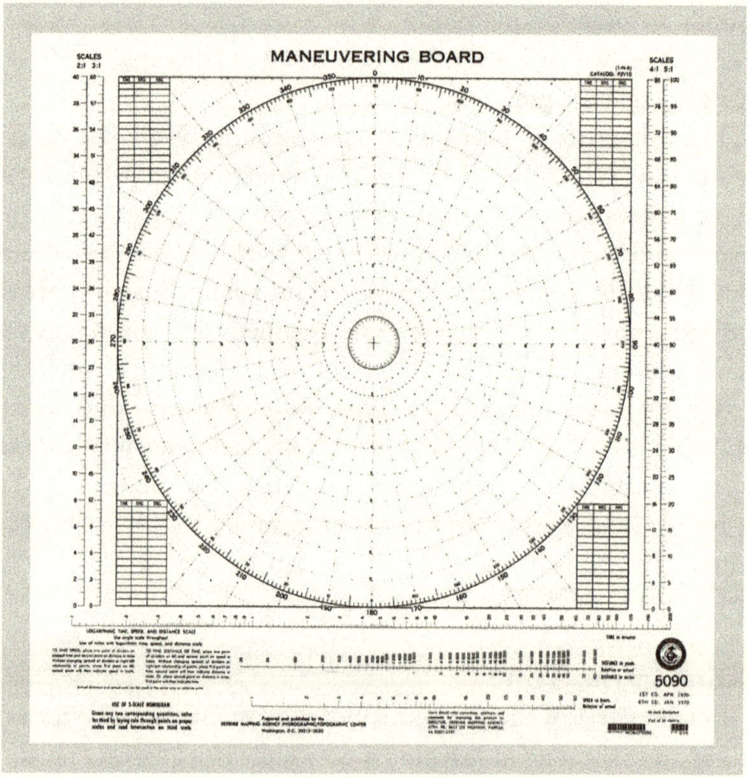

Figure 8-3.The Maneuvering Board plotting sheet.

The men on the bridges and in the Combat Information Center (CIC) must perform Maneuvering Board calculations quickly and accurately. They must plot (on a Maneuvering Board coordinate sheet, shown in Figure 8-3) the relative movement of their ship to the others in the formation. Otherwise, the sailor may be lost and/or the vessels may collide. The plotting of the relative motion of a ship in relation to another ship is not a complex process: A radar is used to locate a ship (or ships), a compass and a parallel ruler are then used to plot the movement of the ship in relation to your ship. The challenge is making the plot accurate during stressful conditions.

The OCS Operations class had many hours devoted to Maneuvering Board drills and tests. Because of my previous practices with the Board, I did very well. My first exams were graded as 100%. After much practice, the process became second nature to me. Several other candidates in Kilo One who were new to the Maneuvering Board never got the hang of it and with each day, they fell further behind. I felt sorry for them. They were not lucky enough to have had prior practice.

Our instructor, Lt. Stewart, called me aside and asked how I had picked up the Board so quickly. I informed him, "I haven't, Mr. Stewart. I worked all of Dutton's examples and problems before I reported to OCS. A Chief at my recruiting station warned me about the Board's difficulty. He loaned me Dutton and the Board material."

Mr. Stewart, looked at me for a moment, and said, "That might be a good practice for all the recruiting stations to take on."

Later, ineptitude crept in and I made several erroneous plots on exams, but not before I had padded my grade average to assure a passing mark.

Several of my buddies flunked out of OCS because of their inability to maneuver the Maneuvering Board. I am certain their future was affected by this failure. One of my good friends who failed the OCS operations class had finished law school. One afternoon, our platoon marched back from marching practice to discover this man's bunk bed mattress was gone. So was he. Was I more intelligent and facile than my friend? Not at all. I was another example of Malcolm Gladwell's concepts of getting an early start and putting in the time. Thank you Chief Bos'un.

In the early spring of 1963, all OCS candidates were asked to fill in forms to indicate in which branch of the Navy we would like to serve. We were allowed three choices, with preferences noted for each. My lawyer friend was going to choose JAG, but he ended up swabbing decks on a tin can (destroyer). Some chose air. Some chose the Supply Corps, some submarines. I chose UDT, air, and destroyers in that order.

Northeast Winters

The academic and marching schedules at OCS precluded students from doing much physical training. Nonetheless, I found time to run and lift weights several times a week. I rarely swam. It took too much time. My "lemon" was giving me no trouble.

Nonetheless, during a two week Christmas break, I returned to New Mexico, and met with a urologist who was assigned to Sandia Base. He had little to offer other than: I had an injury with (possibly) faulty blood vessels and (possibly) damaged nerve endings. I was probably okay. *Just take it easy, Mr. Black. Need any aspirin? They're free at the base pharmacy*. Thanks, doc. I'm thankful I didn't have to pay you for your advice.

Northeast winters were cold. Wind off the near freezing waters of Rhode Island Sound made my runs around the base a miserable experience. Later, I wised up and ran around the basketball court inside the gym. I was in good shape and looking forward to the UDT qualification test.

Cross those t's, Dot those i's, and Slash those Zeroes!

The Navy had its ways and traditions. (It still does.) Some of us learned about them the hard way. The instructor for the engineering class was a Master Chief Petty Officer. His job was to teach us in a few weeks the engineering plant of a warship. A very difficult assignment for all, we could only skim the surface of the subject. After OCS graduation, those men who were assigned to the Engineering Department on a ship would be given intense on-the-job training. OCS did not so much teach us what we needed to know, as it taught us what we did not know.

One convention emphasized in all classes was the correct punctuation of numerals. Chief Nickell made this rule clear:

"Gentlemen, here are your exam papers. They're marked and graded. We'll review the answers."

After a few Q and A appraisals, one of our mates raised his hand. Chief Nickell asked, "Yes, Mr. Rawlings?"

Charles Rawlings was a cool Floridian. He was one of the smartest men in Kilo One, acing all the tests. He also had a dry wit, "Chief, all my answers are correct, but you gave me a zero."

Chief, "Yes, you failed to put a slash through your zeroes (as in Ø). Your answers are all 0's. You also failed to put a decimal point and a zero at the end of each number (as in Ø. Ø). I had no choice but to give you a zero on the test, and I hope you learned something today."

"Yes, I did learn something. I noticed my grade of zero has a slash through it. But you also made an error, Chief."

Uh oh. None of us had ever contradicted one of our instructors.

Chief Nickell kept his cool, "What was that?"

"Your grade on my paper is marked as a zero with a slash (Ø), but not zero point zero (Ø. Ø). Which one is it, Chief?"

Charles was irritated but the mistakes were on his test, not Chief Nickell's. Nonetheless, Charles was not accustomed to failure but he was cool about the confrontation. He kept a smile on his face. Chief Nickell responded that the convention was standard practice and tried to leave it at that.

"Very well, Chief, but I don't understand why you marked me off only once. After all, each answer had three errors. No slashes, no decimal points and no trailing zero. I should have gotten a *minus* 200. Sorry, that would be minus 200 POINT ZERO!"

Touché. Everyone laughed, even the Chief, who then responded, "Good point, Mr. Rawlings. Let me see your paper."

Charles arose from his desk and walked the paper to the front of the room. There, Chief Nickell scratched-out his grade of "Ø" and replaced it with (– 2 Ø Ø. Ø). "Any other questions, Mr. Rawlings?"

"No, Chief. We've both made our points."

Later, Charles was called in to talk with the department head of Engineering (a Lieutenant Commander) and the Chief. He was informed his grade of zero had been changed to 100. The department made that decision because of Charles' perfect scholarship record as well as the manner in which he dealt with the problem.

Common Sense, Tolerance, and Flexibility

The OCS administration showed admirable tolerance and flexibility about these kinds of situations. One student was close to failing the final exam for the Orientation Class—the easiest class in the curriculum. A failure would have meant his dismissal from OCS. He was a math whiz and was making high grades in the other classes. But he was not adept with subjective material or writing. He was given the benefit of the doubt on some short answer questions on the exam.

He was one of my best friends (Bob) and told me his Alabama academic training was in numbers not words. I understood his situation. I had college friends at UNM who became IBM engineering marvels, yet struggled with required language courses. One of my fraternity brothers—a premed student—was a crackerjack in biology and chemistry but had a lot of trouble qualifying for medical school because he could not get through liberal arts courses.

My Alabama friend showed me his final exam. The prose was not pretty, but he was given a passing grade. The maxim for this story is: don't throw out the baby with the bath water. My friend went on to become a great F-4 fighter pilot and won several citations for his performance in Vietnam.

Respect for others' quirks and acceptance of their minor deficiencies can go a long way toward building a foundation of trust. The OCS officers were practical teachers. Certainly, the dropout rate was high, but the officers were open to reasonable compromise. Of course, if a candidate couldn't cut it, he was sent to the fleet as an enlisted man. But my friends were competent—well beyond the norm. Charles had no academic weaknesses. Bob was not so good with verbs. They were given passes by the U.S. Navy and became fine naval officers.

UDT Qualification Test

Toward the end of the OCS program, all officer candidates received a notice the UDT would be conducting a test for men who were interested in serving in this outfit. After classes and before dinner, around 120 men showed up for the screening. I can't say how many of them were really interested. I think some were there out of curiosity, but I was surprised at the turnout.

The test was divided into three parts: two swimming races (breaststroke or sidestroke and crawl (surprise)), a running race (one mile), and calisthenics (push-ups, pull-ups, and a rope climb). Our performance times were made available to us for the two swim tests, the run, and the rope climb.

I placed first in the breaststroke race, second in the crawl, and fifth in the rope climb. My finish in the run was 25th, not great but easily passable. My overall score placed me in the top 5% of the candidates. It was enough to be granted an interview, which took place the next afternoon.[3]

The tests for today's SEALs are more rigorous than the tests I took at the Rhode Island base. I recall the two swims were only two laps each, about 50 yards apiece. The run was a mile. I don't recall any timed pull-ups or push-ups in our tests. I do recall the rope climb was timed. For today's SEALs qualification tests, the candidate must pass: (a) a 500 yard swim, (b) two minutes of push-ups, (c) timed curl-ups, and (d) a 1.5 mile run.[4]

Equally important, a SEALs candidate must score very high on a mental test; more than twice that of a regular Navy conscript. As well, a SEALs candidate is screened for "psychological and personality traits."[5] Considering the potential danger and certain rigor of the job, these tests are practical filters. They are used to sieve the (usually well-meaning) laggards away from the outliers.

The Interview

The evaluators had my college transcript in hand, as well as my resume. We talked about my experience with the Red Cross program and AAU water polo. They noted I had been involved in campus politics. I mentioned I was considering going into international law someday. They asked about my groin injury. I told them it was fine. After all, I had easily passed the UDT physical qualification drills and tests and I was not experiencing pain.

One evaluator asked me about a line item in my "Who's Who in American Colleges and Universities" write up. "What is the Zoot Finster Drum and Violin Corps?"

Candidate, "Eh...just a tongue in cheek group some of us put together, mostly for fun."

Evaluator, "I see. What instrument did you play?"

"I specialized in the raspa."

"The stick with ridges in it?"

"Yes, sir."

"Did it take a lot of practice to master?"

"No, sir. Again, the group was not much more than a farce."

"And you chose to put the entry in your Who's Who write up?"

"Well, it seemed like a good idea at the time." *But not now.*

"So you were making fun of Who's Who."

"Yes, sir." *No sense in lying.* But I did not feel confident about this turn of events. *They might think I would make fun of, say, the American flag.*

"Tell us why you think you could lead a UDT team?"

"Because I've been in leadership positions and performed well enough."

"UDT is not a college student council."

"Sir, I counted over 100 men at the test yesterday. I suspect I have as much leadership experience as any of them. All of us have to start somewhere."

"What makes for a good officer?"

They had me on this one. I could have spouted out *Harvard Business Review* malarkey and probably gotten through this question. I replied, "I don't know for certain. Common sense is important. In the military I think the principal ingredient is to take care of your men. If you do, they will take care of you."

"Anything else?"

"Show respect for those you lead and they will respect your leadership. Just make sure you're the leader."

I left the interview thinking it did not go well. I replayed the questions and answers in my mind time and again, even jotted them down in a notebook. My last response about "respect" bothered me. It seemed too pat, too much like a quote from Bartlett's. But I had done my best. The die was cast.

The Second Interview

The next day, I was elated to learn I had made the short list for UDT school. I was invited back for a second interview. The interviewer, a full Commander offered, "We liked your physical test scores. We liked the interview yesterday. (*Whew!*) This is the last you'll hear from me in person. You may or may not be selected. You may or may not hear from us about your acceptance or rejection. Whatever, you'll know for sure when you receive your orders to report."

We spoke for a few minutes. He asked again about my football and gymnastics injuries. I replied, "Commander, I passed the physical to get into the Navy. Do you want me to take another one?"

"Your swimming, running and rope climbing scores were sufficient. Nonetheless, if you're selected, you'll have to take another physical. For the final candidates, you'll all go through a compression chamber test, and we'll put you in the Bay in a diver suit and hard hat. Good luck, Mr. Black. You may or may not be seeing us again."

"Thank you, Commander. I hope I do."

Pressure Testing and Hard Hat Diving

Pressure Testing. Several of the 120 men who participated in the initial test were selected to undergo two more tests. One test (the hyperbaric pressure test) consisted of sitting in a pressure chamber for a while to determine if we could withstand increased (underwater) pressure. Several of us were placed in the chamber at the same time along with an observer. Outside, other men were peering in from a curved window that distorted the images of the observers. From my vantage point, I felt like I was a landlocked goldfish inside a dry fish bowl being observed by weird looking terrestrials. Below is a general description of what it is like to undergo a pressure test:[6]

This test is performed under the supervision of a diving-certified medical doctor. All testing subjects enter a pressure chamber, accompanied by the doctor, and the tank is sealed. Typically, there is in the chamber an object such as an inflated volleyball or water polo ball. Upon sealing the tank, pressure is increased, while the tested subjects equalize their eardrum pressure. If a subject is unable to do so, the test stops, and pressure is slowly released. Pressure builds within the chamber until the chamber is equal to water pressure of a certain depth, such as 60 feet. At this point, the chamber feels very warm and dry. The ball has become compressed enough that it has taken the shape of a bowl. It appears to have been emptied of air, due to the greatly increased air pressure inside the tank. Sounds inside the tank at pressure sound as if they are "far away".

During the controlled release of pressure from the tank, the air in the chamber becomes quite chilled and a fog forms in the chamber, often precipitating as a sort of dew. Once pressure is fully released, the candidates are examined with an otoscope to check for ruptured eardrums. Candidates with ruptured eardrums are either rejected as unfit, or removed from the testing cycle until healed, depending on the severity of the injury.

Because of the sensations a person experiences during this test—coupled with a very tight space possibly leading to claustrophobia—not all men passed the test. The protocol was for a candidate to raise his hand if he wished the test to be stopped. I did fine, not because of any badge of courage, but because the exercise did not bother me. After all, I was never in danger and I could hold up my hand at any time.

Hardhat DivingTest. The second test had us placed in a hard hat diving outfit. To gauge our reactions to being in deep water and (again) in tight quarters, we were submerged into the nearby bay. This test was also conducted to allow us to evaluate a hard hat diving billet in relation to UDT.

I had one memory of hard hat diving: The 1948 John Wayne movie, "Wake of the Red Witch." My recollection is the scene in which John is deeply submerged and his diving helmet is filling with water. John is quizzically looking up toward the surface as if he is puzzled about the maladroit source of the water swirling around his mouth. I saw this movie about the same time I saw the movie about WWII frogmen. I knew I wanted to be in UDT and with equal conviction, I knew I wanted no part of being outfitted with a huge metallic helmet, a heavy canvas diving suit, and worst of all, lead weights attached to feet, chest, and back.

I knew enough about hard hat diving to understand that two filaments from the surface ship were attached to the diver: an air hose and a rope. The rope kept the diver in touch with the surface and also prevented his weight from breaking the air hose.

We were lowered into the bay on a small platform with a rope attached to it, *but no rope was attached to the helmet*. I became aware of this fact because I was not the first guinea pig. I watched earlier men take the plunge. For my descent, the pull of the current in the bay was so strong it threatened to take my feet off the platform. If I lost my grip on the ropes of the platform, I would end up like John Wayne. Was it dangerous? I thought it was and upon surfacing, offered my opinion. One of the attending sailors responded that he heard my complaint all the time, "So far, we've never lost a man. Next diver!" I couldn't help but laugh...after the fact, of course.

The Selection

During the last days of OCS the officer candidates received their orders. The texts were written as if we were now officers. Mine reads as follows (I'm abbreviating a longer document):

> Proceed San Diego, Calif, report CO NAVPHIBSCOL, Coronado, at NAVPHIBBASE, primary TEMDUINS involving demolition of explosives about nineteen weeks. COMPTEMDIRECT report CO, UDT ELEVEN, primary duty involving demolition of explosives.

I will never forget receiving this piece of paper. My Kilo Company buddies and I were waiting in our barracks for the delivery of our orders, for a blue ink memo that would affect our lives, perhaps to our deaths. As we opened our envelopes, some shouted in glee; some groaned in despair. Some were assigned to their first choice; some were not. Our Kilo platoon leader was assigned to an oiler. The man who bunked next to me was ordered to report for pilot training.

I had finally made the grade! After years of dreaming and preparation, after hours of grinding away, I was headed for Coronado, California, home base for the West Coast UDT operations. I discovered I was one of six of the 120 candidates selected for UDT training.

Figure 8-4. Happenstance marchers.

Shortly, we received our commissions. And for one final time, we marched to the parade grounds for a full review by the big wigs of all companies of OCS. After 16 weeks of marching, one would think we would have been better marchers.

No, as Figure 8-4 shows, we soon to be Ensigns never got our muscle memory sufficiently aligned to keep our hands and feet allied in the marching formation. Granted, we weren't soldiers or

Marines, men who marched even more than we did. Nonetheless, we could only hope we navigated our ships and boats better than we navigated ourselves.

Running in the Sandia Mountains

I had the luxury of shore leave before I was due to report to UDT 11 (the number designation of my class) in Coronado, California. I returned to Albuquerque in the spring of 1963, determined to settle once again into the rigors of training and exercise.

During my leave, I concentrated on getting my wind back. Each day, I would drive to the nearby Sandia Mountains and take a run on the mountain trails. The high altitude training would make it easier to run on the sand dunes at Coronado beach. The time was well spent. I was prepared, and my gymnastics injury was history. Or so I thought.

Reporting Early for UDT

I decided to leave Albuquerque and report to Coronado early. Formal UDT 11 registration was a week away. I wanted to continue my conditioning drills on the beach and sand dunes, two of several locations for the training. I flew to San Diego, took a taxi to Coronado, and checked in at the BOQ (Bachelor Officer Quarters). The next day, I obtained gear from the supply store and began running on the sand dunes behind a beach called the Silver Strand, or Strand.

The UDT evaluators at OCS had informed the men selected for the program that the runs would take place across sand hills with the candidates wearing (heavy) combat boots. Their descriptions convinced me it would be a good idea to get ahead of the sand dune power curve. Put in the time and things will work themselves out. I checked in with the UDT group and told them what I was doing. I asked for typical times for completing the sand dune runs. This performance information allowed me to set goals for the week.

The runs over the sand dunes were considered by many UDT candidates to be the most difficult test of the physical routines. As mentioned, the runs were not made on the hard, wet sand on the beach. They were made in the soft sand hills behind the beach. For my readers who think themselves in good shape, try that work-out for a few miles.

It was these runs over the sand dunes that did me in. I started out okay, but by the fifth day of my routine, I acknowledged to myself I was in trouble. My pain would not diminish as rapidly as it once did. I had to stop any rigorous physical activity for a day before I could continue the runs. For the runs completed, I fared well against the times given to me by the UDT staff, but I could not sustain the exercise.

I decided to do nothing for the week-end. Monday was the beginning of the UDT training program. By Monday, my pain was gone. I was pumped and ready. Get ready UDT, here comes UDB!

UDT Rigors and Routines

The SEALs training program today is different from the UDT program I went through in 1963. The modern program is more demanding and involves land based commando and guerilla warfare training.[7] As mentioned, our training was oriented towards the water. For the first weeks, only officers participated in the training. Later, enlisted men joined the program.

Also, today's program, called BUD/s (Basic Underwater Demolition/SEALs Training), requires the arriving men to re-do their qualification tests. We did not go through this procedure.

For the first part of the training, the day began at 6 am with one hour of calisthenics. In between each exercise, we jogged around in a circle. No rest for the weary. After this hour, we placed a large rubber boat on our collective heads and with a paddle in hand, jogged about a quarter mile to the beach. (In the SEALs training, the men have the good fortune to lug around a log the size of a telephone pole.) During this time, we sang a chant about the glory of what we were doing (PT means physical training):

PT, PT, PT: so good, so good, so good.
Wine, women, song: no good, no good, no good
UDT, UDT, UDT: so fine, so fine, so fine.

None of us believed a word of the song but its cadence helped us transport the boat and ourselves to the beach. At the beach, we worked with the boats and/or ran the obstacle course. But first, we took the sand dune run. By then, it was close to noon. We would then jog back to the base, eat our chow, have about a half hour of free time and then spend the afternoon in the water or attend lectures about UDT operations. Figure 8-5 shows a typical scene of these activities.[8]

I'm told SEALs training today is partially reversed from our regimen. We swam in the afternoon. Some of the SEALs water work is in the early morning. Also, the word "Hooyah!" and its associated exclamation point was not used. Our joint response to an instructor's order or question was "Yo!"

Figure 8-5. Training scene.

UDT candidates ran everywhere, as do today's SEALs. To chow, back from chow, to the beach and back from the beach. In between, and at any time, an instructor could yell "Drop!" to any of us. Immediately, one or all of us would drop for a series of pushups until we heard the magic word, "Recover!" Then, we were given the privilege to get back on our feet and continue running.

I quickly discovered a personal irony pertaining to my many years of work in the water to prepare for this program: Initially, a UDT trainee did not need to be a great swimmer. Average would suffice. A considerable time in the pool was devoted to teaching the men how to swim better, a part of the training that surprised me. Why apply to UDT if you can't swim well?

Much of the work entailed paddling rafts, climbing obstacle barriers, and running. For the swimming, the huge flippers (fins) gave most anyone with legs of reasonable strength and stamina the ability to swim adequately enough to pass the exercise goals and tests. Notwithstanding, the water work was quite difficult for some of the candidates.

Initial routines had us swim the sidestroke and breaststroke. Thus, my frog kick did not help me for surface swimming with fins but its variation the sidestroke kick (the scissors kick) was a god-send. It can be executed with flippers to produce a very powerful stroke. As with the UDT try out at OCS, I did well in the swims.

As mentioned, some of the drills had us swim without fins. Several of the candidates floundered around almost helplessly. I was amazed, but they told me they had rarely swam without fins.

The instructors told us they would have us swimming like frogs. I had already attended this school.

My underwater breath holding experience also came in handy during drills in which our masks were pulled off our faces. We had to keep our wits about us as we recovered from the mugging. In addition, some of the drills entailed binding our arms and legs together. We would be required to swim with any stroke we could execute with our appendages bound-up. These drills were a piece of cake for me, as I had been doing them since I was in junior high school, but a couple team mates panicked and had to be hauled from the water.

Another drill had both our arms and legs tied up but we did not swim. We were to remain stationery and find a way to keep breathing. The logical approach was to drop to the bottom of the pool, then push with our legs to take us to the top. There, we grabbed a big gulp of air, sunk to the bottom and repeated the process. This routine was trouble-free for me. It was nothing more than the *bobble-bubble* game I had taught my students during the summers at John Easley's swimming pool. My students and I were not bound by ropes. But my muscle memory required the same actions. My putting in the time, my motivated efforts and my work to reach my dream were paying off.

Hope is the Failed Man's Bread[9]

The performance of the fourteen officers in training could be divided into two levels. The nine men who came from OCS, the Naval Academy, or from a previous training program (those who were injured and had healed) were at one level. All of us were in top notch physical condition. The men who had been "put back" to rejoin a team were tougher and more motivated than any of us. They had experienced at least some of the rigors of the training and were determined to make it through this time around

The five who came from the fleet were on another level. They were in fair to pathetic shape. It remained a mystery to me why the requirements of admittance were both rigid and ragged. I learned that an enlisted man might be granted orders to report to UDT training if he would re-enlist. But the few out-of-shape men in our group were officers and I do not recall their extending their commissions to obtain orders to come to Coronado.

Later, I met and became friends with a fleet officer who had joined UDT just to get off a ship and gain a billet ashore. He was a fine basketball player in college but he could not swim worth a lick. After flunking out of UDT, he was assigned to the Coronado Base as Athletic Officer. He led the base team to a championship in a San Diego Navy league.

I entered the first day of training fit and ready, but later my right testicle began giving me problems. With enough aspirin ingested to erode my stomach, I kept going as long and far as I could. But I was slowing to a jog, then a walk during the sand dune run. The swimming work was not the problem and did not seem to put much stress on my groin area. The sand dune running was doing me in.

My pain had now increased to the extent that it interfered with my movements. A UDT instructor, who had been running backwards (!) in the sand observing the runners, put his hand up, "Hold it, Mr. Black." I stopped.

The UDT training philosophy (as well as the present day SEALs) is to make absolutely certain anyone who passes is an warrior outlier. Any physical or mental weakness could lead to catastrophe during a combat engagement. At the same time, these training guys were silently cheering for us. They wanted us to succeed, but only if we had the strength and tenacity to do so. No free passes.

The instructor informed me he noticed I was limping. Did I have a leg injury? What could I say? That I was fine? That I just needed a day or so of doing nothing to let my body heal?

"I injured my groin last week."

"We thought something was going on. Your performance has been getting worse, not better. Can you walk back to the bivouac?" (Where we began the run, and where a medic was on stand-by.) I replied yes. We left the dunes and returned via the hard sand on the beach.

The medic took a quick look at my privates, put me in a medical wagon and drove me to the Coronado base infirmary. After a doctor examined me, I was placed in a military ambulance, which transported me across the bay to the San Diego Navy Hospital. My career as a UDT frogman was hanging in the balance.

Still in a confused state of denial, I refused to accept what was happening. I had done well so far. If I were not injured, I was confident I could make it through the program. The trouble was that I could not make it through the program without reinjuring myself. I had spent a long time working to fulfill a dream. In such a short time, the dream was over.

A Dream Denied

I remained at the hospital for a while. I don't know how long. I was doped up. But I recall my return to Coronado, where I met with a Navy Captain, one of the high ranking UDT members assigned to the school. He had the dubious distinction of finishing my dream.

"Mr. Black, you're too far behind your mates in UDT 11. The medical report from the hospital did not clear you for a roll-back to the next school. You've done well so far. If you can pass a physical, you have our assurance you can get into the program again."

I asked him if I could stay at Coronado, rehabilitate, then start an exercise program to be ready for the next class. He was sympathetic but said my request was out of the question. In hindsight, I agree. That practice could have resulted in a BOQ full of injured wannabe frogmen waiting for their next opportunity. (Now that would have been prime duty.)

He wished me luck. I was out the door. Three years of Navy life was in front of me. Nothing else was on the horizon. As John Milton said, "Our final hope is flat despair." For the first time in my memory, I could relate to Milton's idea.

---

[1] Thomas Fuller, *Gnomologia: Adages and Proverbs*. Secondary source: Leonard Roy Frank, *Quotationary*, Random House, New York, 2001, p. 299.

[2] Elbert Hubbard, *An American Bible*, p. 219. Secondary source: Leonard Roy Frank, *Quotationary*, Random House, New York, 2001, p. 724.

[3] The performance figures may be off a few places for the rope climb and the run. They are recollections, but are close to the mark.

[4] Web pages and *USA TODAY*, May 3, 2011, p. 4A.

[5] *USA TODAY*, ibid., p. 4A.

[6] From Wikepedia, with my edits for purposes of brevity and clarification.

[7] It is my understanding the modern day SEALs' four-mile runs are on the hard, wet sand, not the soft sand hills. Pussies! Source: Howard E. Wasdin and Stephen Templin, *SEAL Team Six, Memoirs of an Elite Navy SEAL Sniper*, St. Martin's Press, 175 Fifth Avenue, New York, 2011, p. 66.

[8] Sourced from Wikipedia. Key-in UDT or SEALs.

[9] Paraphrased from saying by George Herbert, in *Outlandish Proverbs*, 1640, p 477. Secondary source: Leonard Roy Frank, *Quotationary*, Random House, New York, 2001, p. 371.

CHAPTER 9

REPAIRING THE DAMAGE

Wanna see an Ugly American? Visit a Navy port town.
—anon

Dressed in fatigues, combat boots, and a helmet, I left the UDT Captain's office to return to my BOQ room. I was to await orders from Washington, DC, which would result in my being transferred to another billet. The commander informed me the orders would arrive soon. Former UDT trainees were not kept around the area. We lent an air of melancholy to the ongoing operations.

As mentioned, a UDT trainee was not allowed to walk around the Coronado Base. Even if alone, he had to jog to his destination. The jog was awkward because of a strapless helmet. Unless held by one hand, or weighed down by a rubber boat, the headgear would bounce around on the head, sometimes falling across the eyes.

As a very recent yet former member of the UDT, I no longer had to run from point to point, so the short trip back to my quarters was taken in a slow stride. On the way to the BOQ, I passed by a Navy Lieutenant and saluted him. He stopped me short, "Mister! You're not running! Drop!"

He thought I was in UDT. Until a few minutes ago, I was. But no longer and it was not a propitious time for anyone to assume so. I was tempted to respond with sarcasm or four letter words, but I kept my temper at bay. He had not recognized me personally, and I had not seen him in our training sessions, so I asked, "What for Lieutenant?"

As I reflect on this episode, I recall emotions of self blame and antipathy. Self blame, in that I had failed in an important quest. Antipathy, in that I was being upbraided by a complete stranger. I felt alienated from a culture in which I could encounter an unknown person on a sidewalk, who by virtue of wearing two silver bars on his shirt collar, could dictate my actions.

The Lieutenant was not impressed, "Name and serial number!"

"Ensign Black, 669864."

"I'm headed for the UDT hut, Mr. Black. You're in deep trouble."

I held my tongue, "May I go now, sir?"

He held his, "You may go, but I'll see you this afternoon at the pool."

"You may be there, Lieutenant, but I won't," as I slowly continued my walk to the BOQ.

I never heard from the officer. I suspect he reported the incident to the UDT command and they informed him of my recent change in status. Admittedly, my contrary nature again surfaced, but I was not up to the task of placating the man after my recent debacle.

I returned to my room, sat down on my bunk and asked myself, *Now what?* I joined the Navy to be in UDT. At this point, I was stuck in a culture that was at odds with my makeup. I liked and admired the military but I had come to learn my independent, egalitarian nature would not work in a structured hierarchy.

Bootstrapping Time

A man can justifiably lament if he is dealt a bad hand by a dealer. He cannot complain if he has dealt himself the hand. It is said, "A bad workman blames his tools." I was a workman, but my faulty tools were of my making. A couple years ago I made a mistake on a trampoline. I had been paying the price ever since. The UDT and

Navy—or for that matter, life—owed me nothing. I had been turned off by encounters with people who had a sense of entitlement about themselves. It would be hypocrisy to take up the cross of self privilege. The Navy did not come to me, I came to the Navy. I owed this outfit my best efforts for the remaining time I was to be associated with it.

I can easily write those noble words now. Back then, I was emotionally bleak. I had passed two Navy physicals since signing up. I had gone months without any problems from the injury. I had passed the UDT qualification test with flying colors. Nonetheless, a filament to my future had been severed. Somehow, I had to find another thread, if nothing else, for the sake of my ego.

Shortly, my orders arrived from the Navy Bureau of Personnel. I had been assigned to a two star admiral's staff. It was operating on a communications flagship stationed in Subic Bay, Philippines. My job was to be a radio officer. I had one week of idle time before reporting to the San Diego Naval Base for training in two subjects: amphibious warfare, and communications and cryptography. I was to depart Coronado immediately. My presence among UDT 11 trainees was no longer welcome.

Communications and Cryptography

The communications and cryptography schools were the tonics I needed. They helped overcome my funk and forced me to direct my thoughts toward other matters.

The amphibious training was interesting. I learned how to climb down rope ladders into LCVPs. I learned how to disembark from an LCVP onto a beach—both intuitive maneuvers. I also obtained information from the amphibious warfare training that would be valuable to me these next few years. But it was the communications and cryptography program that captured my fancy and opened my eyes to a new world.

In those distant days, the encryption of a message was a cumbersome process. The machines used for coding and decoding messages were variations of WWII devices. Based on a secret key known only to the sender and receiver(s), the sender would physically manipulate a set of mechanical rotors, insert them into a modified typewriter and key in the clear text of a message. The outcome was called cipher text and was unintelligible to all except the intended receivers of the message. It would be sent over the air or through a copper wire and could only be decoded by a machine that had set its rotors based on the same secret code.

On more than one occasion, I set the rotors incorrectly. The device was not analog. I was not permitted to *almost* get it right. I had to get it *exactly* right. Having not done so, I would begin from scratch to reset all rotors. Equally humiliating, the receiver would send back a nasty clear text message advertising my incompetency.

Yet I was intrigued by this technology. This binary world had an elegance that I found attractive. I knew it or I did not. I was competent to the task or I was not. It was akin to the Maneuvering Board and the UDT: meritocracy in action.

Such are the ironies of life. My sand dune injury had led to a new life. It was a field of endeavor that soon replaced my passion for UDT (but not my passion for swimming). It was the world of telecommunications.

Hello G.I. Joe!

The flight from America (San Francisco) to the Philippines was taken in a military transport. We stopped in Guam for fuel and to stretch our legs. After landing at Clark Air Force Base, located on Luzon Island in the Philippines, I boarded a U.S. military bus that transported me to my ship, a three-hour ride.

Having spent most of my life on the arid plains of the southwest, the trip through this part of the Philippines was an extraordinary experience. The landscape, fecund and beautiful, was beyond my imagination. The villages were those I had only seen in movies. Thatched huts were placed on stilts to keep the monsoon waters from their floors. Rain! How much Dad talked about it; how little we received. But not here. Later, I discovered my books succumbed to mildew if I did not read them or fan their pages on occasion.

For this short journey, I was America's Non-Ugly American. I sat by a window smiling at the natives, waving to them, occasionally thrusting up a V sign with my fingers, just like Van Johnson did in the movies. The citizens remained indifferent to my diplomatic gestures. Some glanced up to the bus, but most did not. Some waved back, but most did not.

The other bus passengers and I were not the first American saviors to venture into the mountains of Luzon to glad-hand the natives. They had seen more than a few of us making our way from Clark to Subic. But they had not seen me! Come on, wave back to show some international camaraderie. *Hey! That kid responded to my V with a one-finger salute. What's going on?* My provincial naiveté was about to take a U turn.

Commander, Amphibious Forces Seventh Fleet

Upon reporting in at Subic Bay, I learned my billet was with Commander, Amphibious Forces Seventh Fleet. (Stay with me on this brief discourse into military jargon. It will help in understanding later explanations of Vietnam episodes.)

The admiral wore two hats, as he was also Commander, Amphibious Group One. The "fleet" title gave him authority over all *strategic* amphibious operations in the Seventh Fleet, which was operating in the Western Pacific (WestPac). The "group" title made him responsible for conducting *tactical* amphibious raids and landings in the same area.

This second title of "group" had him operate under his first title of "fleet." In an elevated warfare situation, several amphibious *groups* might be activated to report to the Seventh *Fleet* commander. For now, only one group existed. Thus, one set of officers was responsible for both planning and executing amphibious warfare throughout this part of the world. This arrangement allowed me to learn strategic *and* tactical amphibious warfare operations.

The "staff" (as we called ourselves) was short of officers. In addition to my primary duty as a communications officer, I was also officer in charge of the staff's enlisted Radiomen. The other junior communications officers were not assigned any men to order around, but were given other duties. I was also named the staff's Athletic Officer.

The time was summer, 1963. Things were picking up in this part of the world. If ordered, our staff (with a fleet of ships, frogmen, and Marines assigned to us) was designated to take on operations in several parts of Asia. The hot spots were:

- In **Indonesia**, Communists and Muslims were becoming increasingly agitated and angry with each other and the government. The current leader, President Sukarno, was losing his support base. The factions had begun to jostle for more power. In the event of a crisis, it would be the responsibility of the U.S. Navy (including Amphibious Group One and the Marines sailing with our task force) to protect and evacuate American citizens.

- In **Korea**, the North Korean regime continued to threaten its South Korean neighbor. In the event of a crisis, it would be our responsibility to be the first to debark troops to counter the North Korean aggression.

- In **Vietnam**, the situation was deteriorating. South Vietnam's President Ngo Dinh Diem was losing support of the population. The South Vietnamese army was being outfought by the South Vietnamese Vietcong and North Vietnamese Vietminh. Diem picked the officers for the army from his cadre of friends and relatives—a recipe for disaster. Increasingly, the U.S. installations (there were no combat troops) were coming under fire.

Other places were stable, but subject to our attention.

- In **Okinawa**, the situation was secure. Japan was making noise about America leaving the island, but at this time, there was not much going on. Sections of the island in which the United States had military bases resembled a giant American shopping mall, accompanied by tenderloin cafes.

- In **Japan**, malcontents were making noise about America leaving the country, but at this time, there was little protest activity. As in Okinawa, sections of Japan in which the United States had military bases resembled a giant American shopping mall with red-light houses.

- In **Thailand**, the situation was stable. American ships sailed into the port of Bangkok to show the flag and buy tons of Thai silk. Excuse the slang, but a WestPac navy joke was, "Bangkok is called Bangkok for a good reason." From what I read today, the joke is still accurate. I grant that it's a seedy statement, but it reflects aspects of the city that are part of its culture.

- In **Singapore**, the British were in control. American ships sailed into the port to show the flag and drink Singapore Slings at the Raffles Hotel.

- In the **Philippines**, a few Communists still made some flak and a few malcontents lobbied for America to remove its military bases. Overall, one could travel through the country without a bodyguard.

Olongapo: The Wildest City in the Western Pacific

I reported for duty to my ship, the *USS Estes*, which was docked on a pier at the U.S. Subic Bay Naval Base. It was Sunday afternoon. All was quiet. Most of the ship's personnel were ashore, either living it up in the adjacent port town of Olongapo, or otherwise living with their families in Subic Bay housing tracts. My home was to be a berth in a stateroom with three other Ensigns.

Two of my shipmates were in the stateroom when I arrived. After introductions, they took me into Olongapo, the rowdiest place I have ever visited. The streets of Olongapo resembled a wild west movie with public drinking and open solicitation for sex. Figure 9-1 shows a part of the main street of Olongapo. I snapped the photo during the daytime, before it mutated into a huge brothel.

Figure 9-1. A street scene in Olongapo.

The town was packed with sailors and Marines. The bartenders poured their drinks almost exclusively to servicemen, as very few natives were customers. A barmaid was also likely a hooker. She vied for tips, took on any sailor at a moment's notice, and set up a more permanent (loosely speaking) liaison after the bar closed. The floor shows varied between a Filipino Frank Sinatra and a strip tease artist, with nothing to strip.

Some of the rougher shows had open sex on the stage. It is hard to believe, but one of my shipmates told me of one show that involved a donkey. It is also difficult for many of us to come to grips with these aspects of human behavior. I include this vignette not to repulse or titivate, but to illustrate the sleaze of many navy port towns.

Some semblance of order to Olongapo's ribald nightlife was established by the Olongapo police. Acting in concert with the U.S. Navy Shore Patrol, they occasionally came into a bar, checked that no one was being murdered or mugged, and went their own way. After their precursory inspection, the sailors and whores reengaged in their cominglings. Fights were frequent.

My two new friends knew I was to be the officer in charge of the staff's enlisted Radiomen. One said, "You better get used to this. Every port we visit has an Olongapo. You'll have your hands full getting your men out of the brig or keeping them from going AWOL." The advice turned out to be an understatement.

My shipmates knew the town well. They had their favorite concubines. As the evening wore on, as the San Miguel beers took their toll, we ended up at a bar where their girl friends worked. Toward midnight, they informed me we had missed curfew. We were supposed to have been back onto the base no later than 12 midnight. *No*! This was my first day at my new post and I was already *absent without leave*.

I was dumbfounded but my buddies were not concerned. They informed me of their approach to this situation: We were to sit at a table at the back of the bar, near an exit. At this vantage point, we could enjoy the band and the floor show, which consisted of Filipino singers, but no whores or donkeys. We would continue to buy a lot of beer and generously tip the help. In turn, they would alert us to an incoming Shore Patrol party who might be knocking on the locked front door.

Our escape, which occurred twice, took us through the back door exit, up a ladder, and onto a big tree. There we sat or grappled until one of my shipmates' girl friends came out and said, "All clear!" We would return to our table to once again inure ourselves to a Filipino rendition of "I Left My Heart in San Francisco."

I still marvel at the bizarreness of it all. Three grown men, officers in the U.S. Navy, clinging to the branches of a tree behind a bar located in Asia to elude the cops. I liked these two men. They became my friends, but I never again let them set my schedule when we went on liberty.

Unfortunately, one of them got into trouble in Hong Kong for missing morning muster. I left him in a bar around midnight, and headed for the ship. In Hong Kong, the only requirement was for all hands to be aboard for morning muster. No curfew was in place. Frank (not his real name) was admonished by his department head and confined to the ship for our remaining time in port. He had an entry placed in his record about the incident. Lucky for him he was not a career officer.

Anyway, when the Olongapo bar closed its doors at midnight, we were the only Americans in the place. It was crowded, but the clientele were Filipinos and Chinese. The atmosphere was more subdued and much more civil. The tenderloin town was tenderloin for the sake of the Americans.

Finally, around 3 am, the bar closed. My friends' friends gathered us up, and secreted us to their homes. There, I spent the remaining hours sleeping with my head on a kitchen table, while my buddies ensconced themselves onto Filipino futons.

Reveille for all. My buddies pushed a cup of coffee into my hand, "Come on U.D., you're going to meet the Admiral and Commander Miller this morning." We easily made it through the security gate. The Shore Patrol guards let us onto the base as if we were daily commuters. There was a steady flow of Americans going through the gate, a pedestrian rush hour. I learned later that the midnight curfew only pertained to public places, such as bars. My friends and I would have been within the rules if we had left the bar before midnight and spent the remainder of the evening in one of their concubines' homes.

I was semi-functioning at both meetings. The Admiral was gracious and officious. Commander Miller, the head of the communications department of the staff and my immediate boss, offered, "Don't sleep in between your watches. No napping when the sun is up." It was a strange greeting. I nodded at his orders, while I nodded.

I also met with Captain Sheppard, the Chief-of-Staff, a position just under the Admiral. The CoS did most of the work. The Admiral had less contact with his staff, especially enlisted men and junior officers. The arrangement reminded me of a king who delegated day-to-day operations to a very busy prince. Captain Sheppard was the prince, and as told later, he was a prince of a man.

Dog Fighting and Cock Fighting

With the Michael Vick publicity, many people are now aware of the prevalence of the perverse "sport" of dog fighting. In Olongapo, both dog and cock fighting were legal and popular. It appeared

Olongapo provided a venue for every vice in the human inventory. Later, after I returned to the States, Olongapo added drugs to its repertoire and many military men took up the habit.

I attended one dog fight and one cock fight. The abuse of these creatures was as disgusting as anything I have seen. Malcolm Gladwell uses the phrase, "morally repellent" to describe dog fighting.[1] A pathetic aspect of the travesty was the evident trust a dog had in its master. The animal would look up to the owner, seeking support. The owner would cheer and encourage the critter to damage itself, often beyond repair. One dog was so badly injured his owner picked him up from the pen, took him outside the arena, and shot him. I did not have my camera to capture this event.

I made it a point to bring my camera to the cock fight. Figure 9-2 shows two roosters and their owners. The men are provoking the birds. Getting them aroused for combat. Notice the cock on the right, and the blade that is attached to its leg (I've placed a circle around it.) The owners had armed their pets with avian stilettos. The bloodbath was brutal.

Figure 9-2. Cock fighting in Olongapo.

I often wonder why we humans place ourselves at the top of the pecking order? These vulnerable creatures—subservient to our cravings and submissive to our commands—become puppets. They depend on us. They look to us for protection. What do we do? We manipulate them to vent our lust for hostility.

Other Tenderloin Towns

It made almost no difference where our ships visited, an Olongapo awaited us. Japan, Okinawa, Formosa (Taiwan), Korea, and Hong Kong all had their tenderloin districts. The exception was Singapore. The authorities there kept a tight lid on sailors' romps through the streets and their women. If one looked, one could find some tenderloin, but the wild aspects of Olongapo were not permitted in Singapore.

While I was in charge of the Radiomen, I had several occasions to bail my rowdy sailors out of a brig. Once, while on Shore Patrol duty, I watched a drunken sailor (who was unknown to me) buy a baby duck from a street vendor.[2] He took the tiny creature in his hand, looked at it for a moment, put the head of the bird in this mouth and bit it off at the neck. He then spit out the head, and topped off his feast with a swing of beer.

What possesses men to such atrocities? Do the Olongapos of the world feed this sort of behavior? Or do these kinds of people feed the Olongapos? I arrested the man for lewd behavior and put him in the brig. I wish I could have done more to him.

In Kobe, Japan, one of my men missed the ship's sailing, a serious offence. He was a modest, quiet person, and a competent Radioman. I was surprised by his absence. He was married to a Filipino girl. They had a home in Olongapo.

I adopted the practice of taking a role call well before the ship got underway. Having discovered the man was missing, my Master Chief Radioman said, "I think I know where he is, Mr. Black."

"Let's go, Chief!" As we ran down the gangway, hailed a taxi, and took off for the man's hideaway. He was not there. His "girlfriend" told us he had left her at a bar the night before with another girl. This quiet, unassuming man was unfaithful to a wife *and* a girlfriend. Still waters run deep.

The Chief and I made it back to the ship, and we sailed without this closet lothario. A couple days later he turned himself in to the local naval attaché office. He was flown back to Subic, taken before Captain's Mast, where he was demoted one rank, and placed in the brig for a few days. He was lucky he did not receive a harsher sentence but this was his first offence. One of my other men, after missing several musters and getting into fights, was court marshaled and dishonorably discharged.

The Prostitution of a City

Sailor towns are as old as navies. They have always been wild and I had fun in them. I was not a prude but my love to a beautiful and extraordinary woman kept my liberty times circumspect. Still, aspects of these cultures were, charitably speaking, over the top. I witnessed the debauching of a fine and pristine Indo-French city. Before the Marines went ashore in Danang (March, 1965), I had an opportunity to walk through the downtown area. I had come in from my ship by helicopter on a courier run. I had a few hours before returning to the ship and took a stroll. Danang was quiet and clean. The streets were lined with old style, white stucco houses. The bars were few, no fights, no chewing off the heads of baby ducks. The cafes were peaceful and even quaint, reflecting the bistros of France.

After the commitment of American combat troops in March, 1965, the city was transformed. I revisited the same downtown area later in 1965. Our ship was anchored in the bay and several officers and I went on liberty for a few hours. The serene scenes of a few months ago were gone. The place was another Olongapo.

Liberty and Aggression. Nature, with its wise approach to abet the propagation of a species, has programmed us to consider sex as fun. As well, through sex, humans are programmed to bond, with associated familial ties, to their partner. Some sex experts state testosterone buildup can lead to aggression on the part of a male. Therefore, sex unto itself is a healthy release.

The mores and religions of many cultures forbid extramarital sex, often for good reason. I make no claim to know where to draw the line on prostitution. But this I do know: If my men had not had access to sex during their tour overseas, they would have been unhappy and more unruly. As an officer of the enlisted Radiomen, I had two notions about the open prostitution in most of the ports:

It made my life easier when my men were onboard the ship, it made my life more difficult when my men were on the shore.

The problem with prostitution in this part of the world: It was accompanied by harmful acts, such as too much drinking, drugs, fights, a huge black market of pilfered American supplies, pimps exploiting their whores, the weakening of relationships the sailors had with their mates back home, and the births of many illegitimate children, discussed shortly.

To give you a sense of the change of Danang, and an idea of the character of these sailor cities, Figure 9-3 shows an encounter in Danang, after it had been transformed. The man with his head looking down was one of my shipmates. He was trying to retrieve his hat from the pimp to his left. The woman to his right had teasingly taken his hat in an attempt to lure him into the whore house. The boy at the bottom right of the photo was observing the events, maybe absorbing on the job training. On this occasion, my friend took leave of the temptation. After all, it was not yet noon.

Figure 9-3. Solicitation in Danang.

Your writer is no wilting flower, but I could not help but feel sad about the transformation of a once elegant city. The worst aspect of this profligacy was the thousands of illegitimate children who were left fatherless when the men returned to the States. One of my roommates had a son by a prostitute. During his tour, he took care of the child and her mother. He was later killed in action. He told me he had made provisions for his son in the event something happened to him. If he did, this child was one of the few fortunate ones. Most of these children lived lives of ostracism, even among their families. Some ended up "peddling or begging on street corners."[3]

Do you recall the one-finger salute I received on my first day in Asia? We sailors were not very effective ambassadors.

However, after the departure of the Americans, the Vietnamese did not suddenly clean up the cities. In 1981, it was estimated 50,000 hookers plied their trade in "...Ho Chi Minh City—a sharp increase since the war."[4] Some of the high ranking Communist comrades ran brothels, often protected by cops with payoffs. Those who are guiltless should cast the first stone.

Fall Out for Morning Exercise

Backtracking to my arrival in WestPac, I had reported aboard the *USS Estes* and was getting to know the ropes. During the first days of my part time job as the staff Athletic Officer, I proposed—with the Chief of Staff's approval and a staff-wide directive—a morning exercise program. Fitness programs were part of my job description and after all, we were a military combat unit. Warriors, even those riding the waves, should look warrior-like. In hindsight, I may have taken this job too seriously. Read on and email your thoughts.

Some of the Navy officers had a soft look about them. They had been exercising at the officer's mess table more often than they had been exercising at the gym. Not so for the Marine officers on the staff. They looked as if they could go into combat at a moment's notice.

I had been observing the enlisted men. None was fat, but many had a dissolute look about them. Watching them embark on their last liberty before I took over as their personnel officer, I noticed their shoes were not quite shined. Their whites were somewhat white, but their pants and blouses were wrinkled, worn one-too-many times onto shore.

I thought some of them had been in Asia too long. So did my head Radioman, Chief Jamieson. (Watch the movie, *The Sand Pebbles.* It depicts the life styles of these sailors.)

Some of the men were called "WestPac sailors." They attempted to stay in the Western Pacific for their entire time in the Navy. They extended their tour only if the Bureau of Personnel granted them another billet in Asia. A few were illegally married or were living unmarried with their mate. They had a home off-base.

Some of my sailors had adapted an off-beat attitude about Asia and the Navy. Their Asian ladies took precedence over most everything, including their families in the States. One of my men had a wife and kids in Arizona, yet stayed in the Western Pacific for three successive tours.

As an important aside: My descriptions of the females in WestPac port towns might be considered stereotyping. In fairness and accuracy, the vast majority of the native citizens were as morally ordinary as the folks in America's towns. The deep pocketbooks of American military men brought out a segment of the population to service the men's desires and needs. Some of the women were dependent on this income to support their families and many of them came from villages far away. They sent a lot of their supposedly ill gotten money back to their families—many members depended on these women for their basic needs. As mentioned, those who are not guilty should throw the first stone.

One of my Radiomen married a lovely woman who came from a prominent family living in the resort town of Baguio. She was as lilly-white, so to speak, as our sisters back in America.

To implement the staff-wide fitness program, each morning I assembled the men on the helicopter deck at the stern of the ship. There, we went through a half hour of stationary exercises. While underway, the exhaust from the ship's engines and smoke stacks lent a downtown LA effect to our movements.

I was doing more harm than good. In addition, the requirement for a daily tonic was ignored by every officer on the staff. This situation was called to my attention by one of my Radiomen. He was a WestPac sailor, a first class petty officer, and a fine Radioman.

After a smoke filled session, he came to me, "Mr. Black, these exercises don't have any officers but you in them. We thought the program was for all the staff."

"Good point, Jordon. I'll bring it up with the Chief of Staff."

Each morning, while at sea, the Chief of Staff held a meeting with his five department heads. If other officers had a topic of general interest, we too could attend the first part of the meeting. After dismissing the men, I dropped by Captain Sheppard's cabin to explain the situation. He was sympathetic and ordered me to bring up the issue in the senior staff meeting.

The next morning Captain Sheppard informed his officers, "Mr. Black has a topic of interest to all." I made my pitch about the absence of officers in what I thought was a staff wide program. I could have heard a pin drop. I left, thinking I had probably committed a military *faux paus.* I imagined the Commanders and Captains, sitting on their high ranking buttocks thinking, *Ensign Black is an arrogant ass.* Not so gentlemen, just doing my job.

Except for Officers. The following morning the enlisted men and two officers showed up for the exercise program. With one exception, the senior officers on the staff had ignored my observations about the staff-wide fitness program. They were too high in the military hierarchy to grovel around on a smoke-laden helicopter deck with lowly enlisted men who might share their fates in combat conditions.

I was one of the officers. Captain Sheppard was the other. *The staff's senior officer* (other than the Admiral) walked up to me and said, "Mr. Black, reporting as requested."

With that singular, graceful statement and his presence before the enlisted men on that helo deck, I am convinced every one of them would have jumped overboard for that man. Captain Sheppard, like the Marine officers I came to know, had a common sense understanding that an officer leads his men, not by self-imposed *separation* from them, but by *inclusive* direction and leadership.

God love that man. He was no spring chicken and was due for retirement soon. Yet there he was, doing jumping jacks with us. He was beloved by officers and men alike. You can see why. Captain Sheppard was a special person and a special officer. In my mind, he was an outlier officer and warrants having his picture in this book, as seen in Figure 9-4.

Figure 9-4. An outlier officer.

The men stayed with me for those few miserable times on the helo deck. Unless they were on watch, they showed up for thirty minutes of smoke induced misery. The next day, after the Chief of Staff's splendid gesture, we were making our way into the fantastic harbor of Hong Kong. I announced, "Men[5], I have good news. In addition to your being granted extra liberty this week, Captain Sheppard has given me permission to terminate this program. Frankly, it's not fair, and besides, the smoke is killing us. No more jumping jacks. Get dressed for liberty. Dismissed!"

My status with the enlisted men went up a few notches.

Drawing the Line

Regarding the relationships of officers with their enlisted men, I learned there was more of an elitist air in the Navy officer corps in relation to the enlisted ranks than in the Marine platoons that I came across on ships or beaches. A sense of shared fate and closer daily ties among officers and enlisted men also held for the UDT and holds today for the SEALs.

No question, officers and enlisted men want separation from each other. And separation is needed for military units to properly function in combat situations. It's one thing to have a drink with your men, it's another to get drunk with them. It's one thing to be approachable, it's another to be a pal. It's a thin line to draw, but many officers drew a thick line—forming an elitist barrier between them and their enlisted men. I saw it time-and-time again, sometimes manifesting itself in, *I'm better than they are* bigotry.

After I returned to the States, I paid a call on one of my WestPac friends, a Commander who had been assigned to the Bureau of Personnel in Arlington, Virginia. I sat in his office, waiting for him to clear up some matters before heading out for liberty. I was there for about a half-hour. During that time, several enlisted men came and went, delivering or picking up papers. I noticed Jim never uttered one word of well done or thanks.

Afterwards, while we were having a beer at the Navy Yard I said, "Jim, I noticed you never said 'well done' or 'thank you' to any of your men."

Jim looked at me in total puzzlement, "Why should I? They're doing their duty."

His approach was too cold for me, too elitist. Jim might have suffered from insecurity and his behavior was an example of anxiety reaction. He might have been hiding behind his rank, or he might simply have been maze-dull. Whatever Jung would say about the matter, I thought Jim drew the line without regard to common respect for and courtesy to his enlisted men.

Take care of your men and they will take care of you. Today, the SEALs know this truism. So do the Marines. So did Captain Sheppard. Jim did not. By the way, Jim never made Captain.

I made it a point to spend social time with my senior petty officers. I never socialized directly with their subordinates, only with my petty officers. On occasion, we met each other on liberty and had a beer or two together. A few times, we took turns buying each other dinner. I think they were both respective of and loyal to me. I was to them.

It was a simple relationship between a tin horn Ensign and his Chief Petty Officers: My job was to make sure they did their job. Their job was to make sure I stayed sufficiently out of their way so they could do theirs.

I do not mean to belittle my role as a junior officer in relation to the enlisted men under my command. My support of my petty officers was often important to them and their men's comfort and welfare on the miserable WWII ships we were on. I went to bat for them. They went to bat for me. It was that simple.

One time I walked into a bar in Inchon, Korea where several of my Radiomen were in the process of getting very drunk. Several Korean ladies were hanging-out with the sailors while parts of the ladies' bodies were....well, just hanging-out. They spotted me, "Mr. Black! Come on over! Let us buy you a beer!"

"If there's any beer left, you bet!" As I seated myself into a festive mixture of sailors, whores, smoke, and beer.

Chief Jamieson, a brilliant Radioman, and a humorous, decorous man with a wife and child back at Subic, was once again acting as the care taker for his flock. He was sitting with his men, looking over them. Some so young, he was almost acting as a baby sitter.

"How are you, Chief? Anything I can do at this end? Need extended liberty?"

"Thanks, Mr. Black. No, especially not extended liberty! I've got a problem and could use your help. One of our new boys, never been out of Oklahoma till now, wants to get married to his honey in Olongapo."

"Ah, love is a many splendored thing, especially the first time."

"Exactly, Mr. Black."

"Tomorrow, before we get underway, bring him to my stateroom. We'll talk."

"Thanks, Mr. Black.

"Thanks for letting me know, Chief."

Officer Assistance

To understand why the Chief was coming to me about this problem, many of the young, low-ranking enlisted men considered an officer to be a special person. The officer may not have been liked, but he was still special, someone to behold, usually someone to listen to. Strange to me, but I still encounter gray (enlisted) panthers today, who upon learning I was an officer, take on a diffused demeanor of respect. (I think it is absolutely weird but then, I'm a non-hierarchical person.)

When push came to shove, the U.S. Navy could not forbid a sailor or officer from marrying a foreigner. This foreigner—usually a lady of the night (a sailor did not frequent embassy parties)—was well aware of the benefits of instant U.S. citizenship. She often granted her favors to young, naïve sailors who had only recently tasted the sexual spices of life.

I spent more than a few hours suggesting to these boys (maybe 18 years of age, sometimes surreptitiously younger) that they wait a while before saying, "I do…and come to Tulsa to meet my folks."

I usually asked them to grant my request of waiting just one more visit to the port-of-call of their sweetheart before they committed themselves to the marriage altar. As their immediate officer, with whom they did not communicate much, my one-on-one session was a big deal (thus Chief Jamieson's request). Once they agreed to my idea, they never married their lady of the night. Not one, I batted 1,000.

Did I do right by the sailors? By the ladies? I did right by the sailors. I did not do right by the ladies. My responsibility was to my sailors, not to the ladies.

Liberty Delayed

After the cancellation of the lead-laden exercise program (possibly inspired by Captain Sheppard's realization he would no longer exercise on the helo deck), we prepared ourselves for Hong Kong, a dream like port selling exotic and erotic combinations of women and wares.

Our wallets were flush and our testosterone was over flowing. Hong Kong was about to be the recipient of the pent up demands of navy sailors who had been at sea for a long time. Hong Kong was ready. Our ship was noise on the spectrum of this city's experience with horny and thirsty sailors.

Not so fast. My men were still off shoots of The Sand Pebbles' semi-slovenly sailors. I had told my petty officers I would expect our men to not only show competence in their jobs in the communications center, but to show pride in their external appearance. My petty officers agreed, but they also offered that there was a thin line to their being hard-asses on trivial points about dress in relation to the men doing what was important: competent performance of their radio jobs.

And their jobs were a big deal. Later, their superior performances were instrumental to many successful operations in Vietnam. They were the cog of the Pacific amphibious forces' operations. If their communications machines did not work, this part of the U.S. Navy did not function.

My petty officers were giving me a vital hint: Don't go overboard with the uniform bullshit. And it was sound advice. I discovered the further behind the combat lines, the more the Navy concentrated on trivialities. The closer to the combat lines, the more the Navy did not sweat the small stuff.

Once again, my petty officers kept me off the shoals before I did some damage to my hull. But in my defense—and after taking their advice into account—I think I proffered some repair to my men's lives, to their hulls and engines, if you will.

After a precursory inspection, the officers in the other four departments on the staff released their men to liberty. I was a new arrival. I was an unknown to my men, as they were to me. I informed my standing on-watch petty officer (a second class radioman), "Nadeau, these men are not to go on liberty until they are properly uniformed."

"Yes, sir."

I informed Nadeau within ear short of the men, "They've got twenty minutes. I'll be waiting." The men went below to polish up.

Within a few minutes, the men had re-assembled for another inspection. They passed—not with flying colors, but they passed. I now had an opportunity to make some points—all within the confines of my petty officers' advice.

"Nadeau, I'll talk to the men." (I was still wrestling with this aspect of naval hierarchy, but went along with it. After all, it was the Navy's party, not mine.)

"Yes, sir."

"Men, you're as fine a group of radiomen as I know. Okay, I don't know any other radiomen. (A few laughs.) I'm new aboard and I don't know much about radios either…or about you. But your petty officers tell me you're first rate, that you're the best in Task Force 76 (the number designator for all amphibious forces in the Seventh Fleet).

"Know this: I'm not going to give you a hard-ass time about a shoe shine. But on the other hand, when you walk off this ship, you represent the U.S. Navy. But of more importance, you represent yourselves. No one is going to judge you by anything but your appearance. Give it some thought: Your appearance is all you have.[6] People don't see into your mind. They only see your face, what you wear, how you act.

"You need to take care of your appearance—we all do, including me. I called you back to muster this morning because your appearance did not do justice to the best Radiomen in the South China Sea."

There was silence on this part of the main deck. A breeze was passing around the ship's superstructure, muted by the background noise in Hong Kong harbor. The men looked down or into the distance. None looked at me.

Was my talk corny? Did the men think it a condescending sermon? I couldn't tell. But I thought my crew needed to hear what I had said.

After this brief pause, I ordered, "Now get your asses off this ship and come back in one piece!"

Elitism? Egalitarianism? It's a thin line. Whatever it may be, the next day Radioman First Class Jordon, my covert path into the minds of my men, passed by me in the Comm Center, "Nice going yesterday, Mr. Black. You were the talk of the table last night. We hoisted a beer to you."

Jordon: A hindsight thanks to you...some fifty years too late.

My Men

Figure 9-5 shows your writer and some of my men on the shores around the South China Sea. These sailors were either Radiomen or members of boat crews who were later added to my compliment of men. (The staff had two boats reserved for the Admiral and Chief of Staff, more on this subject later.)

Figure 9-5(a): we had completed a working party detail of transporting gear from our flagship to a site on a beach in Vietnam (before the war heated up and we had to change our behavior). The men were not on liberty and were to return to the ship to continue their ongoing duties and watches. But we were not on a rear base in California. We were in Vietnam. The men had been on a hot stinking ship for weeks without beer or a lady of the night. I bought each man one beer and said *One beer only men; we're still on duty.* My action was against Navy rules, but don't sweat the small stuff. I also said, "Well done, here's a toast to us." By the way, the sailor with two beers was not a Radioman. He was the coxswain for our boat. I don't know how he ended-up with two beers, but he got us back to the ship in one piece.

Figure 9-5. WestPac sailors.

Figure 9-5(b) is a shot of Radioman First Class Jordon. I took a liking to the man. He took a liking to me. He often passed me useful scuttlebutt that was not available in officers' quarters.

I ended-up in charge of several enlisted men who did not fit neatly into the five departments. One such man was Chief Hicks, shown with his back to the camera in Figure 9-5(c). The Chief was a Corpsman and the only "doc" on our staff. His job was mostly one of dispensing aspirin to our crew. Each ship on which we sailed had a full medical staff aboard so Chief Hicks' presence was somewhat superfluous.

A good natured WestPac sailor, he had a Filipino family in Olongapo. Later, I learned he finally received orders to return to the states. Instead, he retired. As a going away present to me, just before I returned to the States, Chief Hicks presented me with a handmade Acey-Ducey board, a variation of a backgammon board.

The other sailor (in whites) in Figure 9-5(c) is Radioman First Class Angstead. (As I said, other than sharing a beer on shore, I socialized only with senior petty officers.) My main man, Chief Jamieson offered this advice to me, "Mr. Black, Angstead is a good man to get to know. He will give you a feeling with what's going on below." (Below, as in the quarters where my men lived.) "While underway, we Chiefs have our separate quarters. Angstead lives with the men. He can keep us posted."

"Thank you, Chief. No problem with my going around you to talk with him. No chain of command problem?"

"Not at all, Mr. Black. We're all in this together."

Angstead, Chief Jamieson, and I became friends. While ashore, we sometimes had dinner together during liberty hours. Was this breaching of the social line between officers and enlisted men a breach of Navy decorum? Possibly, but not for me. *Treat your men with respect and they will do the same.*

The Lemon Sours

For the next year or so after the UDT injury, my groin continued to plague me, but I no longer had to submit my body to the rigors of UDT training. I continued to exercise, and formed several programs and teams as part of my duties as Athletic Officer. I was the player/coach for our basketball team, but found I was increasingly reducing my playing time because of the pain. It finally reached the point that I paid a (yet another) call on a doctor. This time, I came across someone who offered a cure.

Slicing the Lemon. The surgeon's statement remains in my memory, even though the results of his declaration do not, "It's time for cutting, Mr. Black."

He was a good humored, no nonsense Texan. He and I joked about our drawls. He also joked about castration. I did not. I had seen enough castrations during my times on a cattle ranch to appreciate the finality of the procedure.

During a cattle branding session, calves were castrated. It entailed cutting through the testicular sack, severing any remaining members of the blood and nerve families that had survived the initial assault, pulling out the ball and depending on one's hunger, throwing the defunct nut into the trash or grilling it on the branding iron pit.

He told me my initial injury had likely been mistreated but the sand dune run was the final blow. The removal of what remained of my right testicle would likely allow me to return to a life with a semblance of normalcy.

His prediction, however tenuous, was good news. I had left the San Diego hospital several months ago, but my pathetic testicle refused to stay behind. Like a welfare recipient, its debilitating effects tagged along for the ride. It followed me to the Far East, to basketball games, to running, sometimes even to walking. I was the working model for the cliché, "playing with pain."

I had come to believe the supposed wisdom of the doctors who had examined me: my condition was not treatable. I had never considered that the removal of my testicle would solve the problem. How could I? How could any self respecting, macho, prideful, vainglorious man even consider the idea of looping off part of his masculinity? Forgive the pun, but it just did not connect.

My doctor disavowed me of my fears. He told me the removal of my right testicle would not affect my sex life. He also offered his opinion that my right testicle would no longer give me pain. A facetious observation as I would no longer possess the organ. I took it as a line from his quaint wit and sort of laughed.

Whatever his peculiarities toward humor, the surgeon removed one half of my testicular assemblage. I was no longer bilaterally symmetrical.

After several weeks of healing and rehabilitation, I was supposedly cured in that my lemon could not swell, as it no longer existed. I assumed I could go about living my life as I once did. I believed the change would be transformative to my outlook on life—recounted later. I thought: *With a few months of conditioning, I would be ready for the next UDT program in Coronado, California.*

Coming Up

However, for the next couple years the Vietnam War heated up, keeping me onboard ships and often away from swimming pools and training facilities. Frustratingly, my love of swimming, but past injuries, kept me from my forgman aspirations. This situation led to a job that sparked my interest, leading to pursuits away from UDT. As my son would say, go figure.

Aside from a few sidebars in this book, UDT leaves the picture. The doctors in Subic Bay would not release me for UDT duty, as told in Chapter 11. Because of my billet aboard ship, swimming as a continuous presence went away, at least for a while. During this time, my ship and its personnel entered into the Cold War in Asia and participated in fights in Vietnam.

For these next three chapters, my focus on the *individual* outlier will be moved to *group* outlier behavior. Later, these examples will meld-back into the idea of the individual outlier.

---

[1] Malcolm Gladwell, "Offensive Play," *The New Yorker*, October 19, 2009, p. 59.

[2] During ports of calls to foreign cities, the ship's crew and officers would be assigned temporary duty to augment the local Shore Patrol personnel. If you are adventuresome and want to sample the seamy and often hilarious side of life, spend a night or two on Shore Patrol duty. The duty was rotated

among senior enlisted men and junior officers. I stood duty in several cities, usually wishing I was somewhere else, yet fascinated by the antics of humans on the loose.

[3] Stanley Karnow, *Vietnam: A History*, Penguin Books, New York, 1997, p. 43.

[4] Karnow, p. 47.

[5] The enlisted ranks were collectively called "men." The officer ranks were collectively called "gentlemen."

[6] This idea is not mine. I read about it many years ago. The subject of one's appearances is usually treated with derision. Outside show vs. inner worth, and so on. The trouble with this idealistic notion is the simple fact that people do not observe our inner worth. They observe the outside show. In the long run the old adage, "Appearances are deceiving" misses the point.

Section III

The Hot Cold War

Chapter 10

Waiting and Watching, and Showing the Flag

Let us, then be up and doing,
With a heart for any fate;
Still achieving, still pursuing,
Learn to labor and to wait.
—Henry Wadsworth Longfellow[1]

My body was attempting to return to normalcy. After the operation, and as my job permitted, I setup running and swimming routines with the intention of returning to UDT. But as mentioned at the end of the last chapter, I had little opportunity for working out and had not yet passed a physical.

During this time (in the mid-1960s) I was still assigned to the amphibious fleet that sailed from one part of Asia to another, either to threaten to deploy frogmen, land Marines, participate in training exercises with our allies, or to show the flag. With numerous stops in between, we sailed south past the equator to Indonesia, north to Korea and Japan. All the while, our amphibious forces waited, watched, and prepared.

We were a model for Franz Kakfa's thought: "Perhaps this quiet yet unquiet waiting is the harbinger of grace, or perhaps it is grace itself."[2] We were in a graceful period, but the quiet was not a harbinger of peace.

In 1965, the wait was over. So was the period of grace. We committed combat troops to Vietnam, began raids on coastal villages, destroyed hamlets, wiped out rice paddies with B-52 bombs, and sprayed Agent Orange on the enemy and ourselves.

In this chapter, my participation in this period of grace is described. My experience in Vietnam is recounted in Chapters 11 and 12.

Indonesia

Shorty after a fanciful week in Hong Kong, the amphibious task force, with frogmen and Marines in accompanying transport ships, (including a helicopter carrier) made sail for Indonesia.

As mentioned in Chapter 9, the Communists and Muslims in Indonesia were not getting along and the rulers were losing control of the country. Open fighting had erupted between the Communist PKI and the Indonesian military. In order to be ready to evacuate American citizens and embassy personnel, our task force placed itself off the coast of Jakarta, the capital of Indonesia, and the location of most of the Americans in this country.

In these waters, we waited for two weeks, steaming around in circles, until Washington informed us the crisis was over. The communications traffic coming through the Communications (Comm) Center indicated the opposing factions in Indonesia had toned down their confrontations. The task force split up. The Marine transport ships sailed to Subic Bay. Our two star Admiral flagship headed for the port of Singapore. Rank had its privileges.

Later, our task force returned to this region when opposing factions tried to take control of the state to ease Sukarno out of power. As a precautionary measure, we landed Marines (in helicopters) in Jakarta but did not become involved in evacuations, beach assaults, or fighting. Still later, after I had left the Western Pacific, Suharto took over and held office for 31 years.

Crossing the Equator[3]

Our excursion to Indonesia took us across the equator. Here, the ship's hands took over to execute the famous Crossing of the equator ritual. The ceremony commemorates a sailor's first crossing of the equator. Originally, the tradition was created as a test for seasoned sailors to make certain new shipmates were capable of handling extended and rough times at sea. Sailors who have crossed the equator are nicknamed (Trusty) Shellbacks. Those who have not made the crossing are nicknamed (Slimy) Pollywogs. The ceremony entails the Shellbacks putting it to the Pollywogs.

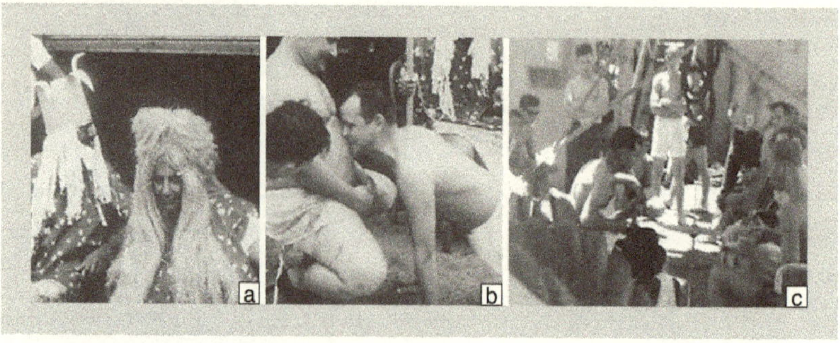

Figure 10-1. Scenes from crossing the equator.

Equator-crossing ceremonies typically feature King Neptune, as seen on our ship in Figure 10-1(a), with the Pollywogs paying homage to the King's court as seen in Figure 10-1(b). The Pollywog (Tom, a Navy Lieutenant and friend of mine) had to rub his face across the lathered-up belly of a fat enlisted man. I said the Navy was elitist, but for a while, officer Pollywogs could be subservient to enlisted Shellbacks.

The ceremony was a welcome diversion from days at sea, entertaining for all, even us pollywogs.

I snapped the photo in Figure 10-1(c) after the gentle bedlam had subsided. The ship's Captain granted the crew an hour or so of this informality. A man on the left is playing a guitar and singing. A man on the right is playing a bongo drum (after all, it was the 1960s). But this relaxed atmosphere lasted only an hour or so. I never again witnessed the informality shown in Figure 10-1(c) on any Navy ship during my almost three years at sea. Nor should I have seen such scenes. These ships were of the U.S. Navy, not Cunard Lines.

Cold War Locales

I have mentioned I was a Cold War warrior. I believed Stalin's USSR government to be a pathological aberration. Nonetheless, his fixation on "acquiring" Germany was a real danger. I thought Mao Zedong or Chiang Kai-shek were choices of a lesser of two despots for ruling China.

I believed in a free market. I believed in the righteousness of America's credos. However, I did not think the United States could or should convert the world to its way of life. I did not think it possible to use military force to create a friendly, neighborly democracy. I believed the American way would eventually triumph over the doctrines of Communism, Fascism, political fanaticism, *et al.* I believed that time was on America's side.

Nonetheless, if it became a confrontational military situation, one in which the enemy might take over a country, I was in favor of countering that enemy. If nothing else, it would allow the country to make its own choices.

Ignoring the revisionists, some wars are necessary. One cannot ignore Pearl Harbor or 9/11. But during my forays into the Western Pacific, I was struck by how prevalent my country had imbued its military presence into regions that seemed far removed from the Cold War. With the exceptions of Singapore, Laos, Cambodia, Malaysia, and Indonesia, we had a large military presence in every other major country in the Pacific Rim: Japan and Okinawa, Korea, Taiwan, Philippines, and Vietnam. Not to mention the garrisons on Guam and other Pacific islands.

The presence of Soviet or Chinese forces in these regions? None.

I could understand having troops in South Korea. And given our Cold War stance, military advisors in Vietnam made sense. China was threatening to take over Taiwan. I thought China had that right. General Chiang Kai-shek was no more the lawful suzerain of this island than anyone else. But he had converted to Christianity, so in America's eyes, that made his crusade all the more virtuous.

Joke aside (somewhat), the huge and expensive Air Force, Marine, and Naval fortresses in Japan, Okinawa, and the Philippines made no sense to me. As of this writing they make even less sense.

I was told by our staff's intelligence department that these military enclaves were needed in order to have our troops, ships, and planes readily available to counter any enemy of the western world. Fine, but in many situations, I wondered: to *which* enemy of the western world were they referring?

I did not argue, although I thought of bringing up Commodore Perry's forced "opening" of non-enemy Japan, the fact that Christians' missions were often accompanied by the military in non-enemy third world countries, of America taking over non-enemy Philippines, that some of the wealth of the western countries was bought at a horrific cost to non-enemy China during the "Opium Years." (Much of FDR's wealth came from his father doing drug deals in Canton[4], an area I visited later in my life.)

During this time, I begin to reassess my views on America's presence in practically every corner of the world. I began to grasp that sure, we had enemies, but we also make some up to foster missionary, political, military, and economic ambitions. I came to believe in Dwight Eisenhower's warning about the military-industrial complex. As of this writing it is firmly in place and has become a sacred cow in America.

But at that time, I thought any hesitations about our presence in Vietnam were mitigated by my view that Stalin was going after the entire pie. Wherever we could counter his thrusts, we should do so. But I began to gain a sense that we were changing; that as a people, we had begun to believe in our own Manifest Destiny propaganda, that the expansion of the United States was "not only inevitable, but that it was divinely ordained."[5] This philosophy was counter to that of our founding fathers, and of our general make up. Looking back, it is clear this mentality was a factor in becoming involved in Vietnam. As of this writing, the idea that America should police the world has become pervasive. It has embedded itself into almost every walk of life in America.

A Necessary War?

A reasonable issue to bring up at this juncture is to ask and try to answer the question: Was the Vietnam War one of those necessary wars? At the conclusion of Chapter 7, I wrote that in my youth, I thought it was, and that it was an extension of the Cold War.

Without diverting this story to what could be another book, I came to believe the war was a mistake. I believe—in the context of the Cold War—it was not a mistake in conducting it. *It was a mistake in how it was conducted.*[6]

However, we should not castigate those who directed America's strategy for this war. Given the times of mid-20th century, they made decisions they thought best for their country. I have thought about this subject many times. I am not sure my strategy would have been any different from what was pursued. Someone once said, "Only in hindsight are humans foresightful."

Nonetheless, these intentions were also founded on an arrogant hubris described in the previous section. The more time I spent in WestPac, the more my opinions moved away from favoring the war in Vietnam.

I followed President Kennedy's actions and remarks during this time. I think he was at odds about what to do. At times, he was cautious. Other times, he seemed to favor more involvement. That stated, shortly after his credibility was shaken by the Bay of Pigs fiasco, he was bullied by USSR Minister Nikita Khrushchev at their summit meeting in Vienna: "Coming out of that encounter, he confided to James Reston of The New York Times, 'Now we have a problem in making our power credible, and Vietnam is the place.' "[7]

Arrogance? Insecurity? Determination to face up to a dangerous opponent? All of the above, with the result of the Vietnam War, and its seemingly everlasting effects on the American psyche.

This writer thought he was well versed in the history and culture of Vietnam, but I had only a superficial understanding of the country. I had no appreciation that Ho Chi Minh was first and foremost a nationalist. He was, secondarily, a Communist. I did not understand the depravity by which France and Diem violated Vietnam, both culturally and physically,[8] that the Vietnamese sought freedom from all foreigners (including the Soviets and the Chinese). I did not appreciate the Vietnam conflict which we belatedly entered was initially a civil war, of one for unification, of one that was initiated by the North Vietnamese after South Vietnam's Diem reneged (with the backing of America and America's allies) on holding elections in accordance with the 1954 (Dien Bien Phu) settlement.[9]

I once read that one way to anticipate and perhaps predict the future is to understand the present. I did not understand the Vietnam of the 1960s. It turns out most of the world's leaders did not understand Vietnam, except for a small circle of men hiding out around Hanoi, patiently waiting for the right time to make their mark.

The Vietnam "quagmire" was much more than what I have briefly explained. I insert this brief *mea culpa*, not in apology, but to set the record straight that I was wrong about my initial assessments of the war. Given South Vietnam's corrupt government, the outlier performance of South Vietnam's enemy (Vietcong and North Vietnamese), and the eventual American citizenry rebellion, the war became unwinnable.

However (and to add to this tragedy), today's Vietnam government is worse than those regimes America propped up during the war. Modern Vietnam is a one party, so-called Communist state. I say "so-called" because it is really nothing more than a dictatorship. It is also an oppressive, brutal autocracy. It jails, even executes its citizens who openly demonstrate for a multiparty nation. Killing peaceful demonstrators? Yes indeed, Vietnam has execution laws for dissidents who come out in favor of democratic changes.[10] We return to this subject in the Epilogue of this book.

Singapore and Sports

Singapore was the polar opposite of a navy port town. It was clean and clear headed. At that time, it was part of the Federation of Malaysia but under the brilliant leadership of Lee Kuan Yew, it separated into a separate country in 1965. The city state was highly regulated. For example, the sale of chewing gum was illegal. But sex could be obtained, if only surreptitiously.

As staff Athletic Officer and player/coach, I set up basketball and soccer games with the British Navy lads, and did not have much time for sight-seeing. Figure 10-2 shows our basketball team. The Brits trounced us in soccer, but we creamed them in basketball. We broke even buying each other beer in their NCO club (noncommissioned officer pub, to which I was graciously invited). They were as cordial hosts as I've ever come across.

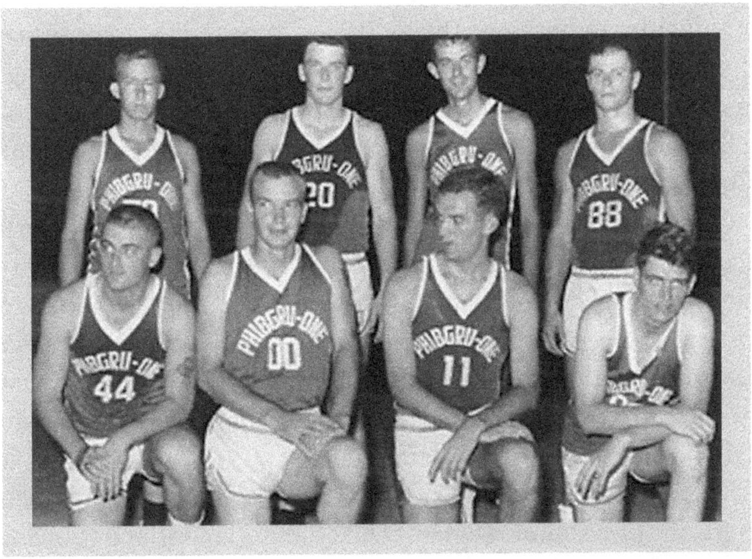

Figure 10-2. The Amphibious Group One team.

Later, these eight men forged together an amazing team. During the years of 1964-1966, we compiled a 48-6 won-loss record. Granted, some of our opponents were Brits. Others were teams from Taiwan and Japan (we had a decided height advantage). But from a staff of fewer than 100 enlisted men (with two officers: number 11 and the tall guy behind me), we defeated carrier teams and teams from large military bases. These feats were akin to Prairie View Community College trouncing UCLA: It just didn't happen. Fortunately, our staff had several Marines assigned to us, acting as guards and aides for the Admiral. One of them was a basketball outlier, and another was not far behind. Number 20 in Figure 10-2 was as talented a player I ever had as a teammate. He was strong as a bull and as nimble as a hummingbird. In all our games, none of our opponents was able to stop him. Number 88 was new to the game, but he was a natural defenseman. I would put him on our opponent's best offensive player and he would without exception, shut the man down.

A junior officer is only as good as his enlisted men. A junior coach is only as good as his players. They made me a better officer and a better coach.

Notwithstanding my athletic duties, I made it a point to pay a call on the famous Raffles Hotel to imbibe in a Singapore Sling. It was a wonderful place and was imbued with the former greatness of the British Empire. It still is, and I will have more to say about Raffles in later books.

Our British Navy hosts were super party givers—and I learned the use of the word "super" on this visit. Alcohol was allowed on their ships, but not on ours, which made for a rather unbalanced exchange of receptions. One night, the British came over to our ship, where we served them cola, coffee, and tea. The next night we went to their ship to take in rum, beer, and gin. Our reception was short lived. Theirs carried on for some time.

The dichotomy of America's Puritanism continues to mystify me. We are one of the most religious, bible touting countries in the world. Just consider that we actually dictate how and when we can purchase and consume a beer! Yet we are one of the most violent industrialized nations in existence. I treasure my country, I am very thankful I'm a citizen, but I dislike this aspect of its makeup.

We staff officers were invited into the homes of Singapore civilians and British officers. My three roommates and I were fortunate to be the guests of a British officer who was married to a beautiful Malaysian Julia Child. She prepared a gourmet curry dish that transported our taste buds to other worlds. God, it was hot! Thankfully, my southwest Jalapeno pepper resilience kept me at the table.

The next day, a British Commander and his family invited us to their home, where we had breakfast. Later, we set out on a motor launch to tour the Singapore Straits, where we had a picnic on a small island next to the large Indonesian island of Riau. This territorial "invasion" was part of a protocol, an agreement between the Brits and the Indonesians.

There will always be an England

Later, a British aircraft carrier paid a call at Subic Bay. Our staff hosted the officers at our Officer's Club, where we could serve alcohol. In turn, they treated us to a grand party on the flight deck of their carrier. It was a regal affair, and was closed by a drum and bugle corps ascending from an aircraft elevator while playing "God Save the Queen:"

God save our gracious Queen,
Long live our noble Queen,
God save the Queen!
Send her victorious,
Happy and glorious,
Long to reign over us.
God save the Queen!

We stood at attention…somewhat, considering the Gilbey's. The wind was blowing gently across the deck. All officers were in full service dress whites. Our wives wore elegant cocktail dresses. As the corps, already audible, became visible on the ascending elevator, a shipmate turned to me and said, "There will always be an England, U.D."

The corps stood on the raised elevator:

O Lord our God arise,
Scatter her enemies
And make them fall.
Confound their politics,
Frustrate their knavish tricks,
On Thee our hopes we fix,
Oh, save us all!

The elevator then began its descent into the hanger deck. The band played on as it slowly went out of sight:

From every latent foe,
From the assassins blow,
God save the Queen!
O'er her thine arm extend,
For Britain's sake defend,
Our mother, prince, and friend,
God save the Queen!

My friend was correct. There would always be an England. But the British Empire was a shadow of its former self. It over reached and never learned an effective empire is one that first comes and then goes voluntarily, not one that comes and is forced to leave. The former allows the occupier to establish leverage for the future. The latter does not.

Nonetheless, this scene: the corps, the music, the gin and tonics, the uniforms, the elegance of the women in their fine attire, the passing of the day into the evening remains crystallized in my mind. I wish you could have been there to have witnessed this grand and prophetic scene.

SEATO Maneuvers

Our ship did not spend much time in our home port of Subic Bay. If we were not responding to a real or imagined crisis, we were conducting training exercises with our SEATO (Southeast Asia Treaty Organization) allies. Depending on the location of the amphibious landings, the participating forces were from the UK, New Zealand, Australia, France, the Philippines, and Thailand. During my (almost) three years in WestPac, we also conducted mock amphibious battles in conjunction with South Korea in the waters and beaches around Incheon (Inchon), and Pusan (Busan).

These exercises were important to our mission. They allowed us to practice and learn. They were instrumental to the success of later beach landings and raids in Vietnam.

The idea of joint operations with other navies was to make certain we could first, sail and maneuver in a combined task force of several ships; second, that we could coordinate the initial beach assaults; third, that we could get all the supplies onto the beach quickly;

fourth, that we could secure the beach head as well as inland turf; fifth, that we could get all our men and supplies back to the ships; and sixth, that we could depart one anothers' company without running into other vessels. The operation required an immense amount of coordination and practice.

Because of the extensive miles traveled by the staff communications ship, every six months it would return to the San Diego Navy Yard for refitting and maintenance. Our staff would transfer to another ship coming to WestPac from San Diego. During my tour in Asia, I served on five ships: the *USS Estes*, the *USS El Dorado*, the *USS Mount McKinley*, the *USS Princeton*, and the *USS Iwo Jima*.

Landing in Mindoro. One of the SEATO exercises was conducted on the Philippine island of Mindoro. As with all these exercises, the operation was classified, meaning none of us could discuss it with anyone who did not have a "need to know." In one the funniest and most bizarre episodes of my naval experience, I learned this need to know was interpreted quite loosely by the sailors. It turned out they believed their Filipino girl friends had a need to know, even to the exact location of the beach where the Marines would come ashore.

On a mid-afternoon, our task force sailed from Subic Bay. The landing area was about 150 miles to the south. The plan was to land the forces early the next day, establish the beachhead, push inland a few miles, establish perimeters there, and reassemble at the ships. The operation entailed the deployment of over a thousand Marines and tons of equipment, including tanks and other vehicles.

The task force anchored off shore, the cargo ships lowered the landing craft into the water and the Marines began to climb down the rope ladders into the boats. I was one of the watch officers in the Comm Center, so I was not topside to see these operations. However, I learned of the following situation via incoming and outgoing messages, and dialogue taking place on the ship's PA system. The traffic conveyed this information: *The landing on the target beach might be impeded by a contingent of civilians. They had assembled near this beach, had erected tents, as well as a small set of bleachers(!), on which a crowd was sitting to watch the action.*

They had not placed themselves directly onto the beach where the landings would take place. They had gained enough intelligence to know the exact position of the assault and had intelligently put themselves, their tents, and bleachers out of harm's way. Here are further summaries of the messages going back and forth between ships and boats: *All personnel and vehicles are to continue with operations as set forth in the landing plan. Civilians are not located in the immediate combat zone. Proceed with operations.*

The boats began their short trip to the shore. They beached themselves and disgorged the Marines, who ran through the surf and into the nearby sand dunes as if enemy fire was raining down on them—all to the enthusiastic cheering of the Filipino crowd. The Navy adage, "Loose lips sink ships" did not come into play today. The sailors' loose lips translated into a movie-like scene. But it was a real life, full size diorama of a variation of miniature, yet peaceful D-Day. We should have charged admission for our staged play.

Later in the day, I was tasked with making a courier run to Subic. I left the ship via the Captain's gig, which let me off at the beach. I had to walk a mile or so to a stop, where a jeep took me to a nearby airfield for a flight to Subic. My short trip on foot had the same flavor as walking through a mini-Olongapo. The tents had bartenders selling iced-down bottles of San Miguel beer. The madams of the streets of Olongapo were also present, shouting to passersby that they had a ready cot and tent waiting for us.

I was in the middle of a La La Land, carrying secret documents with a .45 on my hip. At this point, I would have wagered the girls of the night knew more about the contents in my brief case than I did. Bands were playing rock and roll music while sailors and Marines tried to pretend they were fighting a battle. The scene was dreamlike.

Later in the day, toward sunset, sailors and Marines had begun mingling with the natives. Upon my return, I stopped and had a San Miguel at one of the tents. But I was returning with secret documents, so I kept my intake to one beer and returned to the ship.

As I was waiting for a boat, the Admiral's barge made its appearance on the causeway. Upon debarking, our Admiral invited those waiting to use his craft to return to the ships. I watched him as he viewed the scene. He made no gesture one way or the other about this seemingly unfamiliar and weird exercise.

But it was not unfamiliar. Shortly, I discovered why he seemed so nonchalant. In previous exercises that took place on a Philippine island, the task force was greeted with an admiring crowd. It seemed to have no effect on the efficacy of the exercise, at least to the point of not conducting the operation. It was part of the process. Maybe so, but it seemed pretty strange to me.

Outliers' Efforts.

Nonetheless, the attitude of the Admiral and his amphibious group staff toward this set of circumstances was a lesson to me. We were not to be deterred. We were committed to performing an extremely complex training operation in order to prepare ourselves for the real thing. Granted, the civilians' presence presented a rather bizarre scene, but as I watched the Admiral walk through the mini-Olongapo, it was as if it did not exist.

With motivated and focused effort, he provided the leadership that carved the way for the amphibious forces to conduct a flawless landing of Marines in Vietnam the next year (in 1965). In hindsight, it was a fine example of the performance of the group outlier.

An Unexpected Hurricane

Another strange incident, this time because of Mother Nature, occurred while our ship, accompanied by other ships and a sub, were anchored off the west coast of the island of Okinawa. The anchorage was in a large bay, but with a narrow opening to the ocean. On a Sunday morning several officers, enlisted men, and I had taken a launch to the island to attend a briefing on an upcoming operation to be undertaken with several allies. Without warning from weather forecasts, and during this meeting, a hurricane formed nearby. Later our staff weather man, an apologetic Lieutenant Commander, said he had never experienced such an occurrence. His readings from the ship's equipment and messages from naval weather stations in the Pacific did not indicate a hurricane was just offshore. Of course, during those days weather forecasting was almost as much guess work as it was solid prediction.

We returned to the pier where an LCVP from a troop transport ship was waiting to ferry us to our respective vessels. The surf was high and getting higher. Our small craft churned its way to the anchored ships. It was riding the waves like a roller coaster.

The first ship the LCVP came to was a Landing Ship Tank (LST) in our task force. The LST, shown in Figure 10-3, is a big ship (about 350 feet in length), and was riding the waves in the bay without too much trouble. Nonetheless, as the LCVP approached the ladder (stairs) on the side of the ship, the movement up and down of the small craft relative to the ladder platform was several feet from bottom to top. To complicate matters, the coxswain of the LCVP was having trouble keeping the craft from hitting the ladder platform.

Some twenty men were in the boat. We did a quick survey to find the senior officer. On-board were a Marine Colonel and Major, as well as two senior Navy Officers, who were in the medical and supply corps. As a Lieutenant Junior Grade (LTJG), I was the ranking Line Officer aboard. That is to say, the senior officer in the craft who was allowed to assume command of an *afloat* Navy vessel. On the water, I outranked the other four officers. I had my first, only, and very short lived "Command at Sea."

Without ado, the other officers assumed I was at the head of the chain of command. Nonetheless, I quickly conferred with them and the coxswain. He suggested he take the craft to the bow of the ship, which had the large bay doors open, as shown in Figure 10-3(a) [at sea] and Figure 10-3(b) [on the beach]. I so-ordered, and off we went.

Figure 10-3. LST configurations.[11]

The coxswain had an easier time maneuvering the boat, but not sufficiently to allow him to get close enough for the men to jump onto the LST ramp. The danger was no longer the ladder. The danger was the lowered ramp that ran from the bow of the ship down into the water. A wave crest pushed the boat close to the ramp, which could have resulted in the LCVP's side or bottom catching the ramp and possibly flipping over.

"Coxswain, pull away! No more attempts. Proceed to shore!" I gave my first and only commands as a U.S. Navy skipper.[12]

By the time we reached the dock, the waves were so rough the coxswain had trouble bringing in the LCVP. Lucky for all, we made it ashore and headed for a nearby shore hut. There, by ship-to-shore radio, I informed Captain Sheppard (the Chief of Staff) of the situation and my decision. He responded, "We were watching your craft. Close call. Why are you making this report?"

"Captain, I was the senior line officer in the boat."

"Very well. You are the designated officer in charge of the sailors, including those from the other ships. (The Marines reported to the Marine Colonel.) Get the men billeted. Inform the men and officers we are getting underway. We'll stay in touch through the Communications Center."

"Aye, sir."

If our situation had been a bit dicey, the ships in the bay made our situation look like a cake walk. The unforeseen hurricane was creating such forceful wind and waves that some of the ships were having trouble pulling up their anchors. We stayed at the shack by the shore for a while, watching the ships and the submarine battle the elements. They were making repeated attempts to get away from one another and the nearby landmass of Okinawa. The atmosphere, sky, and waves obscured what was going on, so we took a truck to the barracks where the men were let off. I put a Petty Officer in charge of the men, and went around the base to locate various Quarter Master buildings (clothes, pay office) where the men could draw money and clothes. We might be here for a while. I then checked into a BOQ.

We were on the island for about a week. The task force finally steamed out of the bay. (The submarine had the easiest route, as it submerged and avoided the storm.) The old WWII vintage ships were slow (maximum speed of 11 to 13 knots), and not very maneuverable. The weathermen continued to make mistakes and mis-charted the path of the storm. Thus, instead of moving away from its path, the ships followed it north. After a few days, the force backtracked and decided to steam to Subic. Later, we Okinawa Robinson Crusoes were ordered to take a military flight to Cubi Point, a Navy air base adjacent to Subic.

Navy's Dollars go to Ships. Air Force Dollars go to Officers' Clubs.

During this week, I had the pleasure of sampling the base life of the Air Force. My BOQ room was located at one of the Air Force facilities on Okinawa. My first surprise was that my room had a mini-bar and refrigerator, just like an expensive Las Vegas hotel room. Beer, wine, booze, soft drinks, chips, and peanuts were available for a small fee, which was charged to the room and to each officer's BOQ bill. The treats were replenished every day and the supplies could be tailored for each room. I asked the steward to stock my bar with Coors beer, but he apologized by saying the brand was not available anywhere in Asia. I suspected as much, but given this luxurious place, I gave it a go.

My second surprise was the Officer's Club. It was laid out identically to a large Las Vegas hotel casino: A large theater nightclub for big acts (The Platters, one of my favorites, were performing), a disco for smaller shows, a large restaurant, a coffee shop, bars and slot machines. During happy hour, a mixed drink sold for 10 cents. Other than offering cheap drinks but no women of the night, it resembled the Desert Sands, the Rivera, or the Flamingo in Sin City.

I was on a remote Asian island in the Western Pacific. Yet from all appearances, I could have been in Nevada. America's vast military machine carried with it an ambulatory America. Today, this cultural exportation is even more pervasive.

While I was emulating Bugsy Siegel, my shipmates at sea were wallowing in danger and sea sickness. Later, I learned they spent several days in semi-terror and misery as they tried to elude one of the most powerful hurricanes to hit this part of the Pacific in many years. I had already experienced one of these storms. Before I returned to the States, I would endure another. I was on large ships and they were tossed about almost like corks. It never failed to amaze me how we stayed afloat.

Upon uniting with our ships, we learned two of them had collided in the Okinawa bay while trying to steam out to sea. A personnel transport ship slipped its anchor. Its engines could not prevent the ship from colliding with the task force flag ship, the ship to which I was assigned. Figure 10-4 is a photo I took of the port, stern part of the ship. The helicopter deck was almost totaled. Some of the bulkheads on the port side were hit with such force they split. Part of the damage occurred to a berthing space, and several men were injured. No one was killed.

Figure 10-4. Damage from the collision.

Imagine the force of this collision. The cargo ship was steadily drifting. Its momentum was slowed by the ship's screws and the dragging anchor. Still, it did a lot of damage.

The ship sailed back to San Diego. Our staff transferred to the *USS Princeton*, an old WWII aircraft carrier that had been converted into a helicopter carrier to support Marine air assaults inland while the Marines in the assault boats attacked the beaches.

The few weeks of stay on this vintage, historical ship was a memorable one. It also entailed miserable experiences, recounted next.

The USS Princeton[13]

The *USS Princeton* was twenty-one years-old when our staff came aboard. It was built as a combat aircraft carrier but was reclassified and converted to an amphibious assault carrier, and designated as LPH-5. It was capable of transporting a battalion landing team (1,000-1,500 men). It carried helicopters in place of planes. *Princeton*'s mission was that of vertical envelopment: The landing of Marines behind enemy beach fortifications and to link up with assault forces that had landed on the beaches. Figure 10-5 shows the flight deck of the *Princeton* and the loading of Marines aboard some of the helicopters.

Figure 10-5. Flight deck of USS Princeton.

In October 1964, *Princeton* began operations in the Vietnam waters against North Vietnamese and Vietcong forces. Combat operations continued into 1965 and culminated in May off Chu Lai as the ship carried out its primary mission: vertical envelopment, for the first time in combat history. Some of this time, our staff was aboard. Also, we directed the assault and landings at Chu Lai, recounted in the next chapter.

A Floating City. Life aboard an aircraft carrier entails living in a floating city. The ship is so enormous that basketball courts can be set up on the hanger deck. The mess halls are as large as big restaurants. Every day, I would pass strangers in the passageway, just as I would do on a city street.

I understand the living conditions on modern nuclear carriers are akin to living ashore, at least for officers. Granted the space is tighter, but the necessities of life are a few steps away.

Life aboard a WWII vintage carrier in the Western Pacific was not comfortable, especially during the summer months. I shared a state room built to accommodate six people. Three sets of double bunk beds, six small fold down desks, six chairs, six tiny closets, and one fan made up the furnishings. The quarters were located in the bowels of the ship. Thus, we had no port holes to provide ventilation. I would have given up my stateroom furniture, closet, and cases of San Miguel beer to have had exclusive use of that fan while the ship was underway.

The nights for attempting to sleep were so hot our sheets were wet from sweat. The only saving grace was the fan. Fortunately, four of us occupied the six man cabin, so there were fewer bodies to cool. After the first night of this misery, we set up a schedule. Every half hour, the use of the fan would be rotated. It was the responsibility of the next recipient of the fan's air to wake the current recipient and notify him the fan had been passed. It reminded us of a four man relay race, except instead of passing a baton between us, we passed an electric fan.

One of our cabin residents, LTJG Smith (not his real name) did not sleep in the stateroom, so we were granted use of the fan every third rotation. After a few nights of his absence, and our asking him about his vacancy, he confessed he was sleeping in one of the pilot's ready rooms, those spaces used to brief the flyers about missions. These spaces were cooled by air conditioning and were off limits to all unless scheduled for specific events. However, as the Assistant Logistics Officer for our staff, Smith possessed the keys to these heavens. He confessed he felt guilty for not sharing this luxury with his buddies, but he was fearful that a larger contingent of cool air waifs might be caught napping in the space.

We disagreed, "You bastard! After all we've gone through for you! We protected your drunken ass in Incheon!" (We kept him safe one night from a Shore Patrol confrontation.) "This is the thanks we get?"

We shamed him into letting us sleep in one of the ready flight rooms. We were stealthy about it and were never caught in this off limits area.

It was during this part of my deployment to the Western Pacific that I considered asking for a transfer to Logistics when my friend LTJG Smith shipped out, which was only a few months away. I did not, as I was becoming increasingly fascinated by the world of wireless communications and cryptography. (Later, I was reassigned to this very post to round-out my experience, and told in Chapter 11.)

Ramping-up for War

Much to our discomfort, the heat of the tropical winter of 1963 was being augmented by the tropical heat of spring. Much to the discomfort of Washington, the political climate in the region was also heating up. The overriding concern of WestPac's amphibious forces became Vietnam. We were not alone. We were the tail being wagged from Washington, through the high level U.S. Naval commands in Hawaii. Our two star admiral staff in the South China Sea was the end of the tail. If military actions were to take place, Amphibious Group One, with the Marines and frogmen, was where the buck stopped.

With each passing week, a steady ramp-up of America's war machine was taking place. The number of advisors in Vietnam increased, as Americans helped set up the Strategic Hamlet program. Airplane landing fields were being built to house more American fighter planes. The old LPHs were being replaced by new—from the keel up—LPHs. The *USS Iwo Jima* was the first of her class of this new ship (later, our staff boarded her for a few weeks). The Navy also deployed another class of ship, called the amphibious transport dock (LPD). It was capable of 20 knots and was able to house very large landing craft. Between 1961 and 1964, the "amphibious fleet rose from 113 to 133 ships."[14]

In addition to the growing military prowess of the amphibious forces, U.S. air strikes were increasing. Later, the Rolling Thunder bombings began (early 1965). The bombs were dropped from such heights that they were only accurate to within 750 feet. They did considerable damage but more of them missed than hit their targets.

Amphibious Group One was assigned two PT boats to augment our emerging strategy of using fast attack boats along the coasts and rivers. They arrived in Subic Bay in October of 1963. They were a sight to behold. Initially, they sat in blocks on the pier next to our flagship. My image of a PT boat was from WWII movies: small boats. The PTF-3 and PTF-4 assigned to us were not small, at least in comparison to the old PTs. Figure 10-6 shows these two boats in operation off Pearl Harbor, just before they were transported to the Philippines.[15] The boats were deployed for river patrols in the Mekong Delta in South Vietnam.

Figure 10-6. PT boats.

In the early 1960s, the National Liberation Front (Vietcong) was growing much bolder. They attacked American air bases that were operating in-country. In turn, the Americans would sortie their planes and hit the enemy in retaliatory raids.

Each escalation from one side would prompt escalation from the other side. Meanwhile, South Vietnam's leadership in Saigon was coming apart at its seams. Our amphibious task force was ready to be deployed from Subic. But for what reason? To rescue civilians? To land Marines? No one knew, not even Washington.

Diem

To gain a sense of the impending tragedy and folly surrounding America's South Vietnam ally, I have extracted three quotes from Karnow about the leader of South Vietnam:

- Diem "...defied American advice to reform his administration....the United States concluded that the war could not be won with Diem." (page 230)

- An American official: Diem became "...a puppet who pulled his own strings—and ours as well." (page 251)

- A State Department official: Soldiers and ordinary citizens had "lost confidence" in Diem. (page 269)

A civil war cannot be won if the citizens do not have faith in their leaders. Diem was not a leader. Worse, he was an imperial, Catholic-centric autocrat who feared and hated Buddhists. He existed in his own isolated world.

One of his worst mistakes was his treatment of the Buddhists, which led to our task force scrambling out of Subic Bay and steaming to the coast close to Saigon. On June 11, 1963, an elderly Buddhist monk burned himself alive at a Saigon intersection. In August, four more monks burned themselves to death. Diem's sister in law, Madame Nhu applauded the suicides.[16] Turmoil followed more turmoil.

No Liberty Until?

During the summer and fall of 1963, our amphibious task force spent much of its time slowly steaming around in giant circles off the coast of Vietnam, near Saigon. We had been ordered to stand-by and to be prepared for possible amphibious operations. To this point, the only U.S. military personnel in Vietnam were supposedly noncombat troops. The landing of the Marines would take the war to a far different level. Anyway, standby we did, for days, then weeks, then months.

To relive the boredom, I enrolled in two correspondence courses from the Navy Post Graduate School. My Russian and International Law lessons and their associated discussions with my shipmates made for scintillating conversations at officers' mess.

All ships went on water rationing and "navy showers." (A short time under the shower head.) The steel ships attracted the sun's rays like a skillet attracted heat. The conditions for the enlisted men (sleeping almost on top of each other inside large under-ventilated spaces) were far worse than officers' staterooms. Upon leaving their space after an inspection, I gave thanks to the OCS gods that kept me out of these holds.

One enlisted man took it on himself to extricate his body from this misery. He was a sailor who was assigned to one of the troop transport ships, another WWII antique. We learned he informed his shipmates he was getting off the ship. They laughed and dismissed his comment as a joke. Shortly, he appeared on the main deck with an air mattress in his hands. Before anyone could restrain him, he ran to the side of the ship and jumped. The fall was about twenty feet.

Man overboard! The alarm to all ships sounded via radio and flags. After a few short exchanges between the Admiral's bridge and the vessels, evasive action was taken. As well, the troop transport ship lowered a boat in the water to try to rescue the man.

Figure 10-7. Man overboard.

I took the photo in Figure 10-7 of the rescue boat and (on the horizon) another of the ships belonging to the task force. The rescue boat is a black speck just below the distant ship.

Lucky for all, the man was rescued and none of the ships collided. He must have been a good swimmer, as we learned he lost the air mattress when he hit the water. He also made true on his boast. He was transferred to our ship, where a helicopter flew him to Saigon. There he was flown to the Subic Bay Hospital, where he was admitted to the psychiatric ward. One prison for another, but at least he was on land.

Swimming Off-shore

During this time, the task force senior officers recognized they had to deal with crew morale problems. As told earlier, during 1963-1965 the amphibious task force was steaming from one end of the Western Pacific to the other, sometimes to prepare for the evacuation of American civilians from a hostile country; other times to show the flag, and scare the local politicians or the currently reigning military junta.

With the exception of certain cabins, air conditioning on the ships did not exist. As also described, the enlisted men lived and sweltered in semi-ovens. It was impossible to keep human sweat and stench at bay. Until nasal fatigue came to the rescue, invisible clouds of semisweet but sour dankness defeated any hope for a restful sleep.[17]

The magic words "Swim call!" rang-out over the ships' PA systems. All ships in the task force had anchored just off the coast of South Vietnam. We were awaiting orders from Washington, DC about how to handle the increasingly volatile situation in Saigon (told later in this chapter). What better way to bolster morale than to allow our ships' crews to cool themselves in the Pacific Ocean?

As Athletic Officer for the staff, and with my swimming background, I was ordered to coordinate the swim for our ship's crew. For safety, two of our small craft were lowered into the water to act as a boundary for the swimmers and to check for sharks. We placed rope ladders over the sides for the men to reenter the ship after jumping or diving off its sides, or scaling down the ladder into the sea. I set up an area where the hearty swimmer or diver could launch himself from the main deck, which was about twenty feet from the water. Before long, many of the sailors were climbing up ropes and using this platform for their swim call.

The preparations for the swim were complete. The boats were deployed. Men in the boat were armed with M-1s to scare away or shoot sharks. A huge swim fest was underway. Hundreds of men flocked to the sea. They escaped their hot metal brigs for a short respite into the very world that kept their brigs afloat.

I had been waiting for the settlement of the operations so that I could also dive into the water. The situation was under control. All systems were go. I called the Chief of Staff, my mentor and friend Captain Sheppard, "Captain, all is secure. Request permission to go into the sea sir!"

"Permission granted, U.D. Well done."

Whoever rolled the dice dictating the ships' fortunes or misfortunes during those times, I silently offered a modest request: Grant us occasional moments like this. Grant this cool interlude to my men and me. Make it easier for us to laugh about the irony of a cool liquid world that surrounds our stifling lives.

My enlisted sage, Jordon, posed the question, "Mr. Black, why can't we do this more often?"

We could. It was not all that difficult. We saved fuel by anchoring. The deployment of safety craft was not a big deal. The recess was a great morale booster and gave the enlisted men a brief reprieve from their hell hole living quarters. Later in the day, I posed the question to Captain Sheppard, who directed me to bring up this issue the following morning at the daily senior officer conference. Uh oh. I could picture it now: *Here comes that smart ass Athletic Officer again. Trying out some new fangled program.*

After I presented a brief PR talk about yesterday's swim, including the cool tonic it had on the crew, the ranking member of the group (other than Captain Sheppard) informed me, "Mr. Black, this is not a resort ship. We are not on a pleasure cruise. We are a war ship. We never should have had that swim in the first place."

His response reminded me of the navy joke about an asshole skipper who informs his crew, "Now hear this. No liberty until moral improves." Meanwhile, this Captain was one of the few men on the ship with an air conditioned cabin. He had no appreciation of the repugnant misery in which most of the ship's inhabitants lived.

I disagreed with this man. I held (and continue to do so) the notion of, *take care of your men and they will take care of you.* For later years, *take care of your employees and they will take care of you; take care of those around you, whoever they may be. In the long run they, or someone else, will reciprocate.* This philosophy does not work every time in our lives. But it works enough for me to embrace it as a way to live.

The curmudgeon's view prevailed. We had the one-and-only task force swim during this time. We continued to steam around in circles. In the middle of an afternoon, one of my cabin mates took me onto the main deck. He had taken an egg from the officers' mess.

"Look at this, U.D."

He cracked open the egg and placed it on the ship's deck. It started frying. He was doing a Julia Child routine on a huge skillet. Below this skillet, hundreds of men were doing their own version of frying.

You may now be asking: Is this writer a wimp? I answer no. I merely offer that the reliance on past practices and resultant traditions can sometimes lead to unsatisfactory results. One swim a week would have done wonders for the crew's morale. I gradually came to the conclusion that high ranking officers often lost touch with the idea that one of their jobs was to see to the care of their enlisted men. But then, after leaving the Navy, I saw this same dull witted nonchalance in countless managers in government and private industry.

From the Plains to the Pacific

While at sea, if I were not on watch, after dinner I spent most of the evenings away from my stateroom. My favorite place was the deck above and overlooking the admiral's bridge. It was the highest deck on the ship and contained a small space housing electronic gear. Rarely did ship's personnel come up there in the evenings. I had my own private balcony.

During this time, I spent hours watching the fleeting aspects of the translucent water as the ship made its way to our next port. The water's reflections appeared to be glowing from the reflected moon rays. Yet the water also took on a strange light that seemed brighter than the moon itself. But for only a second or so, then the reflection would disappear and the water would return to a black state—more symbolic of its force and depth. It was a far cry from Easley's shallow ponds.

From this height, the only sounds I could occasionally hear were the waves falling alongside the ship's bow. But if I turned my head at a slight angle, I could also hear the wind passing by. Even more pleasant was the breeze generated from the ship's movements. Granted, the air was warm but it seemed to cool my body. Certainly, it assuaged my spirits.

I have often thought about those nights at sea, about my private deck. Compared to the spaces below, it was almost luxurious. To boot, I was drawing a pay check for my occupancy. Beyond what I had before me, my only wish was to be in the water.

Someone once said, "Things are beautiful if you love them." I suspect this quote could be uttered about almost anything. For me, and among other things, it would be my love for a woman. But at this time, the quote pertained to the Navy. I loved this part of my life. It was indeed beautiful.

During those times on that deck my thoughts often drifted back to the dry plains of my home in New Mexico, of Easley's Twin Lakes, of my midnight swims in the pool, of my childhood dreams of becoming a Navy frogman and my thousands of hours of labor to that end.

I had traveled from the plains to the Pacific to fulfill a quest. It was denied. I sat on that deck for many hours and into many nights thinking about this fact.

While I marveled at the waves, I mulled-over my life. I had come a long way from those plains, but mostly in miles, not in perspective. My problem was where I was headed after I left the Pacific. I had no idea what I was going to do.

I suspect my private deck offered the venue to give me a time and place to work out my plan: Keep grinding away.

I have never been one for originality.

The Maneuvering Board Again

During times at sea, I mentioned I stood watch as an assistant Officer on Deck (OOD). There was little to do unless we were steaming with other ships, or set to rendezvous with another vessel, such as a supply ship. It was one of these times around the coast of Vietnam that my previous homework—yep, putting in the time—with the Maneuvering Board came to my aid in a way that affected my career.

The Commander of our task force at this time was Admiral Lee. Like I, he was interested in international relations and foreign affairs. Some of his personal messages that came through the Comm Center were exchanges about current events taking place around the world. On occasion, he asked us junior communications officers about the messages we took to him. (We were required to read all incoming traffic). I suppose he became interested in me because I liked to talk about such arcane subjects as the Marshall Plan or the Suez Canal crisis. Not many people were so inclined. I think we engaged each other.

On one watch when I was the assistant OOD on the bridge, an enlisted man was brought before Admiral Lee. The day before, the man had pulled out incorrect signaling flags and given them to the OOD, who hoisted them onto a yardarm. The flags were used to direct the other ships in the force about their turns. Incorrect flags from the flagship could lead to collisions. Thus, this event had presented a serious danger to the task force and was highly embarrassing to the Admiral.

The man was scared and with justification. Admiral Lee looked him over for a moment. He then reached over to the man's shirt sleeve, where his seaman, second class cloth insignia was sown. Admiral Lee ripped off the man's insignia, but it took more than one "tug" from the Admiral's hand. The insignia was well threaded onto the shirt. After a few thrusts onto the top of the sewing, the seaman's sleeve and collar began to slide down his arm. The assaults of the Admiral's attacks on the insignia resulted in the badge coming off in the Admiral's hand. The seaman's sleeve was in tatters. It was a messy and ugly scene. Once done, Admiral Lee handed the once proud icon to the man, and said, "Dismissed." The Admiral then turned his attention to read the messages he was holding in his hand.

I looked at the OOD. The OOD looked at me. Silence on the bridge. Justice was served...Navy style.

To be fair, this event seemed out of character for Admiral Lee. He was an engaging, witty, and intelligent man. I was told he gained a third star later in his career. But he drew the line on certain situations. The seaman had put the task force at risk. So had the OOD who had not adequately checked the flags as they were pulled from the flag locker. But the OOD on that watch was also the Admiral's personal aide. It was the final responsibility of the OOD for the flags hoistings, not an enlisted man. Bad luck for the seaman.

Networking aside, it is fair to observe that Admiral Lee did not take kindly to subpar performance on the bridge. Thus, my final Maneuvering Board story takes on a bit of drama...at least for your writer, and I hope for you as well. Our flagship was due to rendezvous with a personnel cargo ship to transfer several persons between the ships. On such an occasion, the radar and the Maneuvering Board were used to plot the ships' courses to each other. The outcome of the Board's plotting was integral to a smooth link-up. The result would be a tie up as seen in Figure10-8, which shows a transfer of an officer between the two ships. He is holding on to the boson's chair rail that is being pulled toward our ship, highlighted with the dark circle.

"Mr. Black, plot a course to PA-27."

What? It was the OOD's job to plot the Board and present recommendations for the speed and direction of the ship. I looked at the OOD. He looked at me and shrugged.

"Aye, sir."

I made the plot, and presented it to the Admiral.

"That was fast. You're sure?"

"Yes, sir."

"Very well. I'll keep your first plot here (in his hands). Continue the tracking. Let's see if your plot holds up."

Figure 10-8. Rendezvous at sea.

The original plot stayed on course. The Admiral later said, "U.D., I'm fast on the Maneuvering Board. You're faster...and as accurate. Well done."

In a nutshell, a Chief Bos'un at an Albuquerque Navy recruiting station helped me in this fortuitous circumstance. I took his advice to heart and put in the time on the Board. It paid off.

The OOD later told me no one had been able to contest Admiral Lee's competence with the Maneuvering Board. I did not know I had contested it. I had no idea of that notion, but Admiral Lee later made sure I was granted the position I requested for my next assignment—which became a lynchpin in my career. I will ever remain grateful to Admiral Lee, as well as to the Bos'un. The Chief laid the groundwork for it to happen.

A few months later, I was again denied a physical clearance for UDT (described in Chapter 11). I decided to extend my time in the Navy for a billet in Washington, DC. Admiral Lee personally intervened to assure my assignment. I owe my transfer to prime duty to this man. Later, back in DC where we had both been assigned, Admiral Lee invited me to his home for cocktails. I wish I had made the effort to stay in touch with this man. He was one of those gems of intellect and wit we rarely come across.

Diem's Murder

In the late fall of 1963 our task force was steaming off the coast of South Vietnam. As a crypto officer, I was tasked with encrypting and decrypting classified messages. The traffic during these times was frenetic and confusing. It was obvious something was amiss (even more than usual) in Saigon, but the messages did not reveal the extent of America's complicity in the Diem coup.

Depending on one's interpretation of the Vietnam War, the coup was either beneficial or detrimental to the cause. Whatever the case may have been, the messages of the first part of November directed our task force to stand down. The unclassified wires informed us Diem and his brother Nhu were dead and that a new South Vietnamese administration was in place.

All was well. Previously, Madame Nhu, the sister-in-law of Diem, had succeeded in imposing a puritan-like life style on Saigon. With the demise of her husband and Diem, nightclubs and brothels once again flourished. Good news for thirsty and horny American advisors.

Henry Cabot Lodge, a principal participant in the coup, sent a wire to President Kennedy, "The prospects now are for a shorter war."[18]

How little did Lodge realize the implications of his complicity. Someone once said, "You can change your horse in midstream to make for a better ride. Just make sure the new horse can carry you to the other side." In this war, America rode one bad horse after another.

Graciousness

After this mini-crisis, our vessel split up with the other ships and made sail for the city of Kaohsiung, a large port in southwest Taiwan. Here, our basketball team defeated the locals.

We were not aware of the Taiwanese custom of exchanging gifts between opposing teams. Before the tip-off for the game, a Kaohsiung notable came onto the court. There, he presented us with a hand-made cloth pennant commemorating this historic event. In Chinese and English, the pennant proclaimed:

PHIB-GRU-ONE and KAOHSIUNG
FRIENDSHIP AND GOODWILL

The present was a beautiful token, one of courtesy and graciousness. Even more, the pennant was accompanied with a large melon. Our team was humbled and pleased.

We had no reciprocal gift. We were caught unaware. My team mumbled, "Think of something, Mr. Black!" It was an awkward moment. As the official waited for the exchange, I waffled. After a moment, I walked to the official and handed him our basketball, making it seem as if it were the only basketball in existence. It had probably been manufactured in Taiwan.

The man might have been in charge of the Taiwanese basketball assembly line factory. He made not one glimpse of surprise or insult. He bowed his head, smiled, and gave his thanks for our "generous" gift. His elegance spoke volumes for his culture. For many years, I kept this pennant close. Somewhere along life's highways, I lost it. I wish I had not.

Kennedy's Assassination

It was during a stay in Kaohsiung that President Kennedy was assassinated. I learned of the event as I was coming on watch at the Comm Center. We were aboard the *USS Iwo Jima*, a new helicopter carrier. It was early morning, and I was walking down the passageway toward the radio shack. On the bulkhead next to the Comm Center entrance was a bulletin board where news items were posted. The area was crowded with enlisted men and officers. They were reading the newscasts about Kennedy's death.

Kaohsiung was one of the favored ports for sailors' bacchanalian romps. The prostitutes were regulated and thus clean. Dope did not exist. Prices were cheap. Rice beer was abundant. All in all, Kaohsiung was a tame and sane version of Olongapo.

The captain of the ship had a difficult decision on his hands. We had been at sea for a while. All hands were looking for several nights of liberty. He made this announcement over the ship's PA: *Liberty is granted in accordance with ongoing watches and work details. You are to conduct yourselves on shore as befits the U.S. Navy. We have suffered a great loss. Your behavior ashore should reflect this loss. That is all.*

That early night in Kaohsiung was one of the strangest times I spent in the Western Pacific. Officers and sailors were ashore, but we were not really on liberty. A quiet air of disbelief—of unacceptance—hung over the potential, lingering festivities in the bars and brothels.

But alcohol takes its toll, both in remorse and revelry. As the evening wore on, the impact of Kennedy's assassination was tempered by rice beer. Kaohsiung's navy area was not capable of restraint anyway. Toward midnight, the town resembled another navy port...which it was.

The next day, we steamed away from Taiwan to our home port in the Philippines. The next year, 1964, would be one of more amphibious training, frequent visits to Vietnam, and the Gulf of Tonkin incident. The year 1965 would witness the escalation of the war in which our amphibious forces would land combat troops on the beaches of Vietnam.

A period of grace was coming to an end.

---

[1] Henry Wadsworth Longfellow, *Voices of the Night*, 1839. Secondary source: Leonard Roy Frank, *Quotationary*, New York: Random House, 2001, p. 913.

[2] Franz Kafka, *Conversations with Kafka*, p. 93, 1953. Secondary source: Leonard Roy Frank, *Quotationary*, New York: Random House, 2001, p. 913.

[3] From Wikipedia, altered with my edits and additions.

[4] James Bradley, *The Imperial Cruise*, New York: Little, Brown, and Company, 2009, p. 280).

[5] Microsoft Encarta. All rights reserved. Key-in "Manifest Destiny."

[6] As discussed in more detail shortly, if you think America did not offer a better alternative to the Vietnamese people, I ask you to look at Vietnam's current despotic, venal dictatorship.

[7] Karnow, *Vietnam*, p. 265.

[8] France was instrumental in expanding the opium use in Vietnam (initially, only Chinese smoked it) and outside its borders. France even built an opium refinery in Saigon, all to increase income. Stanley Karnow's *Vietnam: A History* is a good reference for this subject.

[9] Nothing is simple about the Vietnam War. Asking Communist dictators in North Vietnam to participate in democratic elections was an Alice in Wonderland exercise.

[10] Associated Press (AP), "Vietnam Court Gives Activist 5.5 Year Term," *USA TODAY*, December 29, 2009, p. 6A.

[11] Sourced from Wikipedia. Key in "LST" or "Navy Assault Crafts."

[12] While at sea, and on watch on the Admiral's bridge, as the junior officer, I took orders from the senior officer, usually a Lt. Cmdr, or a Cmdr. The deck below ours was the site where the ship was steered and otherwise controlled. During the times we sailed in a task force, the officers on the Admiral's bridge gave the orders for the movements of the collective ships. In this situation, the deck below us took our commands and navigated the ship. These task force operations are where my Maneuvering Board abilities helped me in my career, a story recounted shortly.

[13] History of the *Princeton* is sourced from: http://www.chinfo.navy.mil/navpalib/ships/carriers/histories/cv37-princeton/cv37-princeton.html. With some editing, the historical text about this vessel is nearly verbatim from the military documentation.

[14] Edward J. Marolda and Oscar P. Fitzgerald, *The United States Navy and the Vietnam Conflict, Volume II*, Department of the Navy, 1986, p. 280.

[15] Marolda and Fitzgerald, p. 207.

[16] Karnow, *Vietnam*, p. 301.

[17] As we learned later, when the Vietnam War heated up, our ships were heavens compared to our comrades' accommodations ashore. Yes, they had their sanctuaries on base, but they also had their days and nights in terrifying situations.

[18] Karnow, *Vietnam*, p. 327.

Chapter 11

Committing Troops

The words of the prophets
Are written on the subway walls
And tenement halls
And whispered in the sounds of silence.
Paul Simon, "The Sounds of Silence", 1964.

And shouted on the National Mall
And in Pentagon halls.

Upon returning to Subic Bay a few weeks after the operation, I paid a call on the surgeon to review my rehabilitation. I was happy about my recovered mobility. I was not happy about the area of my body that went under the knife. It was giving me pain. At times, I could not sleep. Yet I was supposedly cured. What was going on? How could something that no longer existed cause pain?

The doctor had no good news. First, he attributed the cause of the pain to damaged nerve endings, blood vessels, scar tissue, or all of these factors.[1] He offered no solutions except pain pills. I was not happy. I replied I had merely exchanged one set of pain for another.

He said he regretted the after effects of the operation. I offered I did, too, likely more than he did. He wrote a prescription for a pain killer. I asked, is that it? He said, not quite. He said he would not recommend my returning to UDT training. And yes, that was it.

If it appears I am letting this man off too easily, I was not surprised by his diagnosis and assessment. However, I did rethink my earlier opinion about his competence. Anyway, I had begun to consider the rigor of UDT and question if I wanted to risk further harm to an area of my body that had already been damaged. I was aware there were more important things in life than swimming for a living, such as having a family and the pleasures of getting one started.

It is easier to accept bad news if it is introduced into our lives gradually. Maybe that is one positive aspect of growing old. It happens so slowly we gradually accommodate ourselves to its gloomy realities.

The door to my UDT dreams had closed at the time of the sand dune runs in Coronado, California. Deep down, I knew it had. Subconsciously, I had been making that adjustment for over two years. Now, it was time to consciously close the door.

Wireless Communications and Teletype Machines

During this time I became fascinated by the technologies of radio communications and cryptography. The subjects were complex in theory but simple in our practice of them. It was later that I delved into their underpinnings. For now, my hands were full with learning the basics.

Most of the ships in WestPac used the punched tape/teletype system for radio communications. A typewriter type device was used to key in a message. The device produced a perforated tape of the output. The tape would be fed into a printer to produce hard copy, which was used to proof read the message. The tape could be altered to make corrections. It would then be fed into a tape reader for transmittal as electromagnetic images through the air.

A few of the ships with which we communicated had only telegraph transmitters and receivers. But my Radiomen were versatile and several of the senior petty officers were competent telegraph operators. I had retained some knowledge of the Morse code from my Boy Scout days, but I restricted my operations to times when we were playing around and experimenting in the Comm Center.

As a rule, Communications Officers did not get their hands "dirty" with handling the equipment. We supervised the men who operated radio equipment with which we were largely ignorant. Small wonder many enlisted men looked upon officers with derision. As mentioned, an officer was only as good as his men.

The exception to the hands-on rule was the crypto gear. Only officers (and with some exceptions, higher ranking enlisted men) were given the security clearances for access to these machines and their codes. As the Vietnam War escalated, I was given another level of clearance for a higher security classification. For this assignment, a ship had first, a security clearance to the Comm Center, next, a security clearance to a crypto room, and then another clearance to another crypto room. It reminded me of Russian dolls that contained dolls containing more dolls, into yet more dolls.

During times of high alerts, such as Diem's murder, the Comm Center was a place of semi-bedlam. We were up to our necks in punched tape. We had so many messages coming in and going out that we had to hang them on the bulkheads with paper clips for temporary storage. I would not be surprised if some of the traffic never made it onto the airwaves.

The Gulf of Tonkin Incident

The August, 1964 Gulf of Tonkin incident has been covered by the media with thousands of articles and books. Most everyone acknowledges the attacks were used by the Johnson administration to escalate the war. He and his aides were looking for a politically expedient pretext to place combat troops into Vietnam. Without them, most experts agreed the war would be lost. McGeorge Bundy said that looking for such an opportunity was, "...like waiting for a streetcar."[2]

Shortly after the Tonkin Gulf incidents, a Navy officer arrived to replace my boss, who was reassigned to a position in the States.

(I had recently been reassigned to the Logistics Department of the staff, but I also continued to work in the crypto room.) I remember our first conversation as we sat in our shared office on the ship. For this story, I will call him Mr. Baker. He said he had recently debarked from the *USS Maddox*, and had witnessed the Tokin incidents. I asked Mr. Baker about the attacks on the two destroyers. He related this story to me.

While his ship was cruising in the Tonkin Gulf, it was attacked by two or more North Vietnamese PT boats. The boats came close enough to leave bullet indentations on the ship. The destroyer's guns damaged at least one of the boats and kept them at bay.

Mr. Baker snapped some photos of the attack, but he had not yet had them developed. We were in port for a few days, so he took the film to the Subic Bay Navy Exchange. I asked him to make copies for me and he did. I lost some of the photos, but managed to hold on to two of them, as seen in Figure 11-1.[3]

It is difficult to make out the images in the pictures, but they do provide telling information. The top picture shows the explosions of the shells as the U.S. ship's cannons track to the target of a boat, which is not visible in this photo. The bottom picture shows a boat approaching the U.S. ship.

I do not recall if Mr. Baker talked about the U.S. ships being in international waters or North Vietnamese waters. Wherever the ships were, President Johnson used the attacks as a way to justify landing Marines in Danang in 1965—the beginning of America's huge commitment to the war.

Mr. Baker related the story in a matter of fact way. I accepted it as such. We did not think it a big deal. Later, I was surprised to learn the political consequences of the Gulf of Tonkin affair.

In relating this story to you, it is noteworthy that this officer had no axe to grind one way or the other about this incident. It occurred. He took some pictures. He shared them with me. Regarding the attack, he was apolitical. So was I. The PT boat attack was part of the war. Again, it was no big deal. Someone shoots at you. You shoot back. Even better, you shoot first.

Figure 11-1. Gulf of Tonkin attacks.
Photos from member of ship's crew.

Another aspect of his conversation remains in my memory. He mentioned the unsettling effects the noise of bullets hitting the sides of the ship had on him. Fortunately for him and his shipmates, the attack boats were lightly armed and were repulsed by the destroyer's superior fire power and U.S. aircraft.

Figure 11-2. Gulf of Tonkin attacks. Photo from Wikipedia.

Mr. Baker told me his ship may have been attacked a second time two days later (August 4, 1964, the first attack occurred August 2), but he was not certain because of weather conditions. He said the ships were at general quarters and prepared to protect themselves. He laughed several times during our talk, but they were not happy laughs. He said everyone aboard was spooked, and the ship Captain was not going to place his men and the ship at risk by not firing. According to Wikipedia:[4]

> During an evening and early morning of rough weather and heavy seas, the destroyers received radar, sonar, and radio signals that they believed signaled another attack by the North Vietnamese navy. For some two hours, the ships fired on radar targets and maneuvered vigorously amid electronic and visual reports of enemies.

Over the past fifty years, I have witnessed the Tonkin Gulf incident turned into a myth. The Web contains a wealth of information about this affair. Here is one example, with my comments italicized.[5]

The American commitment to the war against Vietnam, which killed over 50,000 U.S. military personnel, and probably over 2 million Vietnamese civilians, was cemented by an incident that appears to involve more fiction than fact. (*This lead-in sentence is incorrect.*)

In the Gulf of Tonkin incident, North Vietnamese torpedo boats supposedly attacked the USS Maddox in the Gulf of Tonkin, off Vietnam, in a pair of assaults on August 2 and 4 of 1964. (*The word "supposedly" is incorrect, and if the writer had done his/her homework, the facts were available that the first attack did occur, including the torpedo boats launching torpedoes—not to mention bullets hitting the ship.*) It was the basis for the Tonkin Gulf Resolution, which committed major American forces to the war in Vietnam. The resolution passed the House of Representatives unanimously, and passed in the Senate with only two dissenting votes.

In retrospect it is clear that the alleged attack was little more than a transparent pretext for war, delivered in a one-two punch. (*The word "alleged" is incorrect.*) First, media descriptions of the August 2nd attack as an "unprovoked attack" against a U.S. destroyer on "routine patrol" hid the fact that the Maddox was providing support for South Vietnamese military operations against the North. Second, the alleged August 4th attack appears to be a fabrication, official accounts attributing the "error" to confusion. (*North Vietnam was trying to conquer South Vietnam by military force. The writer implies that South Vietnam and its ally were not allowed to shoot-back. The phrase "appears to be a fabrication" is incorrect. As Mr. Baker explained, the Americans were genuinely confused.*)

These critics fail to mention the attacks that were being launched by the Communists in South Vietnam, notably the February 6-7 assault against a U.S. base near Pleiku. Eight Americans were killed in this attack. It was a key event that incited Operation Flaming Dart: the bombing of North Vietnamese army camps in North Korea. Prior to Pleiku, the USSR was going to pressure North Vietnam to consider negotiations. After the attack and America's response, the Soviet Union felt compelled to furnish almost unconditional military aid to North Vietnam, including surface-to-air missiles.

Slothful Journalists. It is sad to witness the Tonkin Gulf event dissolve into fabrication because of the political leanings of those who wrote about it, and those who continue to write about it. Reporters are tasked with the responsibility to report about an incident, without biased interpretation. They are ethically bound to convey facts about the event. While watching a TV show recently, I viewed a Tonkin Gulf report, which I paraphrase: *It was determined the government lied about the Gulf of Tonkin Incident.*

Hendrick Hertzberg, a supposedly respected correspondent with *The New Yorker* magazine, writes, "The Tonkin Gulf incident was not even an incident, since an incident, to be an incident, has to occur."[6]

How can we respond to such a careless, indolent, stupid, false, and pretentious statement? Perhaps we can start with: The sentence is clever but counterfeit—a combination that should keep people like this man off a news beat.

In spite of Hertzberg's falsehoods, most respectable media postings state the August 2 attack did occur. There is more debate about the August 4 attack. All true, as verified by Mr. Baker. What is disconcerting are the postings (sometimes a sentence within a book or paragraph, written by the aforementioned slothful journalist, Hertzberg) that claim nothing happened on *either* August 2 or 4, that the whole story was a concoction by the government to justify the 1965 Danang Marine landings. It was certainly used as a justification but the story was not a concoction.

LBJ may have pushed the truth about who were the provocateurs in the Gulf of Tonkin incident to support his plan to commit troops in Vietnam. I do not know if the United States ships were the provocateurs by their possible sailings inside North Vietnam's waters, which is claimed by some to have been a violation of international law.[7] In any case, the "international waters" notion is irrelevant. If a country and its allies are battling another country, adhering to international water boundaries is absurd. It's akin to saying the D-Day invasions were a violation of Vichy France's waters.

Of course, America was not at war. It was acting in an advisory role. With Tonkin, Johnson had the pretext for committing troops. However, I view the Vietcong attack on Pleiku as the main reason for dispatching U.S. forces into Vietnam. The military leaders recognized the enemy was changing from a guerilla force to a conventional army.

General Westmoreland pays a Call

On February 22, 1965, General William Westmoreland asked President Johnson for two Marine battalions to protect the airfield at Danang against possible attacks from the 6,000 Vietcong fighters who were in the vicinity. The request created heated debate at the White House, but LBJ decided to commit American forces to the conflict.

On February 26, President Johnson authorized the landing of Marines at Danang. As part of ongoing preparations, our staff had been working on a general plan. We had to make changes in order to tailor our operation to the Danang location and its local conditions. Our staff put on the hat of Commander, Amphibious Forces Seventh Fleet to plan the landing. Later, we put on the hat of Commander, Amphibious Group One to execute the plan we wrote.

As mentioned, I had been transferred to the Logistics Department of the staff to round out my experience. I was the Assistant Department Head. The department was responsible for coordinating the logistical aspects of an amphibious assault. As such, I worked with officers at MACV in Vietnam to develop and execute the plan. A memo in my Navy file will help explain my duties:

> As Loading Control Watch Officer, and Assistant Logistics Officer on my staff during the ship-to-shore and subsequent phases of the amphibious landings, you acted as staff liaison

> with the Beachmaster and controlled the flow of material to the beach. In each of these landings, you personally acted in a staff capacity toward the correction of problems resulting from congestion of materials on the beach and boat casualties from the landings. In the difficult and sustained operations at Chu Lai (recounted later), your conscientious and determined efforts over the extended period of time were a constant source of strength to me. (Signed: D.W. Wulzen, Commander Amphibious Group One/Commander Amphibious Force, U.S. Seventh Fleet.)

Admiral Wulzen laid it on a bit thick—and this book is after all, an autobiography, with its resultant self promotions. Part of the purpose of the prose was to justify to Washington the granting of a decoration. The job was the polar opposite of my communications billet, which was a cushy, secure place in one of the few air conditioned spaces on the ship. In this new billet, during the landings, I was either on the bridge or on the beach helping to coordinate men and machines flowing back and forth across land and water.

I was also officer in charge of the Admiral's barge and the Captain's gig (our Chief of Staff). The ship's Captain also had a Captain's gig, which was maintained by the ship's crew. Our tax dollars at work: Three large boats, reserved for the use of only three men. (These officers were generous in their allowing the boats' use for ferrying operations during liberty hours.)

MACV representatives often came to our flagship for meetings and briefings. On one occasion, General Westmoreland came aboard. He flew in from MACV to meet with Admiral Wulzen, who was in charge of the Western Pacific amphibious operations. The general received the red carpet treatment, which is shown as a gray color in Figure 11-3. He is seen walking with the Admiral to the helicopter deck. At this time I was standing watch on the bridge. I heard the general being piped off the ship, so I walked toward the stern to take the photo.

Figure 11-3. The red carpet treatment.

America Enters the Quagmire

On March 8, 1965, at 5:45 am, the Danang assault forces entered the harbor of Danang, South Vietnam. (Figure 11-4 provides a map used throughout this chapter.) I was on the Admiral's bridge, acting as Loading Control Watch Officer. We had received conflicting intelligence reports about the enemy. Some sources warned us to expect heavy opposition. Others proclaimed the Vietcong had pulled back inland and would not contest the landings. Obviously, we were at general quarters.

Our staff was aboard the *Mount McKinley*, accompanied by the *Henrico*, *Union*, and *Vancouver*. They carried the 3rd Battalion, 9th Marines. We were protected by several destroyers, cruisers, and a carrier, the *Hancock*.

The movement of the ships into the harbor took on a silent, surreptitious countenance.[8] Most ships' lamps were off. The bridge was dark. The only noteworthy lights came from the radar screens and a plastic illuminated board which showed the positions of the ships. The time was one of quiet reflection, anticipation, and uneasiness. I will never know about the emotions of the other men on the ship, but I was sanguine and nervous, sanguine while on the bridge of the ship, nervous knowing I would later go onto the beach.

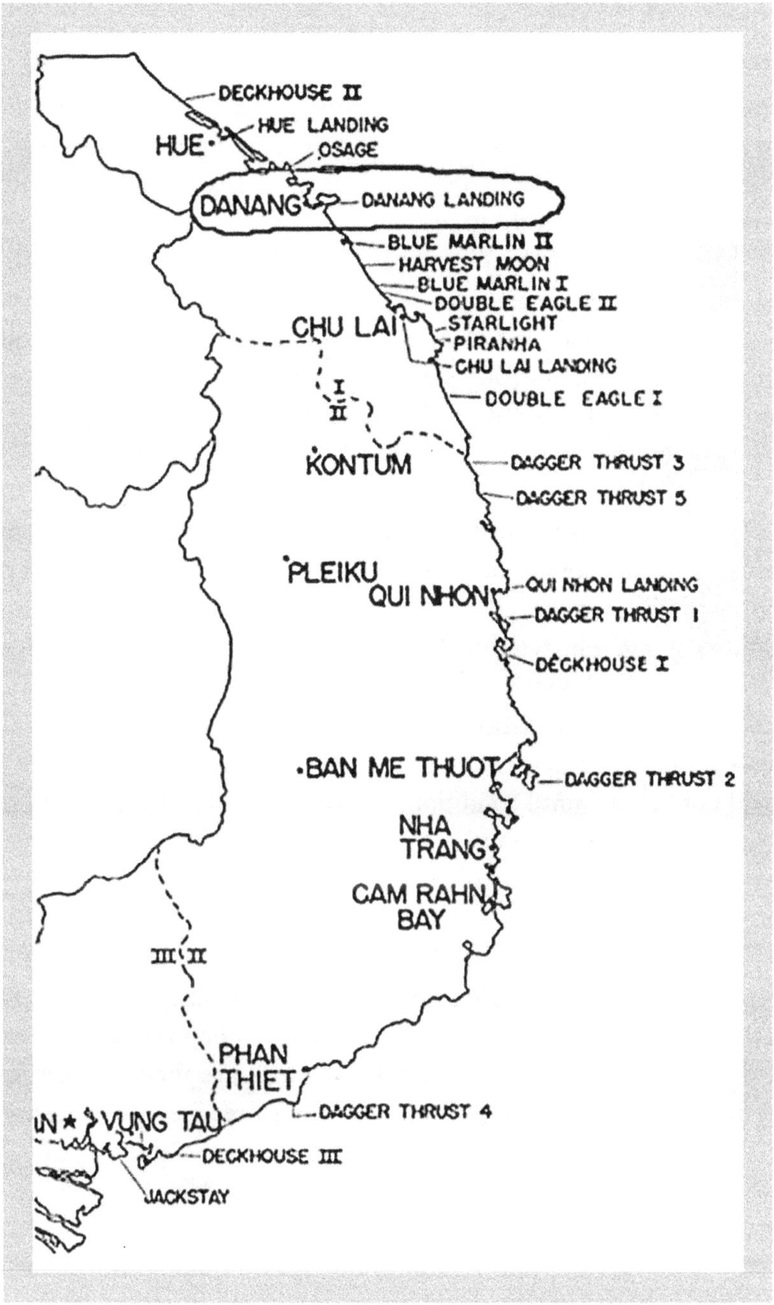

Figure 11-4. Amphibious operations.

Prevalent intelligence reports informed us the enemy would likely not fire on our ships. How could they know? There were some 6,000 Vietcong in the area. Even more, for the past year the Vietcong (and increasingly, their North Vietnamese Vietminh comrades) had surprised us with their cunning, brilliant, and daring tactics. Nonetheless, while I was on ship, I thought I was safe. In my new job as a logistics officer, going ashore might be a different matter.

The ships' company—wearing helmets and life jackets—were at their battle stations. Our many hours of training would finally be put to the test. At exactly 6 AM Admiral Wulzen ordered the traditional amphibious command of, "Land the landing force." Off we went into Vietnam. Off America went into a war that nobody won.

Red Beach II

At the time of the order, beach conditions were favorable. But before all the boats had landed—especially the supply boats—conditions worsened to the extent they became dangerous for small craft beaching. The wind had picked up to around 25 knots and our landing area, Red Beach II, had six to eight feet of surf. The situation put the operation in jeopardy, at least for a quick execution. The smaller and more numerous LCVPs (see Figure 7-3 in Chapter 7) could not be used until conditions improved. We had to rely on larger boats (LCMs) and amphibious tractors (LVTPs). If the landing had been contested, this situation could have presented major problems, with resultant casualties.

During the morning of March 8, we succeeded in landing most of the combat troops, corpsmen, doctors, cooks, chaplains, and hundreds of tons of gear onto Red Beach II. The operations were held up, then resumed, then held up, and again resumed, all without the loss of life. The many intense training exercises we undertook in the Philippines, Okinawa, and Korea were paying off. As mentioned earlier, the landings in Danang in March, 1965, were surely the performances of a group outlier.

I was ashore to act as liaison of our navy amphibious force with the Beachmaster and to relay classified documents between (Marine) General Karch's staff and ours.

I studied the results of the work of our staff. We had done well. The beach surveys conducted by the frogmen proved to be accurate. The landing areas were busy, yet not congested. Security, administrative, and medical areas were being put in place. Except for the high surf conditions, the landing was proceeding flawlessly.

In addition, the beach and the surrounding suburbs of Danang were secure. No enemy was in sight. They were beyond the beach, in the not too distant foothills and jungles. With some minor exceptions, this invisible enemy had remained invisible from the beginning. He had wisely chosen not to engage us. His strategy of asymmetrical combat worked time-and-again during this war.

One aspect of the Danang landing reminded me of the amphibious exercise we conducted earlier on the Philippine island of Mindoro. Certainly, the situation was different in Vietnam because we were coming ashore in an area known to be populated with a competent deadly enemy. We did not know what to expect, although we knew any reception would not include cheering natives selling us beer and sex (those came later). Taking the wise approach, we leaned toward caution.

Figure 11-5(a) illustrates this pragmatic approach to an unknown situation.[9] The Danang landing was a page out of WWII. Many of the tactics and maneuvers to place the Marines on shore were identical to the amphibious assaults in the Pacific, North Africa, Italy, and France. As mentioned, we even employed the LCVP and LCM boats made famous by their presence on the D-Day beaches.

The Danang operations involved only fifteen ships or so, resulting in the deployment of 1,461 troops—a very modest operation compared to, say, D-Day. If you are visualizing the amphibious assault on Danang, don't think *Saving Private Ryan*—it is too expansive and we received no enemy fire on the beaches. You can think about the landing craft and the men coming ashore (albeit safely). Then add the "resistance" of the Vietnamese, as seen in Figure 11-5(b) and you will have the picture of the Danang amphibious landing of 1965. The truth is, we were embarrassed (but relieved) to be coming ashore in full military regalia, ready to kill on sight, only to be greeted by lovely women bearing colorful leis.

Figure 11-5(a). Coming ashore.

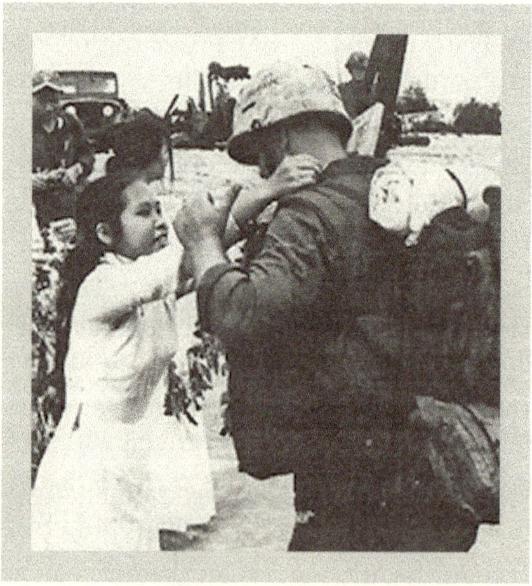

Figure 11-5(b). Enemy resistance.

Informal Liberty

After I had performed my duties on the beach, it was time to return to the ship. The surf came up again, so I was stranded on the shore for a while.

I had not eaten for several hours and decided to find a place for a meal—anything but a military mess. Walking around, I spotted a cluster of small buildings to the south of the beach landing area. As I came closer to them, I discovered one structure housed a café.

The café was open. Unbelievable! In the middle of a war, I had discovered a funky French bistro in the center of the combat zone. Whatever the outside conditions, which were peaceful, my mind migrated to images of baguettes and cheese.

The café was somewhat in business. I was the only patron. But I was not surprised. It was not every day that a hostile, armed-to-the-teeth armada rammed itself onto a nearby beach. Nor was it ordinary for a café to be surrounded by heavily armed Marine patrols. The situation was not conducive to three-star dining.

Seeing this peaceful café in its war like surroundings was an odd experience. The café offered a cocoon of serenity in the middle of a world of commotion. In comparison to the dissonance of the beach operations taking place a few hundred feet away, the cafe was quiet and peaceful.

In retrospect, the situation was a logical consequence of a successful amphibious assault on an uncontested shore. The landing, although going slowly because of the weather, was successful. Enemy resistance was nonexistent. Danang was secure and subject to U.S. reconnaissance and patrols. At some point in a beach assault landing, things return to a sense of normalcy. The landing was at this point when I entered the café.

My entrance into the place sparked considerable comment and activity from the two people inside. The owner of the café appeared to be a Frenchman, who spoke passable English. A Vietnamese woman was introduced to me as his wife and cook.

I did not know if they were afraid of having customers or afraid of having none. I was lightly armed, carrying a .45 around my waist.

The Marines walking around the café had carbines in their hands. Understandably, the café owners were both alarmed and elated. They later told me they had been frightened by the events of the past two days, yet they foresaw a windfall of business from the new visitors.

My ship had been at sea for several days. The food in the officers mess was tolerable but just that, tolerable. Sitting in a French café for a brief spell, I was far removed from Navy food. What could be more French than French onion soup? As I sat down and began to chat with the owner, one of my first thoughts was of a bowl of this soup, laden with melted cheese and sweet onions.

I am not much of a gourmet now, and I certainly was not a gourmet in my younger days. I had no inkling as to the exact recipe for French onion soup. It was a simple matter to me: I liked French onion soup because it was salty and tasted of beef.

My new friend did not catch on to what I wanted for my meal. But after I described the ingredients, he seemed to understand. He issued the order to the cook and brought to the table a Vietnamese beer. Shortly, the soup arrived, steaming from its heat and smelling of its succulent condiments—cooked in a French café, located in a sophisticated, exotic city.

Have you ever looked forward to the first taste of one of your favorite foods? Have you thought about its flavor, as you bring the spoon to your nose to inhale its aroma? Have you begun salivating even before it enters your mouth? Have you ever experienced a gastronomic orgasm, as the food's taste cascades around your tongue and its smell permeates your nostrils? All these anticipations and potential sensations were abundant as I took the first spoonful of Vietnamese French onion soup into my mouth. And as the first taste took hold of my culinary senses, I gagged.

Why is one person's delicacy another's putrescent? How can one person delight in sushi while another is sickened by it? Why are mountain oysters a wonderful dish to some diners and repulsive castrated calf's balls to others? We leave these questions to the world's gastronomic psychotherapists to answer. For this situation, the soup made me queasy for one reason: It was made from fish broth, not beef broth.

The owner and the cook were as distraught as I was surprised. But after gathering my senses, not to mention my tastes, it became evident even to my pathetic palate that it was not the poor taste of the soup that had unraveled me. It was its peculiar taste, its strangeness. After I had gulped down some beer, I began to enjoy my meal—very much. I finished it off. All in all, an outlier soup.

It was time to return to my ship. The surf had died down and the smaller boats could be seen coming from the anchored ships in the bay. After bidding farewell to the restaurateurs, I made my way back to Red Beach II, wiser and more appreciative of the nuances of Vietnamese cuisine.

As the war unfolded, I visited Danang two more times. I made a point to pay a call on my favorite Vietnamese café. The owner and his wife were happy—their café was doing a booming business and was populated with hungry and thirsty Americans. I discovered their French onion soup was prepared with beef broth. Even with a scarcity of beef in the region, the owner told me he had to adjust his menu to a new clientele—a micro example of the macro phenomenon of globalization. I wonder if he made another adjustment after the Americans departed?

Patrolling for Saboteurs

As mentioned, we returned to Danang other times during the next few months. We landed more Marines, and used smaller craft to patrol nearby inlets and rivers. During this time, we were confident the enemy would not challenge us in the air, as they had no airplanes. Our main concern was small arms fire from the shore, and the danger of Vietcong frogmen, or a renegade sampan, sneaking inside the patrol boat parameters and planting mines on our ships. Consequently, during the stays at Danang, most sailors and junior officers were required to spend time on a patrol boat, looking for possible saboteurs. A typical example of the type of craft under surveillance, and one we boarded, is shown in Figure 11-6. I snapped this photo while the crew and I were on a surveillance patrol. The American flag is visible at the stern of our boat.

Figure 11-6. A boat under surveillance.

Fighting with Shadows

As an example of this kind of fighting with an elusive enemy, I found a message in my Navy records (See Figure 11-7). We (as CTF SEVEN SIX, Commander of Task Force 76) sent it to all ships in the area. The causeway under question was searched, as were the hulls of all ships. These almost continual alerts made for tedious duty, but they could not be ignored. And once again, this message demonstrated the asymmetrical approach the enemy took to fighting us: They hit us where we were vulnerable. Until later, they never attacked our strength. It took the human race several centuries and millions of dead warriors to come up with this idea. We had not arrived at this intuitive notion in the Civil War (Gettysburg) or WWI (the doughboy suicidal charges). George Washington practiced it during his times, but we seemed to have forgotten it thereafter.

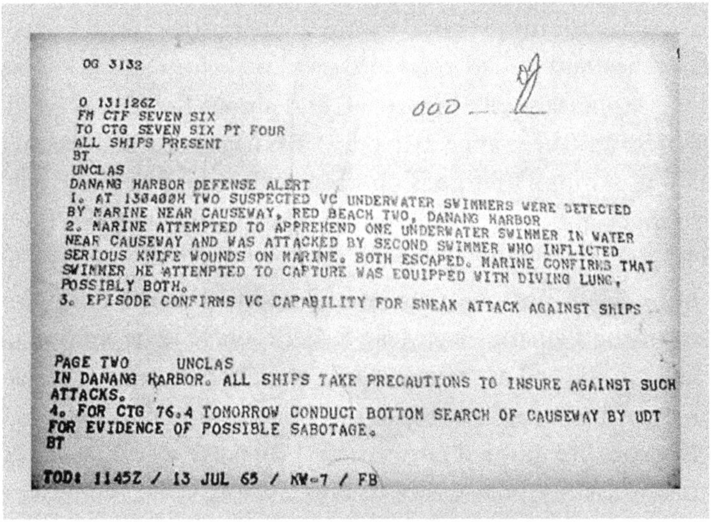

OG 3132

0 131126Z
FM CTF SEVEN SIX
TO CTG SEVEN SIX PT FOUR
ALL SHIPS PRESENT
BT
UNCLAS
DANANG HARBOR DEFENSE ALERT
1. AT 130400H TWO SUSPECTED VC UNDERWATER SWIMMERS WERE DETECTED BY MARINE NEAR CAUSEWAY, RED BEACH TWO, DANANG HARBOR
2. MARINE ATTEMPTED TO APPREHEND ONE UNDERWATER SWIMMER IN WATER NEAR CAUSEWAY AND WAS ATTACKED BY SECOND SWIMMER WHO INFLICTED SERIOUS KNIFE WOUNDS ON MARINE. BOTH ESCAPED. MARINE CONFIRMS THAT SWIMMER HE ATTEMPTED TO CAPTURE WAS EQUIPPED WITH DIVING LUNG, POSSIBLY BOTH.
3. EPISODE CONFIRMS VC CAPABILITY FOR SNEAK ATTACK AGAINST SHIPS

PAGE TWO UNCLAS
IN DANANG HARBOR. ALL SHIPS TAKE PRECAUTIONS TO INSURE AGAINST SUCH ATTACKS.
4. FOR CTG 76.4 TOMORROW CONDUCT BOTTOM SEARCH OF CAUSEWAY BY UDT FOR EVIDENCE OF POSSIBLE SABOTAGE.
BT

TOD: 1145Z / 13 JUL 65 / KW-7 / FB

Figure 11-7. Subterfuge and stealth.

What did it prove? That superior firepower would not necessarily translate into victory. That victory could be attained by wearing-down the enemy:[10]

> "You know," (General Westmoreland) boasted to a North Vietnamese colonel after the war, "you never defeated us on the battlefield." To which the Communist officer replied, "That may be so, but it is also irrelevant."

> "We were not strong enough to drive a half million American troops out of Vietnam, but that wasn't our aim," (North Vietnamese General) Giap explained. "We sought to break the will of the American government to continue the conflict. Westmoreland was wrong to count on his superior firepower to grind us down."

Swimming Again

Following the incident described in the message, we increased the number of boats to check beaches, causeways, and ships. The

Admiral's barge and the Chief of Staff's gig—heretofore in the ship's divots—were put into service for these operations. Both boats were WWII relics and belied their ordinary makeup with wood veneer and fancy rope designs. Figure 11-8(a) shows these two boats and my two crews (three men per craft) who manned and maintained them. The Admiral's barge is on the left. It's the fancy one with the wood veneer and more black paint. The two boats were the same models, just decorated differently.

Figure 11-8(b) shows your writer standing in the gig. We were located in the Danang Bay, near Red Beach II. The engine of the boat had undergone extensive repairs, and before putting it back on line, I asked the Chief of Staff for permission to take "his boat" out for a test run. He granted permission. I then asked if he would grant permission for my boat crews to take a short swim while we were away from the ship. In addition to doing a major engine job, all six men had been involved in general quarters watches. I thought they could use a break away from the heat of the ship. (Of course, I had no ulterior motive.) The Captain brought up the Vietcong frogman incident. I assured him we would be on alert and that we could spot bubbles from any tanks. We carried carbines and pistols with us; we would be just fine and the men (three of whom he knew personally) could use a break. Permission granted.

One of my men snapped the shot in Figure 11-8(b) while I was standing lifeguard for the men in the water. This photo could be misleading. Our routine patrols did allow casual dress. For these operations, all personnel wore standard Navy uniforms. However, because we were not on a regular patrol, and our Chief of Staff had given us permission to take a swim, we donned the appropriate gear.

No Vietcong frogmen bothered us. Other sailors and Marines in the vicinity left us to our own. After days of heat on a floating skillet, disguised as a warship, I enjoyed this swim more than any other I had ever taken. It reminded me once again of my attraction to water and swimming. We returned to the ship refreshed and in better spirits. The bos'un of the Captain's gig personally thanked the Captain for his gesture. It's amazing how a small bit of kindness can foster so much goodwill.

Figure 11-8. Senior officers' boats.

The War Escalates

The prophets about the Danang Marine landings proved to be correct. The war escalated. The dam was broken and troops poured in.

At that time, I thought the introduction of American troops was a good idea. It would have been a sound decision if not for the corruption and incompetency of the South Vietnamese leaders, and of equal importance, the contrary obstinacy of the North Vietnamese. They would accept no compromise. Later, they drove Soviets, Chinese, and Americans to distraction with their intransigence. A lesson learned is that one cannot negotiate with ideologues. In the end, the North Vietnamese triumphed, but at what cost to them and to us?

I had been reading news dispatches about American citizens becoming concerned about the course of the war. Some letters from the States informed me my friends and relatives were beginning to have doubts about our involvement. Protests were forming. For now, they were modest. In a few years, they would rock the country.

USO: Americana comes to Vietnam

After the Danang operations, and the conclusion of several other landings and raids up and down Vietnam's shores, I attended a USO show. Several movie stars and Playboy Bunnies had been flown from the States to an aircraft carrier, which was anchored off the coast of South Vietnam around Phan Thiet, (see the lower part of Figure 11-4). The festivities took place on the flight deck and were attended by hundreds of military personnel.

I liked festivities. I still do. I liked Playboy Bunnies. I still do. But the setup seemed out-of-place. Within sight of us were the beaches and jungles of sites where Charlie (the Vietcong) was patrolling and waiting patiently to kill us. As I listened to the music and watched the Bunny tails, I wondered if Charlie could take-in any of these merriments? I suspected he could hear the music as it was piped into huge speakers located on the deck.

The show was a welcome diversion. As well, mental and physical breaks such as USO shows and saloons in safe sanctuaries are keys to encouraging warriors to return to combat. They help re-stoke our engines of aggression and give new strength to vent our hostility toward an enemy. They give warriors a much needed mental break.

I do not deny the debilitating effects prolonged combat can have on a warrior. Nonetheless, Charlie had no USO shows or safe haven bistros to which he could escape for a much-needed furlough. While we USO patrons on the carrier were putting Coppertone on our bodies, our enemy was pulling leeches off his. While we were reveling in fun, Charlie was planning his next asymmetrical attack.

Both sides in this war experienced adversity. For the American warrior, it was part time and lasted just over a year before he was given a break to visit home. For America's enemy, it was full time and lasted five or six years before he was granted leave to see his family.

If what Napoleon said was true, "Adversity is the midwife of genius,"[11] then our half-baked, commuting to war mentality was doing little more than breeding an enemy of guerilla warfare geniuses: combat outliers.

Hue

Shortly after the Danang landings, we deployed a few troops in Hue, an historic city fifty miles north of Danang. We also made other beach landings and conducted hit-and-run raids along other coastal areas or nearby islands. Again, Figure 11-4 provides a view of the locations of major amphibious operations. I have highlighted Danang with a circle to help orient you to the first major operation in relation to the others that followed. (And Hue is shown north of Danang.) I did not partipate in all the actions listed on the map, as they took place after I returned to the States. For the remainder of this chapter, I'll explain some of the operations that took place during my time in WestPac and offer my views about their impact on the war.

By the way of the Perfume river, Hue is located about 12 miles inland from the South China Sea. In the early spring of 1965, several boats from our task force were dispatched to the city to examine the characteristics of the river and to gain a better understanding of the port facilities which might be used by our forces. I was in charge of one of the boats.

The trip took a meandering route south to the city. The river was narrow, with the banks a couple hundred feet on each side of us. We were in unexplored territory. The North Vietnamese and Vietcong had not yet contested this part of South Vietnam, but our intelligence department briefed us about Vietcong troops deploying to the area during the past month. Understandably, as the city was a key position between North and South Vietnam. In addition, Hue was a cultural center for Vietnam in general and Buddhists specifically.

During most of my time in and around Vietnam, I received extra money for serving in a combat zone. With a few exceptions, I questioned Uncle Sam's generosity. Other than my duties of going ashore as a Logistics Officer or my courier runs, I was safe aboard the ships. The trips in the boats were a different matter, but in hindsight we crew members were safe. As well, we were lucky. At this time, the enemy had pulled back from confronting the U.S.

forces. Shortly, the Vietcong and Vietminh would begin their bold attacks on our troops.

For the Hue operation, we did not know what to expect. Unlike being on a ship at sea or anchored in a bay, we were vulnerable to enemy fire from the banks of the river. I took the photo in Figure 11-9 as we made our way downstream to Hue. Our charts indicated we had just passed by the village of Thon An on our starboard side. The picture in Figure 11-9 shows our view from the port side of the boat.

Figure 11-9. Curious villagers.

I can't speak for the other men in the boat, but I was nervous about our being such easy targets. We were lightly armed and at this point in the war, we had no flack jackets—just helmets. I carried a .45; my boat crew had M-1s; the two Marines on the boat carried M-14s. We did not have much firepower, but it turns out we did not need it. We encountered only curious civilians. I am sure they were taken aback by our small armada, but other than the stares, they displayed no feelings toward us; no hand waves, no "Hello, Joes." But then, no one-finger salutes either.

The small contingent stayed at Hue for a few hours performing our work. We were told by intelligence to "get your asses back to the ship" before sunset. Needing no prompting, we got an early start, made our way through the sand bars at the end of the river, and came into the South China Sea. No less for the wear but certainly a bit relieved.

In contrast to my cocoon, many of the marines and soldiers who served on shore came under enemy fire. Not many of America's warriors actually encountered the enemy personally. (When they did, the fighting was often brutal.) But many were subjected to mortar fire and booby traps. As mentioned, I was lucky to have been in Vietnam before the Vietcong and Vietminh began attacking U.S. personnel with frequency.

This brief visit to Hue was the only one I made to this part of Vietnam. The next year, in the spring of 1966, the new leader of South Vietnam, Nguyen Cao Ky, sent forces into the city to quell citizen and Bhuddist priest uprisings that were underway against his government. Parts of the beautiful old city were damaged as America's ally divided into camps to fight each other. The Communists did nothing to interfere with this self-defeating madness. Why bother trying to inflict damage on an enemy who was inflicting damage on himself?

Much later, in 1968, the Americans decimated Hue with their bombs during the Communists' Tet Offensive. The bombing resulted in many casualties to noncombatants. In addition, Uncle Ho and his minions helped Uncle Sam and his B52s "clean up" the city:[12]

> During the months and years that followed the (North vs. South Vietnamese) battle, dozens of mass graves were discovered in and around Huế containing 2,800 to 6,000 civilians and prisoners of war. Victims were found bound, tortured, and sometimes apparently buried alive. A number of U.S. and South Vietnamese authorities as well a number of journalists who investigated the events took the discoveries, along with other evidence, as proof that a large-scale atrocity had been carried out in and around Huế during its four-week occupation. The killings (by the North Vietnamese) were perceived as part of a large-scale purge of a whole social stratum, including anyone friendly to American forces in the region.

You Have the Watch, We Have the Time

Returning to my time in Vietnam, the years of mid-1963 through early-1966 witnessed the continued incompetence and corruption of assorted South Vietnamese regimes and the passing of the war baton to American troops. Increasingly, the American warriors did the fighting.

Yet the United States continued to dig itself into a hole. With a few exceptions among America's leaders, the idea of defeating the Vietcong and the North Vietnamese with more troops and bombs held fast. It was an illusionary WWII strategy pasted onto a post-WWII reality. Bombing an industrialised country in Europe that relied on the force of massive amaments was one thing. Bombing an agrarian nation in Asia that relied on stealth was another.

The adage spoken by insurgents, "You have the watch, we have the time," had not yet sunk into the the minds of most Americans.

Chu Lai

In May of 1965 the amphibious task force executed another major landing. This time it was Chu Lai, an area 56 miles south of Danang (again, see Figure 11-4). Danang's airfield had become too busy to handle air traffic. Thus, we landed a large contingent of Seebees with supporting Marine protection. The Seebees' job was to construct an airfield as soon as possible because the congestion at Danang was becoming a critical problem.

The landing was unopposed by the enemy. We went ashore onto an uninhabited coastal area. Figure 11-10(a) shows a view, looking inland from the beach. It was desolate. I did not spot a single Vietnamese in the vicinity. Figure 11-10(b) shows the view looking back toward the beach. The LST had docked to a causeway and was off-loading construction equipment. The Marines had already pitched some tents along the beach.

As the operation proceeded and as the maneuvers settled in to a routine, I took a few minutes from my beach job for a walk inland. I was accompanied by one of my boat crews and two Marines. As seen in Figure 11-10(c), I saw little more than sand hills and scrub brush. Charlie had once again pulled back, waiting for a more opportune time.

For my readers who were deployed to Vietnam later in the war, I suspect you are beginning to wonder about some of our off-the-cuff, ad hoc approaches to various operations and maneuvers. As examples, the Chief of Staff allowing us to take a swim around Red Beach II; our lightly armed fleet that made its way up and down a river to Hue. And for this part of the story, the scenes in Figures 11-10(c) and 11-10(d).

Figure 11-10. (a) Looking inland, (b) Looking to the sea. (c) Checking around, (d). Getting ready.

We thought our landing would be unopposed, but we did not know for sure, or for how long. As a precautionary measure, the Marines set up outposts around the beach area. Initially, the goal was to get the guns ready as soon as possible. Afterwards, foxholes and sandbags were put in place to offer some protection to these outward posts. Figure 11-10(d) shows a Marine setting up his machine gun at one of these posts. For a while we were all safe. Before long, the Vietcong decided to disrupt our operations. Later in 1965, marines and South Vietnamese attacked the 1st Vietcong Regiment that was located in the hills you see in Figure 11-10(c). The Vietcong lost 407 men; the South Vietnamese lost 181; the marines lost 45.

Loose regimen? Off the cuff operations? I had no helmet; my gun was on the boat at the beach. In hindsight, we were hassle-free about some aspects of our work, but we did not embrace a death wish. We did not think we were in imminent danger, and we didn't sweat the small stuff; nor did our senior officers. We improvised, trusted each other and exercised common sense. We went to war with what we had and made the best of it. (Besides, to address my wife's retrospective concerns about my folly, my seaman and marines were armed.)

The work of the Seebees was amazing. Within a few days, they had in place a runway constucted of steel, intermeshed platings. Before we left, we watched small propeller driven planes take off and land. A few days later, jet fighters were using the facility

The Dagger Thrust Raids

Figure 11-4 also shows several locations of one of our major operations in 1965. It was named Dagger Thrust. The objective was to support another campaign, Market Time, in which U.S. and South Vietnam forces raided Vietcong bases, small unit locations, and supply sites. While the raids did not succeed in capturing or killing many of the enemy, our forces were successful in capturing tons of supplies. After one raid, the Commander of the Pacific Fleet (CINCPACFLT) send the participants the message, illustrated in Figure 11-11.

Another message from the Commander of the Seventh fleet said:

> I wish to extend my heartiest well done to all the officers and men who participated in the Dagger Thrust operations which were conducted at Lang Ke Ga and Phu Thu. You have taught the enemy that the Vietnam coast is open to our highly professional amphibious/Marine team and he will be continually looking over this shoulder in fear of your

thrusts. This daring and successful operation adds more pages to the glorious record of Seventh Fleet amphibious/Marine operations. Congratulations to all hands and best wishes for continued success. Rear Admiral J.W. Williams, Jr.

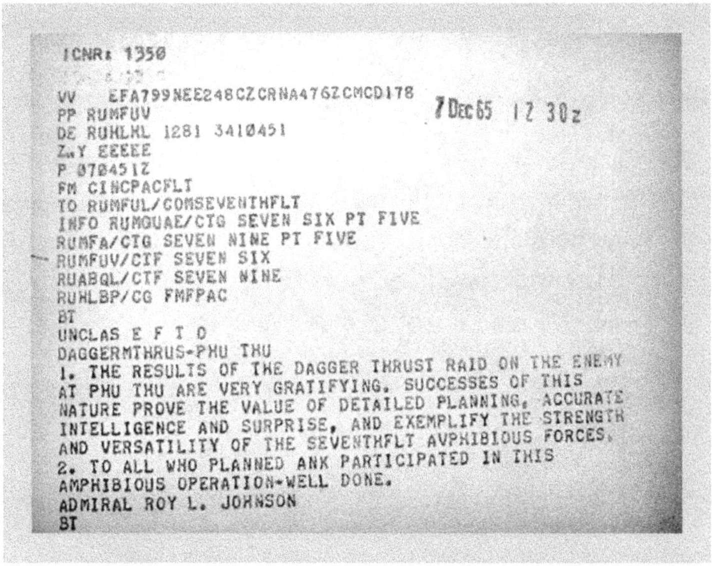
ICNR: 1350

VV EFA799NEE248CZCRNA476ZCMCD178 7Dec65 12 30z
PP RUMFUV
DE RUHLHL 1281 3410451
Z.Y EEEEE
P 070451Z
FM CINCPACFLT
TO RUMFUL/COMSEVENTHFLT
INFO RUMQUAE/CTG SEVEN SIX PT FIVE
RUMFA/CTG SEVEN NINE PT FIVE
RUMFUV/CTF SEVEN SIX
RUABQL/CTF SEVEN NINE
RUHLBP/CG FMFPAC
BT
UNCLAS E F T O
DAGGERMTHRUS-PHU THU
1. THE RESULTS OF THE DAGGER THRUST RAID ON THE ENEMY AT PHU THU ARE VERY GRATIFYING. SUCCESSES OF THIS NATURE PROVE THE VALUE OF DETAILED PLANNING, ACCURATE INTELLIGENCE AND SURPRISE, AND EXEMPLIFY THE STRENGTH AND VERSATILITY OF THE SEVENTHFLT AVPHIBIOUS FORCES.
2. TO ALL WHO PLANNED ANK PARTICIPATED IN THIS AMPHIBIOUS OPERATION-WELL DONE.
ADMIRAL ROY L. JOHNSON
BT

Figure 11-11. Kudos for an operation.

Admiral Willians was correct about the coast being open to our thrusts and dominance. However, the enemy chose not to engage us in naval and coastal battles. The war would be waged inland. With the huge support of China and the Soviet Union, the heavy influx of fighters from the north, the incompetence of the South Vietnamese leaders, and the fickleness of American citizens, it was only a matter of time before before our watch ran out of time.

---

[1] Later research has revealed that an acute injury and/or operation may cause small nerve fibers to spout, not only to transmit pain messages to the brain, but to produce their own pain. It is one known cause of chronic pain.

[2] Karnow, ibid., p. 426.

[3] Similar photos are on the Internet. Key-in "Gulf of Tonkin" and do some surfing. The photo in Figure 11-2 is from the Wikipedia page.

[4] The Wikipedia article is to be commended. It takes an objective (and in my view) accurate view on the matter. Key in "Gulf of Tonkin" in your browser and go to the Wikipedia link.

[5] Also from Wikipedia.

[6] "The Fifth War," *The New Yorker*, November 30, 2009, p. 23.

[7] And this possible violation of international law is subject to interpretation about the "rights" of belligerents to sail inside a nation's waters during wartime.

[8] To us aboard the ships, yes. But to those on land, watching a mini-armada sail into the bay, it was hardly furtive.

[9] Terrence Maitland and Stephen Weiss, *The Vietnam Experience: Raising the Stakes*, Boston Publishing Company, Boston MA, 1982, pp167 and 177.

[10] Karnow, ibid., pp 19-20.

[11] Jules Bertaut, *Napoleon in His Own Words*, 2, comp, 1916. Secondary source: Leonard Roy Frank, *Quotationary*, Random House, New York, 2001, p. 10.

[12] Wikipedia, key-in "Hue."

Chapter 12

Winding Down in the Western Pacific

I wish they were on our side.
A comment commonly uttered by American officers.[1]

Until the spring of 1966, when I returned to America, most of my later time in WestPac was spent in and around Vietnam. During a few short stays at the staff's home port in Subic Bay, I gave swimming lessons to the base children. I also conducted a class for adults. The students were all females. The Navy men were expected to know how to swim.

On our ships' visits to liberty ports, my job was meeting with the locals, principally to set up athletic games between them and us. After the games were over, the hosts usually feted us to cocktails and dinner. I was directed by our Chief of Staff to take care of the "pleasantries" at these banquets, as he was usually meeting with his naval counterparts on more serious matters. My previous lectures and talks with my swimming students in New Mexico and the Philippines helped put me at ease during these exchanges.

I had come to terms with myself that I was not going to be a UDT/SEALs team member. I had not lost my love of swimming. I knew I was a frogman, but not a Navy Frogman. In the back of my mind, I kept thinking about communications, about the world of cryptography. In addition to my readings on the Russian language and international law, I studied Navy manuals about radio communications theory. I wanted to know more about how those devices located in the Comm Center and on the upper deck of the ship did their work.

A Train Trip in Japan

One of my fondest memories of my stay in the Western Pacific was a courier run I made from Sasebo (a city on the southwest Japanese island of Kyusho) to Yokouska, a large U.S. Navy base 30 miles from Tokyo. The purpose of the trip was to deliver classified documents to several ships of Amphibious Group One that were docked at Yokouska. The trip entailed an overnight train journey.

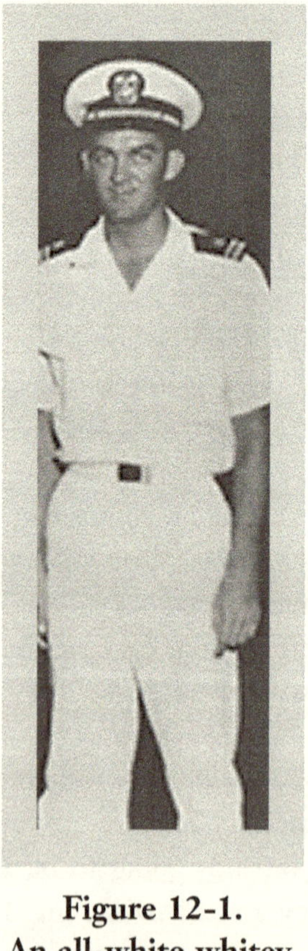

Figure 12-1.
An all-white whitey.

Because I was on official business, I wore a standard Navy uniform. It was late summer, so I was outfitted in service dress whites: white hat, white shirt, white trousers, white belt, white shoes, white socks, and white shorts. For this journey, white stood out, including my white skin, as seen in the photo in Figure 12-1.

This courier run presented special problems. I was transporting classified material over 600 miles on a commercial train through a foreign country. The staff's intelligence officers briefed me on three key points: One, I was to keep the material with me at all times (I ate and slept with it, my worst bed companion in memory). Two, I was not to indicate it was sensitive material. ("Hey fellow travelers, look what I've got!") Three, I could not carry a sidearm for protection. (The reason I should pay attention to point two.) I boarded the train and off I went.

As the train moved farther away from Sasebo and crossed over to the island of Kochi, I contented myself with reading and watching the country side. The train made occasional stops to let off and take on passengers. We nodded politely to each other. Proceeding farther across Kochi, I noticed more people looking at me. They weren't hostile looks; they weren't *you bombed Hiroshima* looks. They were looks of curiosity. I was also curious, but I couldn't speak Japanese to ask questions.

My problem was solved when a man, about thirty years of age, approached me. Ever so differentially, he bowed his head just a bit, and asked (in English obviously) if I minded if we talked. I was worried he might not understand my southwest drawl, but I said, of course!

He then asked if his daughter could also talk with me. She was sitting on the other side of the train car with her head down toward her lap. I wondered whose idea this talking exercise was, the father or the daughter? He said she was enrolled in English language lessons at school but had never spoken English with anyone but Japanese teachers. I said, of course!

For the remainder of the day, I spent my time speaking English with girls, boys, men, and women, some who spoke the English language almost as well as I. We had accents, but we had fun in dealing with them. I think all were delighted with the experience.

One of my newly found friends told me that in this part of Japan some of the passengers had never seen a white man—other than on TV. He laughed and added, nor a white man in a white American Navy uniform. I asked him if they might dislike me because of the WWII American bombings of Japan. He said no.

Their graciousness assured me he was correct. With each stop, one or more of the passengers would quickly jump off the train, run to a nearby stand, purchase a melon or rice cake, jump back on the train, and present me with their gift—just for my English lesson. Their expressions of gratitude and civility were disarming. I was also stocking up on an impressive cache of rice cakes and melons.

I had my evening meal in the dining car with three business men who were on their way to Tokyo. They introduced me to the rice drink sake, lots of it. Since that night, I have never touched the stuff.

I went back to my sleeping car, shut and locked the door, took off my whites, put my brief case to bed with me, and fell into a deep sleep. The only thing more pleasant than sleeping on a rocking train in the middle of the night with a brief case is sleeping on a rocking train in the middle of the night with something other than a brief case.

I awoke and spent the day helping my fellow passengers speak English. I continued to accumulate melons and rice cakes, until I hit upon a plan. I asked my traveling companions if they would teach me a few Japanese words and phrases. They said, of course! In my gratitude I was able to off-load some of my food.

Around midday, I had made my way to the Yokouska naval base, and had found the ship whose commander I was to pass the classified material. I presented myself to the Officer of the Deck, "Request permission to come aboard, sir."

"Granted. You've been among the Japanese."

"Yes. How did you know?"

"Ha. You come bearing gifts," as he pointed to my arm load of melons and cakes.

In the evening I went off-base for a drink. I came across what became my favorite saloon in WestPac—because of its name and the fact that it played country and western music. It was named The Shit Kicker Bar. I sat at the bar in my wrinkled service dress whites, drinking Japanese beer, and listening to Hank Williams. Hank was singing "Jambalaya," but I was thinking about rice cakes and what a fine 24 hours I had just experienced.

Admiral, I'd like you to meet my Pig!

During one of our times in Subic, the staff had a rare joint party attended by its officers and enlisted men. I say rare because it was the only one we had in my three years in WestPac. The event was held at the NCO club (non-commissioned officers). The

Navy would never lower itself to host lowly enlisted men at an officer's club.

The affair made for a weird mingling of cultures. Many of the enlisted men brought their Olongapo girlfriends, who were steeped in hustling and call girl protocol. We officers brought our American wives, who were steeped in decorum and calling card etiquette.

The casual cocktail banter was unlike anything I have ever heard. Heretofore, innocuous questions such as, "What do you do for a living?" had to be parsed more carefully. The answer of, "I fuck for a living," is just not the type of cocktail talk one comes across in the presence of Navy officers' wives.

But the talks and exchanges of stories between two dichotomous cultures—a third world country's lower class with the U.S. Navy's best—became easier and more natural as the night wore on. I was amazed.

My favorite man on the staff, Captain Sheppard (our Chief of Staff) got the party rocking by first going onto the dance floor to dance with his wife. For the next song, he asked the girlfriend of the bos'un of his gig to jitterbug. As I mentioned, Captain Sheppard was not young, and he was heavy around the waist. But there he was, just as game on the dance floor as he was doing jumping jacks on the helicopter deck. Boogying with the best of them! What a fine unpretentious man. I can still picture him on that dance floor, rocking and rolling with a lady of the night. We all joined in for what became a special event in our lives.

At one point in the festivities, I was talking with Admiral Lee and his wife. One of the men who manned the Admiral's barge approached us, accompanied by his Olongapo honey. The sailor was not quite sober but not yet drunk. After the hellos, he said:

"Admiral, I'd like you to meet my pig, Imelda."

The enlisted men (and my officer cabin mates) called their WestPac concubines "pigs." I have no idea about the origin of this lofty title. I first heard it used in the Comm Shack when two Radiomen were conversing about their off-duty lives. I asked one of the men about the moniker. I asked if it was meant as an insult.

"Naw, Mr. Black. I think as much of my pig as I do my wife."

"Your wife?"

"Yes, sir, in San Diego. Anyway, we use the word without thinking too much about it."

"I see."

Admiral Lee batted not an eye, nor did his wife. I batted both of mine, but I kept them sufficiently open to observe his response:

"It's a pleasure to meet you, Imelda. And I'd like you to meet my pig, Mrs. Lee."

Mrs. Lee was equally cool. She shook Imelda's hand and began to talk with her. Mrs. Lee did not ask what Imelda did for a living.

I have told this story to many of my friends. After (finally) accepting its veracity, we sometimes exchanged views about the Admiral's options: Walk away? Make a scene? No, Admiral Lee had become an admiral for many reasons. On display that night was a keen awareness of the event and its participants and the need to "go with the flow." Nonetheless, the élan by which he and his wife made their responses continues to provide me with a model: Keep your wits during unusual encounters. Stay aware of the moment and your time in that moment.

Commuting to War

As mentioned, in 1965, I came to the conclusion that America was not going to win the war in Vietnam. I had not based this belief on the principal reason for the failure: the loss of America's citizenry support, but on my observation that the Vietcong were fighting for their very existence, while we were fighting for Cold War turf—their turf.

As mentioned in the last chapter, America had adapted the European imperialistic, colonial practice of "commuting to war". We did not live among the populace. We were not part of their culture. We knew almost nothing about them. We were not in a position to influence them. We lived in our sanctuaries of ships and base camps and ventured into the countryside during "working hours" to conduct a war; a war Charlie was conducting twenty-four hours a day, every day of the week, every week of the month, every month of the year. As dedicated as each U.S. sailor, soldier, and Marine may have been to his part-time work, we were no match for the obsessive, fervent commitment of the Vietcong and Vietminh to their causes.[2]

I came across this quote and accompanying photo (Figure 12-2) on the Internet.[3] The writer describes a bar at a U.S. Swift boat base (Qui Nhon) that was located off the coast of South Vietnam:

> The highlight of our visit had to be the absolutely palatial, and extremely well stocked, off duty clubs of the base...at least by Chu Lai and Cam Rahn Bay standards. They even had "genuine leather" cups for the favorite past time in all navy bars...!Liar's Dice!...

Figure 12-2. A commuter's lounge for a war.

Charlie the Outlier. Just across the bay from this Swift boat sanctuary—and other American after-hours watering holes springing up in Vietnam—the Vietcong and Vietminh were hidden away in the jungle. They sat on the ground, eating their rice rations, fighting off bugs and disease, while putting together detailed three dimensional mud replicas of America's modern day castle keeps. We ventured forth from our castle keeps to engage the enemy, returning in the evening to a safe haven of showers and chow. Meanwhile, Charlie labored away in his dismal digs.

With meticulous planning, and with what can only be characterized as super human mental strength, our enemy was putting in the time and effort into actions that would eventually lead to our withdrawal from their country. It is fair to say that the Vietcong and Vietminh could have been a case study for Malcom Gladwell's outliers.

A Chinese proverb says, "One can conquer a country on horseback, but one cannot rule a country on horseback." In this war, we stayed on our horse, while the enemy never had one to begin with. He was on the ground. And the ground is where the outcome of this war was decided. Not the sea. Not the air. The ground.

Bombing and the Ho Chi Minh Trail

Not the air? One of America's horses was the airplane. As the war escalated, we used bombing to damage the North Vietnamese economy, kill its soldiers, interdict the flow of supplies and personnel into South Vietnam, and deflate the morale of the enemy. We succeeded in these objectives, but not enough to have made it worthwhile. In many of the enemy's minds the objective of deflating morale with bombing had the opposite effect. It steeled the enemy's resolve.

As one example of the magnitude of the assaults, during Operation Rolling Thunder, conducted from March 1965 until November 1968, around 800 tons of bombs were dropped onto targets every day. The American forces staged 7,000 air raids against roads, 5,000 against vehicles, and more than 1,000 against railway systems.[4]

This force is almost beyond comprehension. Yet with its resultant mayhem and damage, it did not significantly affect the enemy's ability to make war. Why? Because North Vietnam was principally an agrarian economy. How do you bomb a rice paddy?

Even more telling, the enemy forces in South Vietnam "...needed no more than a total of fifteen tons of supplies a day from the north to sustain their effort in the south."[5] The USSR and China were providing 6,000 tons daily to North Vietnam.

America's airborne horses were doing little more than swatting flies. In spite of this bombardment, the infiltration rate from the north to the south "...soared from thirty-five thousand in 1965 to one hundred and fifty thousand by late 1967."[6]

Only Resolve and Resilience?

We cannot ignore the resolve and resilience of the Vietcong and the Vietminh. I have made reference to these qualities several times. I've spent considerable time trying to learn more about the Vietnamese people and how a backward, third-world country took the fight to the point of 1975: the withdrawal of American forces. I've spoken of their resolve, resilience, and other factors. I will not repeat them here but will add some other thoughts.

The American troops were not alone in coping with their spirit and morale. The Vietcong and Vietminh troops suffered as well. The air attacks were terrifying. Some of the insurgents did not see their families for five or more years. Rarely did letters reach them. I think it is fair to say if North Vietnam had been a democracy, Ho Chi Minh would have been voted out of office. But it wasn't, so he wasn't. The North Vietnamese citizens could not vote. They had no choice but to follow the dictatorship. Without question, they were much more committed to the war than their American counterparts, but their options were few. Still, thousands of Vietcong surrendered or simply walked away to return to their homes.[7]

Another factor cannot be ignored. During the Nixon/Kissinger years, the North Vietnamese leaders were offered to take the path of pulling out of South Vietnam to allow the people to use elections to decide what would happen. The Americans eventually offered concessions about the Vietcong in South Vietnam: They would be allowed to become part of this process.

The leaders in Hanoi were not going to repeat the mistake of 1954. As told earlier, North Vietnam was persuaded to stop fighting the French in order for nationwide elections to take place. The elections never happened. Even North Vietnam's allies, China and the USSR, went along with this later violation of the spirit of the Geneva meetings. "Not again," said the Vietnamese and remained intransigent, fixed to their efficacious dogmas.[8]

Yet another factor is that in the end, North Vietnam brilliantly exploited China and the USSR's fixation on the Cold War against the "imperialists," all to the North Vietnamese nationalist advantages. For many years, they succeeded in playing the two countries off against each other. Reading this part of Vietnamese history reminds me of a John Dryden quote, "Beware the fury of a patient man."[9]

Did America Abandon its Ally?

As the war in Vietnam was winding-down, your writer was vicariously tracking its exit from the world's stage while I was in the sanctuary of Washington, DC. Many past and present media pundits contend we left South Vietnam to wither on an unhealthy vine. Further, that we abandoned an ally.

I agree the vine was unhealthy. Its illness stemmed from France's imperialistic lassitude, leading to a corrupt Vietnamese leadership. It was coupled with America's fear of France becoming ensnared in Vietnam, instead of Cold War Europe—so we lent help. The vine could not repair itself. It could not become healthy. It had become ensnarled in a weird form of international welfare. It had become so dependent on America's succor it could not produce its own roots.

I disagree that we abandoned an ally. But this is only a recent understanding on my part. Until I did some research, I had in my mind the haunting image of Vietnamese citizens being pushed away from helicopters that might have taken them to salvation in Los Angeles.

By 1972, the Saigon leadership had a huge advantage in military firepower over the Vietcong and Vietminh. The ratio of men/women under arms was five to one in favor of South Vietnam! During this time, South Vietnam had the fourth largest air force in the world.[10] America made many mistakes that caused it to lose the war. But given the South Vietnamese government, no amount of artificial respiration could have saved the victim—because the respiration was indeed artificial.

Why Are You Here?

During this time in the Western Pacific, our ship twice visited Bangkok, Thailand. This country was a SEATO ally and participated in joint amphibious operations with SEATO navies. Consequently, some of our stay in this area was for business. But the trips were also for pleasure. We looked forward to visiting exotic Bangkok. The city was famous for its jade, silk, food, fantastical palaces, and night life.

Figure 12-3. Bangkok scenes.
(a). River scene. (b). Canal view.
(c). Typical waterway. (d) A new meaning to "deep six".

Thai silk and silken ladies aside, the city suffered from repressive, almost repulsive congestion and smog—far worse than the LA stereotype. This aspect of so called exotic Bangkok took me aback. So much that I was never inclined to pay a call there again. But for those times:

To reach the city, about 20-water miles inland, our ship meandered its way up the Chao Phara River. The trip was a visual treat. Through larger sections of the river, we passed by somewhat distant buildings, such as the pagoda shown in Figure 12-3(a). As the river narrowed, it was fed by hundreds of waterways and canals. Many Thai citizens made their homes along these waters, as seen in Figure 12-3(b). During the stay in Bangkok, one of my favorite recreations was renting a small motorboat (with a guide) and exploring these arteries. Like Bangkok's streets, they were congested, as illustrated in Figure 12-3(c). The variety of businesses found on the canals was as diverse as any place one might find on Main Street,

USA. I snapped the photo in Figure 12-3(d) of a funeral parlor. I assumed the Bangkok funeral directors moved the dead inland for burial, as I saw no floating coffins in the canals.

The most spectacular sights in Bangkok were its ancient castles and palaces, which I leave to *National Geographic* to explain. The most interesting encounter I had during my visits to the city was with two young Thai men. They had come to our ship as part of an open house. This reception was a public relations program established by our staff to promote good will with *anyone* who came across the gangplank: Man, woman, child, Communist, Socialist, Bolshevik, itinerant insurgent, misguided student, someone looking for a cup of coffee. We took them in. No security gates, no bag searches, no frisks. It was a different era.

Our visitors were handed-off to officers or senior petty officers, who escorted our guests around the ship talking about Uncle Sam's naval arsenal. We conducted these open houses in most foreign ports. They were well attended and well received. Cookies and lemonade; tours on a naval warship bridge, grasping the triggers of anti-aircraft guns; sitting on a chain of the ship's gigantic anchor; walking a five story superstructure of a craft that was bigger than most buildings in Bangkok. What could be more enticing? It was Disneyland without entrance fees and free refreshments to boot.

During one of the tours, while escorting the two young Thais, I was explaining the ship's 40 mm deck guns, when one of the men asked, "Why are you here?"

I was not certain what he was asking. I answered the question by saying we wanted to visit Bangkok. Not good enough, "No, why is an American warship here?"

The young man was eager for confrontation. Perhaps he was showing off to his friend, who never said a word. I replied, "We were invited by your country."

"No, why is an American warship in this part of the world?"

"America and Thailand have a mutual defense treaty. It entails our military presence in the Gulf of Thailand."

"We don't need your presence. We can protect ourselves. You're here to...."

"...buy a lot of your products." There was no sense in entering into a rational discussion with a provocateur.

He was having none of my banter and seemed agitated by my put offs. But what could I do? If I had been armed, I suppose I could have shot him and used one of those coffins at the canal funeral parlor to take care of the matter. But this was a public relations occasion, so I was not holstered.

He responded, "An American warship is not a tourist ship. You're here to..."

"Have fun. But it's obvious you're here to argue. If you wish to talk politics, meet me for a drink and we can argue all night. Name a time and place. For now, I ask you to show me the same courtesy as a guest of your country as I'm showing you as a guest of the American Navy. You invited us to your city; and we invited you to our ship. Fair enough?"

He was not happy and said he wished to leave. I again suggested we meet later, "We can argue better with a beer in our hand!" He grinned (somewhat) but finally agreed to a get together. Later that day, we met, drank beer, and argued. Not surprisingly, I learned he was a student and wannabe Communist. He was well versed in the short comings of capitalism and imperialism, but oblivious to the banality of Communism, especially in how it was practiced. I grew to like the man. He was earnest and honest in his beliefs, traits we admire. But his education was limited, as were his horizons.

I would call this confrontation a draw. I had others like it in other ports. I would call all of them draws. Once made up, an opinion is almost immune to change.

Taken as a whole, America's colonialism and imperialistic practices have paled in comparison to the Europeans of previous centuries. And the Europeans were pikers compared to the pillages from earlier Muslims, Mongolians, and many others. Down through the ages, if it was not America doing the marauding, it was England; if not England, Spain; then Turkey; then China, and so on. The problem with the Thai student was not necessarily his views, it was his short memory.

Packing Up and Moving On

Thanks to Admiral Lee, I was granted the billet I wanted. By extending my time in the Navy, Uncle Sam would send me to Washington, DC for a two-year stint. My duties would be ashore, with limited night duty. It was a perfect setup to attend law school where I could pursue my interest in international relations and law. I had not lost my love for swimming or my admittedly naïve interest in telecommunications. For now, my focus was finding something to do with my professional life.

Leaving WestPac was not a chore. I was ready for the United States of America. Enough months at sea, enough jungle mildew, enough war rot, enough foreigners and their one-finger salutes. I was ready for pasteurized milk and unpasteurized Coors, not necessarily in that order.

Figure 12-4. Room with a view.

The transport to America was through Japan. I stopped-over for a few days and stayed at a hotel with a view of Mt. Fuji, a few miles away and seen in Figure 12-4 (from the perspective of my Minox camera). It was wind-down time.

During one evening, while I was sitting in the dining room at this Japanese inn, the waiter played Beethoven's Ninth Symphony on a record player. I sat near the windows, gazing at Mt. Fuji across the horizon, dining on raw fish, drinking rice beer, and listening to a piece of music I had only remotely known. It was a fine place for listening to the Ninth.

And America, here I come!

---

[1] Karnow, *Vietnam*, p. 474.

[2] This statement is made as a generalization. I think it is true, but many of our soldiers endured the same hardships and experienced the same terror as the Vietcong. They also displayed as much tenacity and spirit as the enemy. This point is a delicate one. In expressing my opinions about our failure in Vietnam, they have nothing to do with the spirit of America's fighting men. Check out our history. You will not find any war that speaks to America's warriors with anything but respect for their fighting abilities and courage. For the present wars in Iraq and Afghanistan, the valor and tenacity of America's military has been, once again, extraordinary.

[3] http://www.pcf45.com/qui_nhon/quinhon.html

[4] Karnow, p. 468.

[5] Karnow, p. 469.

[6] Karnow, p. 469.

[7] Karnow, p. 618.

[8] One wonders why the West would invite a group of die-hard Communists to participate in elections and other democratic machinations, especially after the deceit of 1954. They were probably laughing in their rice beer at this naiveté.

[9] John Dryden, *Absalom and Achitophel*, 1.1005, 1681. Secondary source: Leonard Roy Frank, *Quotationary*, Random House, New York, 2001, p. 585.

[10] Karnow, pp. 671 and 657.

[illegible] listening to the South [illegible]

And America: here I come!

[illegible]

Section IV

Aftermath

Chapter 13

Confluences and Convergences

A sum can be worth more than its parts,
depending on how the parts are added.
—anon

I left the United States May, 1963. I returned February, 1966. The military plane transporting me from my departure point in Tokyo, Japan, landed in San Francisco, California. After spending a few days with friends, I flew to Los Angeles to pick up my car, which had been shipped from overseas by freighter.

The country I left was at peace. The country to which I returned was at war. Physically, America was at war with North Vietnam. Psychologically, America was at war with itself.

For my immediate horizon, I was at war with myself as to which beverage I would first consume when I sat down in America: Borden's milk or Coors beer. While overseas, the choices of milk were limited, from the powdered variety on ships, to that of Hong Kong's rich semi-cream. For three years, America's bland pasteurizations never touched my palate. It is hard to believe, but I missed the stuff.

About Coors beer, now-a-days, I order it with caution at the local bars in my current residence. Up here in Northern Idaho, *it's Bud big buddy!* But in the 1960s, Coors was the beer of choice in my part of the country, even for bikers.

To clear up any mystery about the order of my imbibing: Coors beer was second. Borden's milk was third. America's succor was first.

Perhaps my most enduring lesson from the time spent overseas was not to take America for granted. It was not America's horn of plenty that gained my attention. It was America's way of life—especially its devotion to the rule of law—that had paved the way for its wealth. I came to understand that many of the world's citizens lived in cultures of chaos, fear, poverty, and despair. They had almost no leverage on life. Many lived in a day-to-day ditch of lawless insecurity.

I knew my country had fissures in its makeup. It had faults. But I also learned that there was nothing more conducive to being a partisan for America than to sample the alternatives. In reflection, I continue to hold this view, but with more reservations.[1]

Main Themes

I have fretted about when and how to end *A Swimmer's Odyssey*, how to approach the final chapters. I have been tempted to write several more chapters about the post Vietnam days to the present time. So much has happened that I want to share with you. Of course, I am doing the writing, so I would remain the hero.

But it is time to wrap things up with two final chapters. In so doing, I return to the main themes of this book: Success rarely comes from chance. It comes from putting in the time. And not just time itself, but motivated, focused time. For sure, chance plays a role, but the chanceful opportunities that might come along are wasted if we expect to be given a ride on the back of good fortune. As recounted several times, any success I had in my life was not because of natural ability. It came from doggedness and (granted) a dose of luck.

Coming Home to a One-finger Salute

In spite of my elation about being home, my first week in the States did not go well. I was confronted and then assaulted by anti-war activists, by U.S. citizens who disliked people who wore military uniforms. This attack may make sense to you, especially if you are against war in general and the Vietnam War specifically. It astounded me in 1966, and it continues to astound me to this day. It is one thing to question America's choices of where or when the country fights. It is another to attack those who are in uniform doing the fighting.

Why? Because those who put on uniforms become pawns in the chessboard of war's strife. We must answer to and believe in the wisdom of the gentry occupying the back row of the chessboard who design our costumes and put us into battle. As pawns on the front line, we must trust those who sit behind us, who are usually out of harm's way. We can only hope they know the right moves.

Figure 13-1. A Navy uniform.

Flying on military transport, I was dressed in Navy service dress blues. Figure 13-1 shows my uniform, taken as our ship was entering Hong Kong two years earlier. I had just been promoted to Lieutenant, Junior Grade and the Vietnam War was into the future.

Thus, I had not yet earned any chest gear in this picture (often, decorations for just being there).

I was met at the airport by my college fraternity brother and his wife. They were introduced in Chapter 8. Jim and Tina were tonics to my spirits, as was the tonic of America, not to mention gin and tonics. Jim, a product of the Navy, who was born in Shanghai, China, told me he wanted to reintroduce me into America—that I was likely, as he diplomatically put it, "too slant-eyed." Therefore, an immediate stop was in order at his favorite bar near the LA airport and Manhattan Beach.

I had read the receptions the Vietnam War veterans encountered on their return from this war were unlike any war we have known in this country. Even in unsuccessful campaigns, I had not read of the civilian populace mistreating veterans or showing animosity toward the men and women who were in uniform at the time. On the night of my arrival in Los Angeles, I encountered several people who were openly hostile to me. Only then, did I realize how deeply divided our nation had become over the Vietnam War.

I was surprised by the pervasiveness and passion of the anti-war climate—and it was just getting started. A sad aspect of this dissent was not the protest against the war. Regardless of my beliefs about Vietnam, I supported and respected anyone who took a principled stand against this or any war. As I mentioned, my problem was the hate shown toward people in uniform. After having served almost three years in Asia, much of it in and around Vietnam, I came to resent the animosity shown toward me during those first days in the U.S. My indignation and ire were on display that evening at Jim's favorite pub.

Peanuts for Peace

The place was awash with happy, drinking civilians. I had not enjoyed an American bar for a long time and was glad for a change of venue. It was a fine feeling—finally home, sitting in an American pub with two of my best friends. The three of us settled onto stools at the bar and began to catch up on old times. I told them about my reassignment to the Defense Intelligence Agency in Washington,

DC. We were happy to be with each other again, and it looked like a pleasant evening was in store for us.

Shortly, I noticed peanuts flying past me or hitting my back. Their origin was from a table behind us, just a few feet away from our stools. Jim and Tina also noticed the peanut barrage, but they ignored it. I asked, "Did you notice someone is tossing peanuts at us?"

Tina responded, "Just ignore them. They're throwing peanuts because of your uniform."

As mentioned, I had read about protesters in the *Stars and Stripes* and in letters from home—so I knew about them. Still, their emergence into my life took me aback. I had not given a thought about wearing my uniform into a bar in America. It had become part of my body, a part of my identity. I could not comprehend that my wearing a U.S. Navy uniform would provoke insults within the borders of my own country. I had encountered insults while overseas—in Thailand and the Philippines. But those insults were a different matter.

As you likely know by now, I like issues resolved. I don't like them hanging in the air. I like to get matters clarified and move on in life. I would not let their insult go unanswered. I walked to their table and asked, "Why are you throwing peanuts at me?"

One of the peanut throwers responded, "You're not welcome here."

"Why?"

"You're a coward."

What would you have done? You've just had peanuts tossed at you because you are wearing a U.S. Navy uniform. You've just been called a coward. I was nearly beside myself, but I held it in, "My friends tell me you don't like my uniform. What does my uniform have to do with my being a coward?"

The response from one of the men spoke volumes for what I came to learn about the radical anti-war protesters, "You're cowards because you hide behind airplanes and tanks, and kill unarmed civilians."

"So, your solution is to throw peanuts at a stranger in a bar? Someone you don't know? Someone whose opinions about the war you don't know?"

In hindsight, I know I was looking for a fight. Glancing at his beer, then up to me, the spokesman responded. "Just get out of here."

A bartender had come out from the bar and was walking toward the table.

I asked the peanut thrower, "What's your name?"

He responded, "It's immaterial."

"Mr. Immaterial, for all you know I could be a Chaplin. Unfortunately for you, I am not," as I picked up a handful of peanuts from their table. Opening my hand to them, "Here are more peanuts. Take another turn at throwing them at me." I pointed to the spokesman, "One at a time. You first."

I was close to coming to blows with these men, but I tried to keep my wits about me, determined not to let these baiters better me. I suppose my college degree in psychology finally did me some good. But I was close to being out of control. I was hoping for a fight with four-to-one odds against me. (I have never claimed to have good judgment.) None of the four protesters moved a muscle.

Jim had come from the bar. He and the bartender were standing next to me. Jim said, "Let's go, U.D. It's not worth it."

I tossed the peanuts onto their table and walked away. Tina was at the exit door of the bar. We left without any more incidents. I was shaking with anger. Not anger at myself, but anger at their insults.

After getting into the car, we headed for my friends' apartment, Tina started laughing and sang, "Sticks and stones may break my bones, but peanuts will never hurt me!" She helped us put the episode into the background. Jim, the son of a Navy Captain said, "As they say in the Navy, well done! But I'm glad we're out of there."

I have thought about those few minutes in that bar many times. I continue to have second thoughts about my reaction. Fist fighting was part of my childhood culture in New Mexico. Brawls at rodeo dances were as common as the music. I had my share of fights, but I never took a first swing. (Consequently, I usually did not take the last one either.) To this day, I sometimes wish I had punched the guy who called me a coward. But what would that have accomplished? A great deal of satisfaction on my part...and likely an arrest for assault.

It is far removed now, water under the bridge. But for the next nine years, America's military personnel were often treated this way. I guess I was lucky to have been transferred to Washington, DC where people in uniform outnumbered people in civilian clothes, and those in civilian clothes often worked at the Department of Defense.

Nearing my friends' home, we passed another bar named Jack's on the Beach. We talked of stopping at this place, but Jim said, "We're tired. Take our car to Jack's. We promise. There will be happy times awaiting you in the lounge."

I learned later that Jack's was a popular hangout for singles. Fine with me—I was ready for a taste of euphoria, be it a drink or female company. Jim continued, "Maybe you should change clothes. Jack's is a pretty classy place, but you never know, you might run into more anti-war freaks."

"Nope. I'm staying as I am."

"OK, have fun." With this farewell, my friends went to their apartment, and I escorted my misery and myself to a local beach bar. There, I found a friendly crowd. One lovely woman said to me, "Welcome home, sailor!" The evening had a happy ending.[2]

Years Later. That night was long ago: 1966. I stayed in the Navy for a while, and I will tell you a few more stories of those times. For now, we fast forward to 2011. I am now an old man, sitting on an airplane that has just landed at Los Angeles International. The steward comes on the PA, "Folks, we ask you to remain in your seats to allow our war heroes to depart first."

We did as told. Before long, several uniformed men and women walked down the aisle to the exit. As they left, they were applauded and cheered by their fellow passengers, including this writer.

The Defense Intelligence Agency

My assignment to the Defense Intelligence Agency (DIA) placed me in a department dealing with the analysis and dissemination of intelligence reports. This information originated at our embassies and other overseas posts. Because of my clearance, I was given the auxiliary job of a "librarian" for the National Intelligence Estimates (NIEs). This repository was used to store and disseminate NIEs to all units within DOD that did not receive them as part of a CIA distribution list. The documents were stored in a large vault. My boss (an Air Force Lt. Colonel), a senior civil servant, and I were the only people with day to day access to the vault.

Putting in the Time Pays-off Again. What an opportunity. I was in this privileged job because of a few minutes of success with a Maneuvering Board to enable a rendezvous with a cargo ship, and an Admiral's associated approval. That event was the reason for this fortunate position. That and...yes, I think you know and hope you appreciate...just grinding it out.

Artificial Intelligence

I had access to some of the country's most important intelligence estimates. Assessments of Stalin, East Germany, Castro, Vietnam, and hundreds of other subjects were available for me to read at any time. My boss was a happy go lucky, soon to be retired fly boy. He joked that I was not playing with a full deck of cards. As he put it, why would anyone ever want to read the NIE shit? His hero was Johnny Carson. I had only a vague idea of who Mr. Carson was.

My international law and foreign policy studies would be backed up with an impressive library. Granted, I would not be allowed to divulge these secrets, say, in a term paper, but the material placed me in a unique position relative to other students, or for that matter, my professors.

I spent many lunch hours inside the vault. After reading more NIEs than I would care to admit, I slowly came to the realization that the vast amount of intelligence contained in the papers—collected, analyzed, written, guarded, and disseminated at a cost of staggering proportions—was not all that insightful. Or all that secret. As one example, the NIE on Cho En-lai (a high-ranking official in Communist China) offered thoughts that I had read in various newspapers and trade journals. Cho En-lai's biography was no more insightful than the passages from the well-known book by Edgar Snow, *Red Star Over China* (without Snow's sycophantic prose).

One of the departments I headed was responsible for the analysis and classification of photos received from foreign agents and attachés. I noticed my staff examined what seemed to be hundreds of pictures of the same Soviet airplane, one classified as the "Bear" surveillance and targeting craft (the Tu-95RT). I had seen this plane several times as USSR aircraft occasionally flew over our task force in the Western Pacific.[3] One day, I asked the lead analyst (Jim) how many pictures of this airplane had been processed and stored by the DIA. His answer was, "Thousands."

I replied, "If you've seen one, you've seen them all. Why does the DIA not issue a directive to instruct the field to stop sending photos of this plane? The practice seems wasteful."

Jim pulled out a photo of the airplane. He pointed to a small glass-like dome on the fuselage of the body, "A couple years ago, the CIA noticed the shape of this dome had changed from previous pictures. The analysts concluded the Russians may have modified the dome to accommodate upgraded gear." (The dome was thought to be part of the plane's navigation or photo system.)

"I see. Did the dome's change reveal the nature of the equipment upgrade?"

"No. In fact, the change may not have indicated a change to anything but the dome itself. Maybe it was done to reduce wind drag. Who knows?"

Week after week, the department collected, categorized, and stored photos of the Soviet Bear and its variations. This episode is just one example of many other intelligence collection efforts. America's intelligence community was (and is) drowning in data—much of it worthless—with the hope of somehow coming across a rare piece of valuable information.

From my stint at DIA, I learned the major challenge to (and problem with) the field of intelligence is not the collection of data. It is the collection of too much and/or worthless data. So much is collected that it often becomes impossible to correlate/associate seemingly disparate facts into something meaningful, that of information. But what is too much? What is worthless? And how can so much data be correlated to reveal useful information? The answers to these questions may only be known after the fact, after a Pearl Harbor, after a *USS Cole*, after a 9/11.

The IBM System/360

It was at the DIA where I saw my first computer, initially, an uninspiring encounter that soon changed my life. The reports in my department were categorized and indexed by subject, and the results were fed into an IBM 360 computer. The resulting information was sent to hundreds of government intelligence units, such as specialized units in the CIA, the NSA, military branches, embassies, and selected White House staff members.

Because of my job title, I was the department contact with IBM account representatives. They were curious about my experience in Vietnam. I was curious about their huge (room size) machine. They told me about their world. I told them about mine. We became friends and shared many stories across the street from this computer's location at the Arlington Hall Station Officers' Club.

I was not so much impressed with what the computer did as to how quickly it did it, and especially how this seemingly rigid piece of hardware could be "programmed" (with software) to *alter* what it did. It reminded me of a very intelligent crypto device, except it operated with only two numbers: 0 and 1. I was mystified and intrigued. I put aside the cram course for the Law School Aptitude Test, picked up manuals on the IBM 360 and entered into a world from which I have only recently returned.

Because it was the software aspect of computers that gained my attention, Tom, one the IBM reps, suggested I take a course in programming. Thus advised, I enrolled in a software programming class at a local college. The subject was the software package called Autocoder. It was used to program the IBM 1401 (a forerunner to the 360).

I was in my element. I aced the course and I was hooked! Goodbye law school. Hello computers. And hello to one of most fascinating, rewarding, and mentally stimulating experiences of my professional life.

I extended my tour in the Navy on one condition: I would be assigned to a position of software programmer, with no other duties. The Navy was trying to keep me in its fold. As a Line Officer, my request was quite unusual. The practice was to assign only enlisted men to software programming jobs. (In hindsight, this convention was fantastically shortsighted.) But trying to snare me, the Navy granted my request, and my final two years in the Navy were spent as a programmer.

What Happened to Lawyering?

A reasonable question to ask is how could I have abandoned the field of law so easily? I was taken by the idea of computers and software, a different intellectual world than legal mandates. But more, as I learned about the profession of law, I came to question aspects of it. In more than a few instances, a slick attorney could win-over a naive jury, hoodwink a bumbling judge, or kowtow unknowing clients. Sometimes, the lawyer's façade meant more than the law itself. I found this aspect of so called justice to be too analog, not sufficiently binary; too gray, not sufficiently black or white; too subject to subjectivity.

I also began to become concerned about my country's evolution toward a litigious society, where common sense and judgment were subsumed by rigid rules and laws—those not allowing a citizen to make choices. For certain, I had a contrary streak about this idea in my DNA (as recounted earlier), but my early disenchantments have proven true.[4]

Not so for computers. They existed in a world of binary 1s and 0s, of Boolean true and false gates. One could bullshit a jury or a naïve client. One could bamboozle an ignorant home-buyer with a perfectly legal but ethically reprehensible variable interest rate contract. One could not bullshit an IBM 360. I liked the elegance of this form of merit. You had it, or you did not.[5]

Outliers' Success: Opportunity and Effort

Forsaking law school, I enrolled in the Computer Systems graduate program at American University. During this time, one of my new friends in the Washington, DC area (John) worked for the Computer Learning Center, a trade school offering courses in programming and computer operations. A Navy Lieutenant's salary did not go very far in the Nation's Capital and the Center had an opening for a night-time instructor in the FORTAN programming language. I could use the money.

John knew I had written programs using FORTRAN in my daytime Navy job. He suggested I come to the Center one evening to talk with the curriculum director (an Air Force Captain, who was moonlighting). Once again, I got lucky.

Captain Jim Opperman, "I see you're in a programming job for the Navy. It's unusual for an officer to be in programming."

"That was my stipulation for extending my commission."

"Your resume shows former UDT?"

"No. Ex. I was injured."

"You've done teaching and ran a Red Cross program?

"Yes. It was swimming, but I feel at ease as an instructor."

"Vietnam vet. I hope it will be my next tour."

"Captain, be careful what you wish for. It might come true."

"Ha. I've got other candidates for this job, all civilians." After a few minutes of exchanging military stories and jokes, Jim said, "If you want it, the job is yours." The network had kicked in.

I was given an introductory FORTRAN class, which ran two nights a week. I scheduled my graduate studies to fold into the other two nights. I spent weekends studying and preparing for teaching and taking classes.

I put on my grinder's hat and put in the time. It was an intense period of motivated effort. At the risk of repeating myself, I was no more talented than the guy next door. I was more focused and motivated.

My graduate work was not difficult. It required little preparation, as I was actively working in the field of my major studies. But I was fearful I might not be up to par to teach a programming class. I was not going to impart knowledge about the sidestroke or the tired swimmer's carry. I was responsible for explaining and demonstrating an abstract subject. I worried I might not know the answer to a question about the subtleties of the software or how it interfaced with the computer and the computer's other software.

Fear is a great motivator. I took a week off from my programming job to prepare for my first programming class. I read (the classic) McCracken's FORTRAN book over and over. I read IBM's FORTRAN programming guides over and over.

I over prepared. I discovered my students had no clue about the very basics of software programming. But why should they? It was their first programming class. They had recently finished a hurry-up course on, "What is a Computer Anyway?"

Lectures Lead to More Lectures

I believe my experience in teaching the American Crawl in a swimming pool on the plains of New Mexico laid the groundwork for my becoming an accomplished lecturer. Because of the natural setting of swimming, I adapted an informal, less stilted manner toward instruction and lecturing. Admittedly, a college professor in my undergraduate days helped persuade me of the need for a natural approach. During one 45-minute lecture, my classmate and I noted his use of "eh" over two hundred times. His students did not listen to his words. We counted his ehs.

In one of my graduate classes at American University, each student was required to make a short presentation on a topic dealing with computer-based telecommunications. The task was not all that easy as this field in 1972 was just emerging and little literature existed from which to plagiarize material for a presentation. The Internet was in the future. Modems were esoteric instruments. Only one book on the subject was available to any reader but a theorist: James Martin's *Telecommunications and the Computer*. All others dealt with details of interest to a limited population of design engineers.

My Navy communications background was immensely helpful for this short talk. No one else in the class—or for that matter the faculty—possessed the kind of experience I had. Their knowledge came from books. Mine came from practice. As a bonus, I was working in software engineering. Plus, I had experience in lecturing and public speaking. I was stoked and ready.

These confluences came about because of an injury. As my son would say, "Go figure." But I would say it was a matter of having opportunities and working to leverage them.

The week after my presentation, the chairman of the department Dr. Kennevan—who was the professor for this class—gave me a call. He congratulated me on my presentation, asked more about my background, and then talked about the department's need to add a communications course to the program. The field of computer and data communications was just beginning to make a presence in the industrialized world. The increased speeds associated with the newer modems (more accurately, acoustic couplers) were spurring a revolution in how data could be exchanged between computers. Dr. Kennevan wanted AU to be a leader in this field. But the availability of people holding graduate degrees who also had practical experience in both communications and computers were hard to come by.

That summer I finished my graduate studies and was awarded an MS in Computer Systems. The next week, Dr. Kennevan again called and asked if I would consider coming aboard as an adjunct professor in his department to teach night classes in the graduate curriculum. I would be asked to submit a plan for a course that would be based on James Martin's book. I was hardly out of the graduate world, and I was being solicited to teach a class within it.

Now, it seems far-fetched, but in those days, few people had my credentials—as modest as they were. In retrospect, I was a fortuitous interloper into American University's program, and this college's offer proved to be a god-send for me.

As for the preparation of my lectures for the graduate course in telecommunications? Again, fear was a great motivator. I over prepared. My students were bright and keenly motivated, but knew very little about the field. Relative to today's world, neither did I. I am certain my "war stories" about the radio shacks in the ships sailing in the South China Sea and my Vietnam experiences helped me make it through this first experience at "high level" lecturing.

The experiences of my past had begun to converge. The parts, once seemingly unrelated, were coming together to create something I had never intended to pursue (or even knew about). In a nutshell, I was ahead of the power curve in the field of computer based communications. How I handled this initial opportunity would affect the remainder of my life.

Moving to Private Industry

As intended, I left the Navy in 1971, and worked for the Federal Reserve for ten years. My job was in software development. With Navy communications experience on my resume, I was placed on several task forces dealing with the Federal Reserve communications network. During this time, I moonlighted at the American University, the U.S. Department of Agriculture Graduate School, and the Computer Learning Center. I conducted classes for these schools in various subjects, principally programming, computer hardware architecture, and data communications.

The variety of subjects kept me busy staying abreast of the rapidly changing technologies, but these varied experiences would play a major role in my career. My approach to these endeavors was no different from what I had been doing since my childhood: grind away, put in the time, and things will work themselves out. This part of my life brings to mind the idea of baseball player Vernon Law, "Experience is a hard teacher because she gives the test first, and the lesson afterward."[6]

In the fall of 1979, I received a brochure in the mail advertising a public seminar on data communications. I said to myself, "I can teach this course. I wonder if the company needs a lecturer?" Nothing ventured, nothing gained, I called the phone number on the brochure and was placed in contact with its course director. He informed me he was looking for a lecturer in a class titled, "Applications of Distributed Processing in the Minicomputer Network." Whew. It was a valid and complex subject, one beyond the binary bits-and-bytes of data communications.

I was involved in aspects of the topic at the Federal Reserve. With some cramming, I thought I could handle the course. The course director (Ken Sherman) informed me I would be the sole lecturer for a three-day seminar in Hartford, Connecticut, for the dates of January 7-9, 1980. It would not be a once a week three-hour session, as in college class. I would be on the podium for three successive days, seven hours a day. No lab work. All lecture. I wondered how I would be able to speak coherently on a subject for such a long time? Even more, I wondered how a person would be able to absorb it? I soon discovered the answers to my questions, and this work became my profession for the next twenty-two years.

The class went well. Ken asked me to do more work. In a couple years, he and I formed a company with three other men. I left the Federal Reserve and entered private industry. There, I rode the Internet wave for two decades.

Writing Books

Because of the paucity of literature on the subject of data communications, I wrote (my first) book on the subject shortly after leaving the Fed. In those days, it was very difficult to get any kind of book published. The process for a publisher was (and still is) enormously expensive and risky. How I was accepted by the Prentice Hall Company came about because of, once again, the convergence of past experiences. In this case the melding of my software engineering background and (of all things) my undergraduate degree in psychology.

A significant challenge to being a competent software programmer is writing code that not only works, but can be understood by another programmer. To be understood, it must be "readable." That is, a programmer must be able to figure out what the code is doing. Furthermore, if another programmer is tasked with making changes to existing code (a frequent occurrence), the code must be constructed in such a way that the changes can be made with some assurance that they will not create unforeseen problems (bugs) in the overall system. It is a very complex operation.

With my background in psychology, I was aware of a school of thought called Gestalt psychology. In simple terms, this theory states that images are, "...perceived as a pattern or a *whole* rather than merely as a sum of distinct component *parts*...The parts often derive their nature and purpose from the whole and cannot be understood apart from it."[7]

Without delving into the arcane details of writing and reading software code, I concluded the use of Gestalt psychology concepts could help a programmer create code that was more understandable and less subject to error than conventional code. I was so convinced of this idea that I wrote a short paper (while at the Fed) on the subject and sent it to several computer trade journals. During this process, I kept in mind my college mentor Mark Acuff's advice about writing. (Recounted in Chapter 6.)

The trade journal *INFOSYSTEMS* published the article in 1978. It was titled, "Psychology Applied to Software Design". It represented my first success at writing for the commercial world. Granted, I was not paid one red cent for the effort, but I did not care. It was an important step toward gaining a foothold in my profession.

The paper brought forth positive and negative reactions from the industry. Some people thought it an important contribution to the software engineering trade and added support to the emerging field called "structured programming." Others accused me of being a misguided theorist.

Using my experience from the distributed networks lectures, and my recently acquired job as the Federal Reserve Board's data base department chief, I penned another article, which I titled, "An Automatic Pilot for the Growing Distributed Network." I submitted it to the leading trade journal in the industry *Data Communications Magazine*, published by McGraw-Hill. I was pleased to learn it was accepted and surprised to see it was the cover story for the November, 1980 issue.

Because of these two successful articles, I had enough exposure for Prentice Hall to be confident enough to sign me to a book contact. If nothing else, my new publisher knew I could complete a writing project, an important trait for a writer to possess—but one not possessed by a surprisingly large number of so called writers.

The process began to cascade. The *Data Communications Magazine* editors passed my name to their parent company, McGraw-Hill. Shortly, one of their editors called and asked if I would like to write something for them. At that time, modem technology was changing; more people were going on line with dial-up modems. But no books (and few articles) were available on the subject. I suggested I write a guide to modems. McGraw-Hill accepted.

A few months later, after I had presented a public lecture on the emerging technology of packet switching, I received a call from the IEEE Computer Society. Would I be interested in writing a book on the topic? There were no books available that dealt with this subject, as well as the packet switching international standard (called X.25). I said yes.

Confluences and convergences, all coming together to take me through the soon to come Internet revolution. Eventually, I reached a point of confidence with Prentice Hall and McGraw-Hill that my editors only asked I submit a title for a book, and one paragraph explaining what it would be. The next week, I would find a contract for the book in the mail.

The many details involved in writing a book (including the frequent and trivial fights with editors on the selection of a proper pronoun or adverb) led me to swear I would never write another.[8] The one you are reading is my forty-first book, and will soon follow with my forty-first promise to myself to never write another. But it's in my blood. It's likely I will be penning something on a sheet of paper just before another sheet is pulled over my head.[9]

Effects of being Published

My books were not written for students. Even though some of them were used in trade schools and colleges, I did not like to spend time writing questions/answers and especially teachers' guides. My opinion about these guides: If a teacher did not know how to lecture from my books without my hints, the teacher should not be teaching that subject to begin with. My opinion on this matter remains unchanged.

The books were my spring board to what became the most satisfying part of my professional career: lecturing to members of private industry. Because of the books, I began to be solicited for presentations at trade shows and private seminars. My past experience with public speaking was serving me well. And because of my diverse experiences in computer networks, I would often stay at one company (or one city) to present five or six sets of lectures on different topics.

Afterwards, I would head back to my hotel room to continue my research. To stay abreast of the fields. To stay ahead of my students! Some of them (for example, engineers from Bell Labs, AT&T, Nortel, British Telecom, etc.) had patents on (say) one aspect of a technology that I might spend a few moments discussing. If I made a mistake on that single subject, perhaps making only a comment, I would have lost that listener and likely the audience, as word would get around during the breaks that the lecturer had given out incorrect information.

Once again, fear was a great motivator, and for this part of my career, I can safely say I did not over-prepare. My habits, established early in my childhood, were serving me well. My grinding had moved away from my first love, swimming, and to my second love, computer networks.

It had been a long and physically painful road since the accident on the vaulting horse and the sand dune injury to where I was now. As I sometimes say, "Playing with pain" is often an unavoidable part of life. I continued to experience pain from my ill-conceived vault. But that very mistake catapulted me (forgive the pun) into a world that also transported me. It transported me into the amazing worlds of computer networks, wired worlds, the Internet, and the global electronic village. The Internet changed my life.

---

[1] I have placed many essays and reports about this issue onto my Web site (UylessBlack.com) and its associated blog (blog.UylessBlack.com). I hope you take the time to sample them and send me your thoughts.

[2] Yes, but with one exception. I was punched in the face by a patron at Jack's on the Beach because I had on my uniform. As I said, the first week in America did not go well. (By the way, on this occasion, I punched back.)

[3] The planes flew quite near us, a few hundred feet overhead. Its crews and we would wave to each other. I still recall seeing the smile of a co-pilot as he looked at me while I was on the admiral's deck. I wondered what he was thinking. For myself, I was also thinking, *How weird is this*?

[4] In Chapter 4, I told the story of the water pump at John Easley's swimming pool being able to pull down an unwary swimmer. Thus, we lifeguards were especially vigilant during the Sundays when we drained the pool for cleaning. We lost no swimmers. Cut to the present. Federal regulators, due to deaths in *private* pools and spas because of drain pumps, require *public* pools (which have had zero fatalities) to close their pools until "user friendly drains" (my words) are installed. The announcement was made the week before Memorial Day. (From *The Wall Street Journal*, May 28-29, 2011, p. A3). It's the old saw, "Anything worth legislating, is worth over-legislating." That's the mantra of law-making in modern America. Just look at the Health Care and the Financial Reform legislation: Legal overkill to kill personal initiative and responsibility.

[5] These disparagements are made generally. I've a niece who, as a practicing attorney, continuously does good things for her clients. Nonetheless, I hold to my premise that America is often held hostage to a litigious culture. For the skeptics of my claim, take a look at *The Death of Common Sense*, by Philip K. Howard, New York: Warner Books, 1994.

[6] Vernon Law, "How to Become a Winner," *This Week*, August 14, 1960. Secondary source: Leonard Roy Frank, *Quotationary*, New York: Random House, 2001, p. 260.

[7] Microsoft Encarta. All rights reserved.

[8] Truth in disclosure: I've worked with about ninety different editors for my 41 books and assorted videos and design guides. With only a few exceptions, they have made my work better.

[9] For my nontechnical work, I had to learn another way to write. Technical writing relishes brevity; the sparse use of adjectives and adverbs, perhaps incomplete sentences. Kaky, my close friend and sister-in-law, gave me the (2x4 hit to my forehead) clue, "U, maybe you could be a bit more descriptive?" She placed me on the path to become a different (and I hope) better writer.

Chapter 14

Frogman Finales

Ah yes. Glory!
The old man sat on the front porch, regaling in his past.
He had become a legend in his own mind.

My swimming days in mud tanks on a prairie ranch in the plains of New Mexico are a distant memory. So too are the all too brief times in UDT. My water polo days are over. I have left this sport to younger and stronger swimmers. Given an opportunity, I take to the water with as much enthusiasm as I had in my youth. My muscle memory is still attuned to mimic that powerful and graceful swimmer, the frog. But time marches on, so do one's physical skills.

I swim in the local pool. I continue to marvel at the beauty of the silent serenity I experience as my body glides underwater. I take pleasure in the smoothing massage of this liquid as it flows around me while I breaststroke or free style from one end of the pool to the other. On occasion, I try my unpatented frog stroke crawl, if only for one lap. The difficult movements sap me of my wind and strength. Years ago, I could effortlessly sprint with this stroke for several laps. But what should I expect from old age? Old age kindles old bodies.

Nonetheless, while years and injuries have taken their toll I still combat the unassailable fact of my growing old. I keep grinding away. I swim. I use the treadmill. I play tennis with younger and more talented players—who often run me to dizzy exhaustion. The wise adage, "If you don't use it, you'll lose it," is especially important for gray frogs and gray panthers.

Outliers' Outliers

In this book, we have examined the idea of the achiever, the outlier. We've seen examples of how putting in the time with motivated effort leads to success more often than it does not. We highlighted Tiger Woods, my brothers, Julia Child, Bill Bowerman, the SEALs, and others; even America's former Vietnamese enemies. I conclude with two more examples:

Andre Agassi: One of the megastars for whom I have admiration is Andre Agassi, the professional tennis player. Even if you do not follow tennis, read his book *Open*. It says as much about how an outlier becomes an outlier as anything Malcolm Gladwell, David Brooks, and your writer have described.

I have watched Andre Agassi since he arrived on the TV scene. Even in his petulant days, I sensed he had an empathy that seemed at odds with his external persona. I thought some of his actions were obnoxious, but I did not discern in Agassi's makeup the surly bullying of a John McEnroe or the asinine personality of a Jimmy Connors. He seemed beyond the horizons of these limited men.

When Andre was a child, his father forced him into "motivated" efforts to play tennis. Agassi's motivation came from fear of his dad, from fear of failure in his father's eyes. Andre was subjected to hitting thousands of balls from his father-designed ball machine. A machine that hurled balls at the child faster than a club pro would hit them. At angles and trajectories that forced Andre to learn—to embed in his youthful muscle memory—how to hit the ball *early* and *squarely*. (Take it from me, it is much more difficult than it appears.)

I almost shutter when I read about Andre's early childhood, of the scary abuse he experienced from his semi-demented, abusive father. Yet, ironically, this grinding led to his becoming one of the greatest tennis players in history. What makes Agassi's story so remarkable is the fact that he hated tennis, he was frightened of his father's obsession with the game, but he kept at it.

Fear is a great motivator. As I have recounted in this book, on more than one occasion, it kept me motivated and focused. But Andre Agassi overcame such mental and emotional barriers that it staggers the imagination as to how he did it.

In our stories, one motivation for outliers has been positive role models: Tiger Woods and his father; Julia Child and her French mentors; your writer and his hero Tudy. Even more, the endeavors of Woods, Child, and Black were joyful and pleasant to undertake. Agassi did not have a positive role model. More astounding, his endeavors were not just unpleasant to partake, they were distasteful to him. Yet he overcame them to become one of the best in what he did.

Michael Oher. The last example in this book of an outlier is the professional football player, Michael Oher. Like Agassi, in spite of his negative surroundings, Oher became one of the best at what he did: playing the position of left tackle on the offensive line of an NFL team. However, unlike Agassi, Oher had a positive role model. The model was Michael Jordon, the professional basketball player.

Oher grew up in one of the most dangerous and poverty stricken ghettos in America: Hurt Village in Memphis, Tennessee. His mother was a drug addict, who was more often pregnant than not. His father had long abandoned the family. As a child, Oher was left to his own to care for his welfare, often to feed and clothe himself.

His life is described beautifully and poignantly in *The Blind Side*, a book written by Michael Lewis. Chapter 11 of this book will leave you wanting to cry in sorrow for the miserable life ghetto children must endure, and leave you shouting in anger at the ineptitude and callousness by which America (the richest country on earth) treats its helpless children who have been consigned to a hopeless netherworld.

Michael Oher got lucky by being mentored by an extraordinary family. But before this family came across the lad, Oher had spent thousands of hours on the basketball courts of Hurt Village trying to become another Michael Jordon. He played from morning until late at night.

When he was seven years old, he happened to be watching TV at a neighbor's home. There, he saw Chicago Bull's Jordon perform his magic against the Phoenix Suns. Oher left the house with the expectation that he was going to be the next Michael Jordon. For the next ten years, he devoted himself to achieving his goal. He is another example of the 10-Year Rule (Chapter 3).

Michael O never became a Michael J. But his grinding on the basketball court gained him quick starts, fast feet, and dexterity. Luckily, he grew into a huge and strong body, yet he moved his frame with the finesse of a point guard. The combination of his size, strength, and mobility earned him a starting position on the Baltimore Ravens' offensive line.

Outliers' Planes

Agassi and Oher carried through the rituals of motivated practice and repetition to achieve phenomenal success in their professions. Once again, for our story, they put in the time; they grinded away.

What do Julie Child, Tiger Woods, Andre Agassi, and Michael Oher have in common? I think you know the answer as well as I: There's no short cut to success.

These amazing people, and others like them, also possess something else that cannot be measured by scientists or explained by journalists. They possess capabilities that cannot be calibrated by machines or defined with words. I like to think we humans possess ephemeral qualities that cannot, nor will ever be measurable.

Serving up Final Self-Serving Tales

I have mentioned several times in this book that it has been written with your writer as the hero. To this self-serving end, this final section returns to the subject of my first love, swimming.

St. Thomas

To escape the pressures of business, my wife and I purchased a second home on St. Thomas Island. Located in the U.S. Virgin Islands, it became our retreat from winter's snow and a break from work. I would schedule my job activities to stay on the island for weeks at a time. Thus, I was able to live my dream of swimming each day for as long as I wished. Even more, I now had the luxury of living a few steps away from crystal clear sea water populated with exotic fish and beautiful coral. It was a long way from the cattle and mud tanks of my dad's ranch.

Our place was a two-floor apartment that overlooked water connecting to St. John Island. Figure 14-1 shows a view from our deck, with St. John on the horizon.

My favorite swim was to snorkel around the peninsula, whose far point is highlighted with the arrow in Figure 14-1. Figure 14-2 is a photo taken of your writer making a descent to check out some coral. For your reference, the spot of this dive was behind the palm tree, shown in Figure 14-1. As seen, I was not using fins. With the exception of a sidestroke, fins continue to inhibit my motions and a sidestroke is not suited for underwater swimming. The sand shoes were worn to protect my feet from unintended brushes with rock or coral.

The difference between swimming in safe or dangerous waters is often dependent on being away from the incoming waves and surf as they cascade onto land. It's often only a few feet. Some rough waters can be swum with relative ease. The experience may not be pleasant, but if the swells are not too high and not breaking, a good swimmer can stay afloat, perhaps even make headway, depending on the direction of the wind and the force of the waves. That said, the power of waves crashing against the shore or a shore's rocks is another matter. They are overpowering, relentless, and immune to the actions of the strongest swimmer.

During one of our stays at St. Thomas, a hurricane landed nearby. Lucky for us, it came ashore several miles north of our home. Still, the effects of the storm resulted in heavy seas and waves that washed over the rock shoal (seen at the tip of the arrow in Figure 14-1). But from the sanctity of our apartment, the water did not appear to be

Figure 14-1. View from the apartment.

Figure 14-2. Exploring the coral.

rough, just moderately deep crests and troughs, easy enough to swim through, especially given the safety of a nearby beach. I needed to stay away from the rocks. Thus, I entered the water from the protected beach and swam to the far right side of the shoal.

I turn to the present tense in describing this adventure: Off I go, with the intention of swimming around the tip of the small peninsula to its other side, where a fine restaurant awaits my soon to be stoked appetite for oysters and a glass of wine. I'll take a wide sweep around the shoal. No sense in fighting the incoming waves that are cascading onto the rocks.

The surf coming into the beach is high but easy to deal with. I'm making my way to the end of the peninsula, swimming about fifty feet away from the tip—an area I've not explored. I'm doing some dives to check out the local coral growths. Beautiful, lots of fish. I should swim out here more often.

Uh oh. There's a pull of a current I've never come across...But I'm in new waters...It's a big current. It's taking me to St. John! I've never been this far out before. Jesus, it's strong. OK, swim at an angle to the flow and head for the nearest land point, the tip of the peninsula. Forget about the waves on the shoal; just get to the shoal.

Son of a bitch. The current is stronger than my stroke. Take another angle. No, that won't work. You're just swimming out to sea. You've got to head for the tip. Use your frog stroke crawl. Swim! You're in trouble.

Good, making progress, but getting tired. Stay with it; grind it out. You're near the tip. Look out! The waves are going to toss you onto the rocks. Pull up, you're away from the current.

Keep calm. *Don't panic*, you know what to do. *Don't choke*, you know how to do it. Trust yourself. Stay focused. Muscle memory; think muscle memory; think repetition. Wait for a trough. There, go! But not underwater, use your crawl to the rocks. Kick! Pull your feet down and pull yourself through the surf. Watch for the rocks. Don't stumble.

There. You made it. Aren't you proud of yourself? Your frogman kick got you out of trouble. But your arrogance got you in trouble to begin with. When will you learn to exercise a bit of judgment and restraint? You're lucky the waves weren't higher.

Swimming with the Sea Turtle

After this encounter with Mother Nature's ongoing ways, and my ongoing stupidity, we took a trip to St. Croix. There, we chartered a boat with a guide to escort us through an aquatic reserve called Buck Island. The area is protected by the U.S. government. Fishing and skiing are not allowed. Another aqueous nirvana, I could not wait to swim in this water.

After entering the reserve, we tied up to a buoy (anchorages are not allowed at Buck Island because the anchors might damage coral). The guide assembled equipment we would use for a snorkeling swim through the reserve:

Guide, "Here is your gear," as he handed us fins and a snorkeling mask.

I offered, "Thanks, I don't swim with fins."

The guide looked at me as if I had intended to free fall out of an airplane without a parachute. "Sir, we going to be in the water, which is over our heads, for an hour. Everyone uses fins on this tour."

"Thanks, but I swim just fine without them."

"You really do need to put them on. I'm responsible…"

"You'll find me keeping up with you. I don't like using fins, they require a flutter kick. I prefer the breaststroke kick."

"You're a breast stroker?"

"For most of my life."

"OK, but I'm attaching a pair of extra fins on this buoy to take with us, just in case."

"You're wasting your time and energy."

"With respect, sir, I've never seen anyone out here without fins."

"There's always a first. Do you want me to sign a waiver?"

My wife broke the impasse, "Trust me, my husband does not need fins."

That did it. We left the boat and entered into a world so stunning I have dreams about it to this day. I also have dreams about one of the most remarkable creatures I have ever seen swim: a giant Leatherneck turtle. We came across the turtle after we had been in the water for a few minutes. The turtle seemed idly curious, maybe it was expecting food. The guide would not allow any feeding of wildlife, but not all visitors had park guides with them. I guessed some swimmers did bring food with them.

The turtle was not afraid of us, only wary. It kept ahead us a few feet, occasionally glancing back. The guide was taking us away from the path of the turtle. He had told us we had to stay on a marked underwater trail. If the Leatherneck did not have to swim the trail, neither did I. I branched off and followed the turtle.

Slowly swimming, languidly undulating through the water, the Leatherneck swam just fast enough to keep me at a distance. The creature was huge, its front flippers were well over six feet in length. Later, I learned most Leathernecks weigh over one ton.

The turtle was not beautiful in the sense of, say, a dolphin. And after all, how often have you come across anyone who talks about a beautiful turtle? It's akin to making a comment about a beautiful frog. Turtles, like frogs, don't fit into most humans' world of beautiful things. But they do for me. Someone once said, "Fair faces need no paint." I thought the face of that Leatherneck turtle, placid and peaceful, was as fair as anything I had come across.

Without ado, the turtle executed a few turtle strokes and disappeared behind a coral reef. I swam back to my companions. No less for the wear, but thankful for having spent a brief time with a beautiful swimmer.

My Final Water Polo Game

Taking a break from the grind of work, in the mid 1970s my girl friend and I were spending a week at a Club Med resort in Cancun, Mexico. In addition to serving prodigious amounts of food and drink, the Club Med staff made sure we guests burned off our calories with a full schedule of sports events. One set of physical activities were good natured contests between the resort staff and the guests. Bets were placed on who would prevail in basketball, tennis, soccer, swimming, sailing, and more difficult sports, such as horseshoes. The staff would not take our money if they won. But if we won, we would be rewarded with free booze (in the form of payment trinkets placed on stands of beads.)

The swimming contest was to be a water polo game. The Club Med guys made frequent comments during the first part of the week that they had a particularly fine team. They down-played their basketball team, as most of the members were Europeans. Sure enough, the guests' basketball team trounced the staff's team.

During the ramp-up to these end of the week games, staff and guests engaged in macho banter about who would win. We baited each other back and forth. During these jests, we were told the Cancun Club Med water polo team had never been defeated by a guest team. They bragged they had never been scored on, until later in the game when the Club Med jocks thought it wise to allow the men (the guests, who were paying their salaries) some satisfaction.

I liked the banter. The Club Med team exhibited well founded confidence. But their swagger spoke of infallibility—a risky attitude for anyone to hold. So, while I liked the joking, I also liked the challenge. I had not played the sport for twelve years. Obviously, I was well rested and ready for action.

But how was I to deal with the fact that I was likely the only good swimmer among my teammates? Some of them had never played water polo. They were in the contest for the fun of it. Some of my team mates showed up half drunk, a recurring situation in this on-going series—which also explained the lopsided win-loss record in favor of the Club Med team. I had no expectation of the guests beating the staff team. But what if our team could inflict a moral victory? Say, an early score?

The game was played near sunset. It was the major happening at the resort for this time of day, so a crowd had gathered to (first) drink, and (second) to watch a contest most of them had never seen. Thus, the events just cited made perfectly good sense: *I've no idea what I'm watching, but I don't care.*

The ball was tossed into the middle of the pool. Overly confident, the Club Med team started a desultory swim toward the ball. I sprinted toward it. I think to their surprise I reached the ball first. I think to their further surprise, I did not pass it back to a teammate. I took the ball underwater, a violation of a rule (but we were, after all, at Club Med). I pushed it down and swam to the bottom of the pool. Holding the ball in my two hands (another rule violation), I used my frog kick to take me toward the other end of the pool. As I was swimming, I saw the Club Med goalie's legs kicking in the water. No matter, I was behind his defense. He was dead meat. I pushed up from the bottom of the pool in front of the goal net and threw the ball into the back of the net: Guests 1. Club Med Team 0! A brief moment of glory.

It was all too brief. Our opponents took our score in ostensibly good stride, then commenced an aquatic slaughter. Afterwards, at the poolside bar, regaling me for my rule violations but complimentary about my score, the staff got our team very drunk with frequent gifts of Club Med beads.

A Last Visit

The mock water polo contest has likely been my final effort at competitive swimming. I've harbored notions of getting into water-shape and giving the seniors swimming circuit a go. But except for casual swims, I think it's time to hang up the Speedos.

One such swim, and the next-to-last I describe for this book, was taken during a ten-day trip through the British Virgin Islands. On a sail boat with friends, we stopped each day at a different island for swimming. I was not much help with the sailing, but the skipper—a fine friend and supportive cousin—kept me busy with hauling lines and checking anchorages.

My companions were surprised by my swimming alongside them without fins. Even now, the legacy of my amphibian friends stays with me. In my youth, they taught me skills I have kept into my old age.

At one anchorage, the boat crew swam to the one side of the island to try their skills of passing underwater through a tunnel. I decided to swim to another side and take in the scenery. During this short trip, I came across a grotto. The entrance is seen in the left photo of Figure 14-3.

The beauty of this locale cannot be appreciated with a black and white image. The sunlit water radiated a sparkling turquoise-blue color, offering lucid views twenty feet to the sea floor. The water's waves presented pristine undulations of translucent mirrors. They awaited my entry into their aqueous cocoon.

As I approached the grotto, I remembered the joys of swimming in my childhood pool on the plains of New Mexico. I had a waterproof camera with me. I switched to video and immersed into an underwater

Figure 14-3. A grotto of fantasy and escape.

dive, making my way to the grotto entrance. This plunge brought back images of my youth, some reflected in the first part of this book:

The dive marked my passage from a world of gentle surf and tropical heat into a sphere of cool translucent silence. The next few seconds—coasting a bit, gliding underneath the water's surface, flexing enough muscles to keep me moving—left me with a sensation of a near effortless soar though a chilled quiet Ether. The water's mass disavowed flying. It did not matter. My anticipation of swimming into the grotto was more exhilarating than flight.

For those brief moments, I once again realized why I had swum for most of my life, why I loved the water since my childhood. This brief escape into my underwater world was as fulfilling as anything I had experienced in many years.

As I entered the grotto, seen in the right photo in Figure 14-3, I slowed my momentum. I surfaced to find myself in a world far removed from anything I had ever seen. Except for the muted surf, my sphere was one of silence and solitude. I was inside an ancient rock cave, a ceiling of antediluvian stone, layered with a carpet of the finest water I have even seen. For a brief time, this place was there for me, and me alone.

The Last Visit

Not long ago, I decided to get away for a few days from the routines of daily shuffles and scuffles. From Portland, Oregon, I drove over to the Pacific Coast, and spent the next ten days traveling down Routes

1 and 101, commonly called the Pacific Coast highways. The final destination was where the highways ended, at San Diego, California.

Other than the trip itself, I had another reason for going south. I had placed on my bucket list the item of, "Pay a call on the beach along the Strand." The Silver Strand, as it is formally named, is where my frogman dreams came to an end.

I'm not a mental masochist. I don't dwell on what might have been. I leave angst to others. Then why visit the Strand? As you may know from reading this book, I like to reminisce, and I was curious to see what the beach (and the obstacle course on the beach) looked like.

I pulled up to the beach, got out of the car and took a walk. I was not surprised that the beach and sand hills (over which UDT 11 ran) had stayed intact, but parts of the obstacle course were different and the rope climbing towers were gone.

I suspected there was now an indoor obstacle course that was better designed than the old one, probably set up to inflict more pain and misery. I took the photo of one part of the Strand, which is shown in Figure 14-4. The ocean can be seen (barely) at the upper-left corner of the picture.

Figure 14-4. The Strand.

As I stood there, looking at the hills and obstacle course, my thoughts were few, mostly about water under the bridge. But also wondering about fantasizes that drive our youthful minds to dream about things that when we grow old, seem very far removed from reality. An old saying goes, "As wishes inspire dreams, so dreams may inspire wishes." Perhaps our old age and attendant frailties lead us to more modest wishes and less ambitious dreams.

The Last Swimming Student

It is unlikely I will take on the teaching of swimming again. I have made overtures at a local pool, but I suspect they think I'm over the wave. It does not matter. For now, my only student is named Milli, a natural-born swimmer.

Milli is a dog, and a tiny one. I first saw her when she weighed two pounds and exclaimed, "Why she's no *bigger* than a millisecond!" (Thus, her name.) My wife brought Milli home, declaring she was ours. I reluctantly acquiesced, only to learn later about the stalwart intelligence of this breed of dog…the French Poodle.

Milli is a small animal with the heart of a lion. She taught me to never judge the spunk and spirit of a dog by its size. She has become my friend. Truth is, I think more of Milli than I do about a lot of two-legged animals. That aside, at this stage in my life, Milli offers me solace, loyalty, and composure. It's been said by a perceptive person, "If you could only be as great as your dog thinks you are."

This idea surely rings true with Milli. She seems to think I am great…as I furnish her with groceries. But she expresses more to me than my merely being her source of food. I like to think that Milli (and dogs in general) take-on a loyalty to their masters. For this story, Milli has come to trust me as her swimming mentor.

Milli's first experience with swimming did not happen until she was three years old. She was quite surprised by the experience, but took to water as if she had been swimming all her life.

As mentioned, Milli is formally (and erroneously) known as a French Poodle. The effete sort of dog shown in "Breakfast at Tiffany's" movies. But history states that Poodles came from Germany—not France, where they were known as "water dogs." Here are some facts about this matter, which I quote from Wikipedia:

> Poodles are retrievers or gun dogs, and can still be seen in that role most of the time. The poodle is believed to have originated in Germany, where it is known as the Pudel. The English word "poodle" comes from the Low German *pudel* or *puddeln*, meaning to splash in the water. The breed was standardized in France, where it was commonly used as a water retriever.

A splash in the water. A water retriever. My kind of dog! I had originally thought I had custody of a fussy land-locked animal. The discovery that I was the owner of a gifted and gritty swimmer was a tonic to me, as I had developed an ignorant antipathy toward the so-called Poodle.

Now-a-days, when opportunity knocks, Milli and I take to the water. After all, she is a natural water dog, and I am a natural swimmer. When possible, I take her surreptitiously into the pools of hotels and condos. There, she swims while effusing surprisingly large amounts of debris from the hair on her small body.

For less contested waters, Milli and I have done a few swims in nearby lakes. There, I have placed her into the water, where she has executed a perfect dog paddle. It's a stroke I never taught to anyone…two or four legged.

Milli defies the 10-year rule of practicing to obtain perfection. Which is a fitting proposition, as Milli will likely be dead before she reaches (our) ten years of age.

Ten years of practice are irrelevant to Milli. She needs no paddle boards, no tutorials on floating, no demonstrations on arm and leg kicks. I put Milli in the water, and away she goes (Figure 14-5).

Figure 14-5. Final swims with my last student.

While swimming, Milli is oblivious to my hovering concerns. Upon reaching land, she shakes-off the water and proceeds to take a nap. She is a rarity in this book. She is a natural outlier...both in swimming and sleeping.

It's a Wrap

I once read a quote by Benjamin Disraeli. He said, "Youth is a blunder; manhood, a struggle; old age, a regret."[1] Most of my regrets are about the blunders of my youth. Perhaps my biggest one was that ill conceived jump into a vaulting horse. But then, had I not made that blunder, my story would have had a different ending. Several of my UDT training teammates were killed in Vietnam. I escaped a possible similar fate, most likely because of my injury on the Strand. It led me into the field of communications, which led me to my life's profession and one of my life's joys.

Irony or coincidence? Who knows? But I do know this: I'm compiling a list of things I want to do before I kick the bucket. My bucket list includes swimming alongside whales and in the company of dolphins. Am I being delusional? I don't think so. We wannabe outliers like to think old age is just beyond our time on earth; that action on our part is another way to push old age farther into the future.

Another old saying states, "We are what we do, and we do as we are." I've tried to convey in this book that what we do, and how dedicated we are to doing it determine what we become, to be what we are.

I've tried to persuade you there is no short cut to success.

I've put in the time. At this late part of my life, I'll go out on a limb and say that anyone who puts in the time eventually deserves the time to do what he wants. What I want to do is to continue to be able to experience the serenity that comes with swimming, to continue to feel the water flowing around me as I frog kick my way to nowhere, and yet everywhere. A feeling that brings calmness to my body and comfort to my soul.

---

[1] Benjamin Disraeli, *The New Generation*, 3.1, 1844. Secondary source: Leonard Roy Frank, *Quotationary*, Random House, New York, 2001, p.21.

EPILOGUE[1]

Sometimes an outlier becomes an outlier
because there is no other choice.

In 1995, as an ostensible birthday present to my wife, I surprised her with a cruise in the Western Pacific. I say ostensible, because it was as much a present to me as it was to Holly. I wanted to check off an item on my bucket list: Revisiting places I had known in my younger days.

I had lectured in Melbourne, Sydney, Singapore, Hong Kong, and Tokyo. I had served with the Navy in Bangkok, Saigon, and Danang. With the exception of the Australian cities and Tokyo, the Royal Caribbean cruise ship would pay a call on these WestPac locales.

I had another motive for taking this trip. I felt an urge to return to Vietnam. I thought revisiting and then leaving the country would provide a better closure than in the past. Yet I believe a person should stop looking in the rear view mirror of life. There is too much to see and experience by looking forward. The backward view consumes too much energy. This trip would do that for me.

When I mentioned this vacation cruise to my friends and relatives, some of them told me I needed the trip for a catharsis. I looked up the word in the dictionary to find out what I might be in need of. After consulting Webster, I concluded my friends had confused me with some veterans whose experience in Vietnam led them to a life of angst. I had not experienced any prolonged mental anguish during or after my assignments in Vietnam.

Nonetheless, I recognized I carried feelings of regret about Vietnam, as did many people who were associated with the war. I felt no guilt about my participation in the conflict. I was called to duty and I answered the call. Nor did I harbor resentment toward the war protestors (other than those who tossed peanuts at me many years ago)—just animosity toward draft dodgers, and people who made cruel remarks about the fighting forces. But not comments about the war itself. I believe the right to protest wars is vital to a democratic republic, and war protests certainly crystallize differing views.

The reason for my regret was the manner in which the war came to an end, the debilitating social effects the war had on our society, and the horrible social and economic consequences it had on North and South Vietnam.

I had another motive for making this journey. It was curiosity. I wanted to know how Vietnam was faring. I wanted to see the country for myself, not read about it in a magazine or a newspaper. I wanted see if the Vietnamese people I met thirty years ago were as tough and resourceful now as they were then. In spite of my distaste for the repressive Vietnamese government, I wanted to revisit these outlier warriors.

Port Visits

Before boarding the ship, we spent a few days in Singapore. I had been there on naval assignments. As a civilian, I had made trips there to talk to network professionals about Internet protocols. I knew the city better than the average tourist. I was eager to show it off to Holly. We did it up right: The Raffles Hotel for Singapore Slings, the Undersea World, the Mandai Orchard Gardens (nearby, I recommend you stay at a fine Sheraton Hotel).

We then boarded the ship for a calm and peaceful cruise to Bangkok. From there, we visited three Vietnamese ports, two of which were Saigon (now Ho Chi Minh City) and Danang.

After thirty years, I recognized very little in Ho Chi Minh City and Danang. We passed by Red Beach in Danang. I harbored a ridiculous hope of coming across the café that served me French onion soup on that historic day in 1965. Of course, it was nowhere around. If it were, my aging mind was nowhere around to remember it.

While our ship was anchored off Ho Chi Minh City, Holly and I decided to take a tour of the Cu Chi tunnels. We had thought of taking a trip into downtown "Saigon" to visit some old hang outs (if they existed), but with our limited time, we thought the tunnels would be a better choice. They are a famous part of the Vietnamese landscape and one of the extraordinary examples of the resourcefulness of the Vietnam soldiers and citizens.

Several people from our ship took the tunnel tour. The group was large enough to warrant a chartered bus. As we lined up to board the bus for the trip to the tunnels, I noticed many of the tour members were about the same age as I. About twenty U.S. Vietnam war veterans made the tour to the tunnels that day. With wives and other companions, our group numbered around thirty-five.

During our ride to the tunnels, one of our companions had some stories to tell us about the Cu Chi area. In the early 1970s, he was a member of a tank crew that regularly patrolled the land over the tunnel system. Later, he was astounded to learn his tank's daily patrols took him over tens of miles of tunnels and hundreds of Vietcong soldiers. Another man in our tour was a member of a B-52 crew. At the tunnel complex, he pointed out several large craters created by bombs dropped from a B-52. He offered that the craters we were viewing might have been dropped by his airplane. We offered he not bring up this possibility to the tour guides. Some were Cu Chi tunnel war veterans.

Our tour group effused a strange aura. For the entire trip, first to the tunnels, then through the tunnels, the visit to the tunnel museum, and the return to the ship, a collective sense of somber yet accepting *déjà vu* permeated our mannerisms, behavior, and conversations. This collective mood was pervasive, almost visible.

A brief word about the Cu Chi tunnels. Some of the tunnels were dug in the late 1940s during the French battles with the Vietnamese Communists and were expanded during the Vietnam Conflict. The Cu Chi system contains over 120 miles of tunnels, and during the war, supported a population of about 18,000 people. The tunnels connect an amazing labyrinth of underground caves, consisting of several levels of sleeping rooms, kitchens, hospitals, arms caches—everything needed for an underground fortress. Many traps had been installed containing punji sticks and deep holes. Loop back tunnels were prominent, offering escape routes for the caves' inhabitants. The tunnels were small; and I had to bend down as I walked through them.

After paying our admission for the tour, we were directed into a room on the first level of one of the tunnels. Previously a kitchen, it had been converted into a tourist briefing room. We filed into the small dug-out and sat down on benches. Several exhibits had been installed in front of us. The most prominent was a model of the tunnel, cut across to show a side view of the levels—like an ant colony exhibit. After we were seated, a woman (the moderator) came to the front of the room and began a lecture.

I mentioned earlier that our group radiated a peculiar mood. During the moderator's talk, the aura changed from resignation to resentment. I glanced at my companions—most were sitting with clenched teeth and strained faces. So was I. The lecture was an abrasive, insulting, and propagandistic diatribe against Americans.

But propaganda to whom? To the audience, the lecture was propaganda. To the moderator and the other Vietnamese in the room, the lecture was authoritative, truthful, and trustworthy; gospel, if you will...based on their experiences. Nonetheless, her diatribe was pointedly directed toward the American tourists sitting before her.

How one stands on an issue, how one views it, depends on where one sits. Corporate bosses, sitting behind their desks, have a different view of their business than the employees who sit in front of these desks. Investment bankers believe they are entitled to millions of dollars for creating financial instruments of absolutely no value to anyone but themselves, while average citizens are repelled by their behavior. Likewise, war adversaries perceive their causes in the light of their philosophies and self-interests. The Americans' views during the war were from the perspective of saving South Vietnam from the Communists and preventing Southeast Asia from falling to the Soviets and/or the Chinese. The Vietcong and the North Vietnamese had different views. Theirs were of liberating half of their country from the imperialist powers' imposition of a divided Vietnam, and expulsion of the colonial authorities.

The moderator emphasized other views on the war. She stated the Americans were criminals because of our aggression, the B-52 bombs, and the use of Agent Orange on non-combatants.[2] Of course, she failed to mention the Vietcong insurrection, the North Vietnamese invasion (AKA aggression), and their murder of hundreds of unarmed civilians (as in Hue, described in Chapter 11). Her diatribe was pure propaganda, but what made her harangue astounding was its being delivered to twenty men whom she flat-out claimed were war criminals.

I was surprised none of us walked out of the dugout and returned to the bus. But not one person moved. We sat through the lecture, showing remarkable restraint. But what were we to do? We were in Vietnam, surrounded by its citizens. We were in their tunnels, in their lecture, and in their show. No one forced us to come to the Cu Chi tunnels.

And what should we have expected the lecturer to say, other than what she said? As I suggested earlier, where one stands depends on where one sits: I had seen equally accusatory and vindictive propaganda about North Vietnamese war crimes on U.S. television.

Thankfully, the lecture did not last long. Shortly, we left the briefing room and started the tour through the tunnels. The tour was a fascinating trip. For the story I am telling you now, it is instructive to note that our encounters with Vietnamese citizens in the tunnels were pleasant and civil. We were treated with kindness and consideration.

Not so with the military personnel. The soldiers in the tunnels, some young, some old, were unfriendly and cold. Our tour guide told us several of the soldiers were participants in the war. What were we supposed to expect from these soldiers, glad handers? We practically destroyed their country, killing thousands of people along the way.

Yet there they were, guiding us through Cu Chi. Having defeated an enemy, they had been relegated to the role of tour guides for that very enemy. They were babysitting a former foe who was returning to review a place of his own demise. They were kowtowing to a past combatant who had become a tourist to his own trouncing.[3]

On our way out, we deposited tips in a bucket. *Thanks for kicking our asses.* The incongruity of the situation was not lost on me, or likely them.

In spite of my distaste for the country's leaders, what I carried away during this return to Vietnam was a renewed sense of the outlier spirit of the common people, a heightened awareness of the force of patience, of the power of doggedness and persistence, of the beauty and dignity of grinding away.

This latter phrase is perhaps a contradiction in words, maybe of ideas, but it rings true to me. After all, grinding away is the essence and spirit of the outlier.

---

[1] Parts of this Epilogue are taken from my essay, "Symbols," and available at Blog.UylessBlack.com.

[2] Irony? I am receiving veteran's compensation for exposure to Agent Orange.

[3] In no way did I hold (or do I hold) a scintilla of respect for the Vietnamese government that came to exist after America's pull-out. The current leaders are nothing more than brutal despots, repressive dictators, jailing or killing peaceful citizens who modestly ask for a multiparty state. I admire the outlier spirit of the Vietnamese. I detest what Vietnam, as a nation, has become.

Post Script

After completing the writing of this book, I attended a high school class reunion, one including Tudy's class as well as mine. I finally located my mentor. We talked about old times, about her teaching me swimming. She was surprised to hear me talk of how much influence she had on my life. But that's what happens with modest leaders. They don't assume they are all that important. But they are. She's not read this book. She gets the first copy.

Acknowledgments

Although I have taken Malcolm Gladwell to task about one of his claims regarding outliers (Chapter 3), I agree with his other thoughts about these rare people. I also thank Mr. Gladwell for his overall (and unintended) contributions to the theme of this book.

I suspect for most of my life I have harbored the notion of the outlier, of putting in the time. After all, that is what I did: grind away. Mr. Gladwell's book gave me the insight to place a handle around my subconscious ideas.

I also thank Mr. Gladwell for his other books. I have read them all.

David Brooks helped me along with his essay (also in Chapter 3), and assisted in placing substance around the idea of Descartes' dictum, "I think, therefore I am."

After reading a draft of *A Swimmer's Odyssey*, my brothers Ross and Tom called me. They were surprised about my childhood admiration of their youthful exploits. They were regretful about my childhood detachment from them because their teenage minds were not focused on the runt of our litter. Their pubescent disregard for me was the natural behavior of older brothers to a younger one. As said in this book, I love them dearly, even if they swim like bricks.

The ranch in this story was operated by my Dad and my stepmother Mary, who owned the ranch when Dad came aboard. In the eyes of a child, I viewed the ranch as Dad's, and my story is told from this perspective. I thank Mary for marrying Dad and providing a venue of several summers for a child to experience an unconventional world for swimming adventures.

My wife Holly helped give birth to this book. She read the manuscript several times. With each revision, she offered comments that improved the prose and the book's structure. She remains steadfast to and supportive of my many hours laboring over the keyboard.

Two former classmates have been supporters of this book, as well as much of my other work. They have encouraged me to keep writing; they like what I write. What more could a person who writes like better? For my high school classmate Sylvia Gann Mahoney, thank you. For my college classmate Joanna Gilbert, thank you.

My friend and tennis hitting partner, Bill Ellefloot, read the first printing of this book. Politely and graciously, he pointed out several errors, those that were not picked up by software checks or editors. I thank Bill for his uncanny ability to detect the subtlest of grammatical inconsistencies. I'd like to hire him as my wordsmith editor, but he is busy running his own company.

Last but not least, for the UDT and SEALs frogmen, thank you.

Readers' Comments

I take a different approach in quoting comments from readers. Most books place these comments on the back of the cover. These brief remarks offer little substance, such as the readers' experiences in relation to the book's topics. By having readers' comments in this section in the book, I can share with you more detailed thoughts and ideas from those who have read this book. I hope you enjoy and relate to them.

These comments (which I received in emails) do not have names attached. In some instances, I do not know who the sender is, as my material was later sent to unknown readers who responded only with an email address, or from a less-identifiable blog response.

If I do have names, for privacy purposes, I have deleted the name of the sender. If you would like to know the sender, if I have his/her identification (and I have domain names for most of these e-mails), I will contact the sender and ask for his/her permission. In this way, you can also verify the accuracy (pro and con) of this correspondence.

Unless a person included something personal, I have altered no words or grammar. I have used "——" in place of profanity or other words that a reader might find offensive. On a few occasions I must substitute a person's name with a noun or pronoun, in which case, I place brackets around my change. Any notes I add are also surrounded by brackets.

I have made the text the same font size and type, and changed minor formats. In some cases, an e-mail was several pages. I took the liberty of cutting down the length of some of the emails, but I altered none of the words.

I look forward to your thoughts about my book and these readers' thoughts as well.

++++

First of all thank you for your service to our country. Trust me I was never one of those protestors, nor have I ever been upset with anyone who has worn the uniform of this Country.

You discussed quirks of fate and one of these most likely kept me out of Southeast Asia and most likely changed my life. I had undergone knee surgery in 1963 and a bone chip had been removed. I took my Army physical in 1966 and the Army doctors said they wouldn't accept me because of the high probability of arthritis and the government not wanting to pay me a disability pension. Whereas your testicle injury proved to be a blessing (???) in disguise (ouch) so too did my knee injury as going to Viet Nam at age 24 most likely would have ended my baseball career. By the way, such arthritis in that knee **never** did materialize.

Anyway I really enjoyed the book. I admit I did skim certain sections about your Viet Nam experiences itself but was extremely interested in your observations about outliers, perseverance, work ethic, and the stick to it attitude.

++++

If I may be so bold, I'd like to offer some the following thoughts to illustrate how many of your points really hit home:

As to the outlier thoughts, I was never the best baseball player on my junior league team, my high school team, my college team, nor most likely any minor league or major league team I played for but I was dogged in my persistence and that nothing was going to stop me...I was a member of learning how to play as many positions as possible, pitching batting practice, catching in the bull pen, and just not taking no for an answer.

I knew I had to do something unique to separate myself from the rest of the crowd and I read as many historical books as possible in the off season each year and took copious notes which I still have to this day. I also read books on language and famous quotations and catalogued those as well....This all came to mind when you were talking about your own experience with The Maneuvering Board and how that gave you a leg up on the rest of the guys in OCS...and also how it led to other interesting things in your life..You also mention later in the book 'success rarely comes from chance as it mostly comes from putting in the time'...Ask some TV and movie stars about their sudden fame and most likely you'll find out most put in thousands of hours honing their craft, flunking auditions, waiting on tables, and who knows what waiting for that 'big break'. Sometimes it never comes but I personally wouldn't consider chasing one's dreams a waste of time..You mentioned chasing the stars but sometimes the moon isn't bad either.

I thought I had led a pretty fascinating life but compared to yours, mine almost seems 'boring'. Congratulations on a live well lived and for your contributions to our society and to our world...You've made it a better place.

[This man went on to play professional baseball and had a long, exceptional career.]

++++

[Comments from reader about the idea of responsibililty (that is part of the theme of this book).] Early on in my Navy career, I learned that when you relieve the watch and state the words: "I relieve you, Sir" then you've got it. You undertake the necessary actions to correct any difficulties that may exist and no court martial would support me in any claim that what occurred on my watch was the responsibility/fault of the previous OOD. I think several examples stated in your [book and blog] may exemplify that notion.

++++

This book is full on every page of wonderful memories, from growing up in a small town in the 1940's and 1950's to the achievement of long dreamed of adventures in the Navy as a Seal UDT. This book is factual, entertaining and a great read from front to back.

++++

Uyless Black in his latest book, *A Swimmer's Odyssey: From the Plains to the Pacific*, takes the reader on his life journey filled with adventure, adversity, and achievement. His belief that putting in the swimming time with effortful study of details and constant motivated practice would give him access to the career he so passionately sought: Underwater Demolition Team (UDT) frogman. He could not foresee that an injury would change his dream.

Black's swimming adventures started in an improbable location, the semi-arid high plains of southeastern New Mexico. He describes how he taught himself to swim in ponds scattered around his father's ranch. Black used his visual acuity to emulate the strokes of his fellow swimmer in the pond, the frog. Other mentors, some more tantalizing, provided Black with new standards of motivation and achievement.

Black's swimming odyssey changed from adventure to adversity. His passion led him to the waters of the Pacific Ocean where he describes his experience in the Vietnam conflict, including the Tonkin Gulf incident, Marine raids, and the historic Danag beach landings. Black's powerful struggle after an injury while in UDT training forced him to redirect his career path gives the reader insight into overcoming adversity.

Black's remarkable visualization of settings, his psychological understanding of the requirements for achievement, and his struggles along the way serve a variety of types of readers. Black's book encourages, enlightens, excites, and edifies. Even the casual reader will find Black's style of writing and content compelling and refreshing. A Good Book; a Good Gift!

++++

Uyless Black's latest book, A Swimmer's Odyssey: From the Plains to the Pacific, is an autobiography, one which provides the backdrop to a treatise on his ideas about what it takes to succeed in one's chosen endeavors. Through series of well written passages about events and periods in his life, he attempts to show the reader that his ideas make sense, and in the process, gives us a book well worth reading.

We're introduced to interesting people. These include friends around the local swimming pool, his very able and memorable swimming instructor, a U.S. Navy Admiral, fraternity guys, computer nerds and one extra special student of his (two if you count a millisecond size dog!). The reader needn't be particularly interested in swimming to appreciate the author's writings of these people and events.

Black presents an intelligent discussion of historical events that were happening during his time in the Navy during the Viet Nam War. Whether writing about his ideas of acquiring and using good teaching methods, attitudes toward his duties in the Navy, what it takes to be successful in the field of computer software development, his admiration of certain individuals in his life, he keeps the reader interested in what he's saying.

For example, Black interleaves the concepts of Malcolm Gladwell's book, Outliers, throughout this writing. The 10,000 hour Rule is brought into the book in a series of case studies, not all dealing with swimming, that provide the reader with substantial food for thought. Black's commentary on a disagreement he has with one of Gladwell's ideas was especially interesting. He discusses what occurred with Nujood Ali, the 10 year old divorced Yemeni girl, and presents his thoughts in a direct and intelligent manner.

Black's point that `putting in the time' is a requirement for success is well presented; he's written a good book.

++++

Uyless Black doesn't wear a cowboy hat and boots, but his latest book, A Swimmer's Odyssey: From the Plains to the Pacific, shows his core values from being raised on a ranch. In his journey from those first years on the High Plains of New Mexico to his pursuit of his passion, becoming an Underwater Demolition Team (UDT)frogman, he never strayed from his core values.

Black's unusual perspective of ranch life contributed to his passion for swimming. His visual acuity, while observing frogs, led to his teaching himself to swim in the ponds scattered around his father's ranch. His remarkable visualization of settings takes the reader from the High Plains to the Pacific.

Black's years in Vietnam delivers a personal look at a war that became politically unpopular. His perspective, still rooted in his core values, shows his belief in putting in the time and constantly motivated practice to achieve his dream of becoming a UDT.

The reader, caught up in the spirit of Black's passion to achieve, feels angst when Black suffers an injury in UDT training forcing him to redirect his life-long career passion.

Black's journey is more than an adventure; it is an odyssey through adversity to the ultimate success that came to him. As Black said, "I had come a long way from those plains, but mostly in miles, not in perspective." A great book; a great gift!

Essays available at Blog.UylessBlack.com

America's Capital: Author's experiences in Washington, DC

America's Cities: Journeys and encounters in USA's towns and cities

America's Finances: A series on issues such as Medicare, Social Security, and debt

Computers and Networks: Essays on Internet net neutrality, copyright issues, and software complexity

Creatures and Computers: Drawing analogies to wildlife and Internet organisms

Customs and Cultures: A look at America and Americana

Eating and Drinking: Surveys of food fairs, cafes, and restaurants

Food Effects and Drug Defects: Reports on toxic foods and drugs' side effects

Foreign Affairs: America's relations with other countries

Foreign Places: Taking roads, ships, and trains through parts of the world

Immigration and Emigration: America's immigration practices and related problems

Politics in America: With several reports on National Press Club speakers

Presidential Places: Presidential homes, museums, and grave sites

Sports and Games: Essays on competition and the beauty of sport

The Deadly Trinity Trilogies: Two sets of essays to compliment *The Deadly Trinity* book

The Cepee Dialogues (available 2013 as book; draft is available immediately to a requester)

Coming to You Live, from the Dead (available 2013 as book; draft is available immediately to a requester)

Traveling America: Taking roads through America and America's cultures.

War Zones: Essays on cold, warm, and hot wars

These books, written earlier in Black's career, offer useful information for historians and researchers

IEEE Computer Society

Physical Layer Interfaces
X.25 and Packet Switching Networks

Prentice Hall

Data Communications and Distributed Networks
Computer Networks: Protocols, Standards, and Interfaces
Data Networks: Concepts, Theory, and Practice
The OSI Model
Data Link Protocols
Emerging Communications Technologies
Asynchronous Transfer Mode (ATM) Networks, Volume I
Wireless and Mobile Networks
SONET and T1
ISDN and SS7
Asynchronous Transfer Mode (ATM) Networks, Volume II
Second Generation Mobile and Wireless Networks
Asynchronous Transfer Mode (ATM) Networks, Volume IIII
Advanced Features of the Internet
Residential Broadband
Advanced Intelligent Networks
Voice over IP
The Point-to-Point Protocol (PPP)
IP Routing Protocols
Internet Security Protocols
MPLS and Label Switching Networks
Internet Telephony
Quality of Service in Computer Networks
Internet Architecture
Networking 101
Optical Networks
Multiprotocol Label Switching (MPLS) Networks

McGraw-Hill

The V-Series Recommendations
The X-Series Recommendations
TCP/IP and Related Protocols
Network Management
Frame Relay Networks

www.ingramcontent.com/pod-product-compliance
Lightning Source LLC
Chambersburg PA
CBHW022114080426
42734CB00006B/129
* 9 7 8 0 9 8 0 0 1 0 7 1 8 *